SPI

Travel With Someone You Trust®

AUSTRALIA

Contents

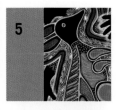

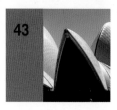

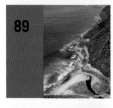

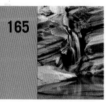

Original text by Pip Moran and Jennifer Muir
Revised and updated by Rod Ritchie

Edited, designed and produced by AA Publishing, a trading
name of AA Media Limited, whose registered office is Fanum
House, Basing View, Basingstoke, Hampshire RG21 4EA.
Registered number 06112600.

Published in the United States by AAA Publishing
1000 AAA Drive, Heathrow, Florida 32746-5063.
Published in the United Kingdom by AA Publishing.

ISBN: 978-1-59508-424-8

Cover design and binding style by permission of AA Publishing
Color separation by AA Digital Department
Printed and bound in China by Leo Paper Products

A04190
Maps in this title produced from map data © New Holland
Publishing (South Africa) (Pty) Ltd. 2010
(except pp194–199 and 216)

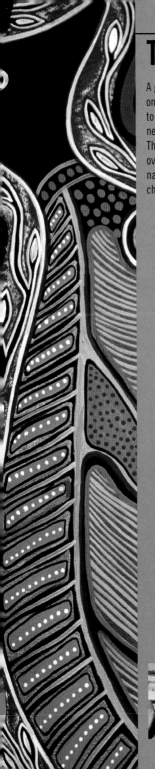

The Magazine

A great holiday is more than just lying on a beach or shopping till you drop — to really get the most from your trip you need to know what makes the place tick. The Magazine provides an entertaining overview to some of the social, cultural and natural elements that make up the unique character of this engaging country.

THE BEST OF

AUSTRALIA

Australia stuns with its riches: its sunny climate and outdoor lifestyle, its vibrant multiculturalism, its fabulous food and wine, its sandy beaches by the mile, its well-known icons – the Sydney Opera House and Uluru (Ayers Rock) – and its unique wildlife, to name just a few.

There is much to see. From the red dirt, brilliant blue skies and extraordinary geological features of the Outback, to the mountain country of the Great Dividing Range; from the pristine wilderness of Tasmania's World Heritage areas, to the coral reefs of the tropical north, Australia offers huge variety in its landscapes and experiences. But visitors to the land "Down Under" will find one constant: few Australians can agree on what constitutes the best of their country.

Best Place to Eat and Drink

It's a safe bet to say that the Blu Horizon Bar, on the 36th floor of Sydney's Shangri-La Hotel (► 64) is one of the better watering-holes, offering spectacular views of the harbour. Sydney is also home to Tetsuya's (► 67), the world-acclaimed restaurant that specializes in refined French-Japanese cuisine, and has an excellent wine list. But Melbourne vies with its northern rival in the fine dining stakes, and Attica (► 107), serves adventurous modern cuisine, as does Pearl (► 108). In Canberra, Ottoman Cuisine (► 85), has brought Middle Eastern food to a new art.

Best Beach

While Bondi is undoubtedly Australia's best-known beach, it's far from the best. Palm Beach and Manly are top beaches, while Tamarama and Cronulla, south of the city, are both popular with surfers. But keen surfers, and beachgoers who like subtropical ambience, should head to alternative Byron Bay on the New South Wales north coast, or trendy Noosa Heads in southeastern Queensland. Both main beaches have north-facing points that allow for a long board ride and good on-shore amenities.

Romantic locations can be found almost anywhere – Cottesloe Beach in Western Australia is one such place. But the most romantic experience of all is a stay on one of the luxurious resort islands that dot the waters of the Great Barrier Reef. The most outstanding of these is Lizard Island, in the far north, offering informality laced with exclusivity, superb food, one of the reef's most beautiful bays – the Blue Lagoon – and the best fringing coral. And the nearby Cod Hole is one of the world's great dive sites.

An aerial view over Sydney Harbour, radiating out from the Opera House

Sydney's Bondi beach

Music festival, Queensland

Uluru (Ayers Rock)

Surfers Paradise,
Queensland

If celebrity is any guide, then the best place in Australia to chill out is the fishing village-turned-tourist resort of Port Douglas, in Tropical North Queensland; you never know who you'll run into while strolling along the golden sands of magical Four Mile Beach.

Best Culture

Aussies have a growing passion for cultural pursuits. The Australian states host an abundance of art, literary and music festivals each year. Sydney hosts the annual Sydney Writers Festival. There are similar festivals in Melbourne, Perth and Brisbane, and smaller literary events are held throughout the country, encouraging and giving voice to its new writers and poets.

For art lovers, the Biennale of Sydney is a "must attend" event. Held in a mix of venues, including the Art Gallery of New South Wales and the Museum of Contemporary Art, this is an exciting celebration of innovative and contemporary Australian visual arts. The Adelaide Festival of Arts, held biennially, is one of the world's top arts events.

The film industry is flourishing in Australia and its film-makers are taking the world by storm. Melbourne and Sydney have annual film festivals that attract world premieres. Contemporary cinema is what this country does best and events such as the Short Film Festival and Flickerfest give low-budget attempts the chance to be screened.

Each major state capital has its symphony orchestra, and the Sydney and Melbourne orchestras give regular performances at home in their respective iconic performance halls, and abroad at some of the world's best venues. Likewise with opera, state and national companies have seasons of new and classic works that play to packed houses.

Also reaching audiences far and wide, as well as locally, is Australia's burgeoning music industry. Rock, pop and opera stars appear in music festivals all over the country.

Best Wild Place

The best place to experience the Outback, and the place where you will come closest to understanding the Indigenous Australians' profound relationship with the land, is the Red Centre. A pilgrimage to awe-inspiring Uluru is near essential. For raw landscape, and an insight into the immense age of this remarkable country, hop from one end of the continent to the other – from the Top End's Kakadu National Park, which contains the finest and most extensive collection of rock art in the world, to Tasmania's Cradle Mountain, with its spectacular alpine scenery.

Best Views

Australia offers some wonderful viewpoints. In Sydney, take a BridgeClimb tour of the Sydney Harbour Bridge. In Melbourne, check out the panorama from the top of Eureka Skydeck 88 at Southbank, while the Gold Coast's Q1 tower offers superb views from 230m (755ft) up.

Canberra is best seen from a hot-air balloon at dawn, and scenic flights over the Great Barrier Reef, and Uluru in the Northern Territory, are unforgettable experiences. In South Australia, admire the raw beauty of the Outback from a lookout in the Flinders Ranges; see Hobart from the summit of Mount Wellington; and the Skyrail Rainforest Cableway provides great views of the Tropical North Queensland coastline and dense canopy of the rainforest.

BEST EXPERIENCES

Here are some "musts" for visitors to Australia.

- Wildlife – if you can't make it to Kangaroo Island, meet some locals at Sydney's Taronga Zoo or Healesville Sanctuary near Melbourne.
- Cruising – on spectacular Sydney Harbour.
- Diving and snorkelling – where else but the Great Barrier Reef!
- Bushwalking – in the World Heritage listed Blue Mountains, near Sydney.
- Driving – along Victoria's Great Ocean Road.
- Sport – watch an Aussie Rules game at the Melbourne Cricket Ground.
- Wining and dining – sample fine wines and cuisine in the Barossa (SA) or Margaret River region (WA).
- Aboriginal Australia – best experienced at Uluru–Kata Tjuta and Kakadu national parks.
- European history – visit the convict settlement of Port Arthur, Tasmania.
- National institutions – head to Canberra to see Parliament House, museums, galleries and the Australian War Memorial.
- For kids – the Gold Coast's theme parks and Phillip Island's wildlife.

THE DREAMTIME...
Indigenous Australia

Two indigenous groups call Australia home: the Aboriginal people arrived – most likely from Southeast Asia – at least 60,000 years ago; the Torres Strait Islanders are of Melanesian origin, and have a rich culture.

For Aboriginal people, the land is imbued with deep spiritual meaning. Few outsiders understand the intricate system that regulates Aboriginal society, and fewer still grasp the philosophy encapsulated in the Aboriginal-English words "Dreaming" and "Dreamtime". Both are at the heart of the emotional and physical attachment Aboriginal people have to their birthplace and the country in general. Ancestral spirits were also an important part of the Torres Strait Islanders' belief – until the "Coming of the Light". The bringing of the Christian Gospel in 1871 deeply influenced the Islanders, and by the end of the 19th century Christianity had largely supplanted traditional beliefs.

Without the Dreamtime there is no meaning, for it was then that everything was set in place for Aboriginal people. In the Dreamtime, the great ancestors walked the earth, creating the landscape and setting in place the Law for the groups they created. From these Dreamtime beings, individuals inherit their Dreaming: totem, complex kin relationships and the law governing them, and the authority and knowledge enabling them to occupy the land and perform the songs and rituals necessary to their country's well-being. When their labours ended, the ancestors were transformed into prominent features in their territory or left reminders of themselves in the landscape.

Landscape in the Dreamtime

At Uluṟu, Anangu people point to scars on the Rock that are the result of the great Dreamtime battle between Kuniya the sand python and Liru the venomous snake. Visitors will be shown the marks made by Kuniya as he moved in with a digging stick to hit Liru. Liru's shield, now a rock, lies where, fatally wounded, he fell.

In the west and the north, evidence of the might of the Rainbow Snake – the Law and the Creation – can be seen in the great monsoonal storms and writhing watercourses. The Kimberley is the home of the beautiful Wandjina who left their imprint on the walls of rock overhangs.

Along the east coast of Australia, mountains were flattened when Baiame, the creator, stepped off their tops to return to the sky. When he left, the southeast wind ceased to blow and a great drought ensued. Flowers vanished, and with them the tiny native bees. But, generation after generation, people kept the faith, refusing to take the honey from the three trees bearing Baiame's mark – the Law said that the bee people needed those hives to see them through the hard times.

A People Politicized

By the late 1960s, the indigenous peoples were becoming increasingly politicized after the success of their campaign to be recognized as Australian citizens. To enhance political and cultural unity, Aboriginal people in eastern Australia took the word Koori, a word for "human", and applied it to all the people in northern New South Wales to Tasmania. Those in other states seized the idea and urban people in South Australia used the word Nunga, those in West Australia Nyungar and in Queensland Murri. People living a more traditional lifestyle still use their traditional names.

The Cost of Colonialism

European settlement had a disastrous effect. Diseases took a dreadful toll and the strangers, along with their farms and livestock, upset the balance between Aboriginal people and their environment. Later, genocide and misguided colonial policies added to the havoc. Equally disastrous was the loss of language – often deliberately suppressed – and disruption to the observance of ritual and Law from the Dreamtime.

Opposite: Uluṟu (Ayers Rock); a young boy with a goanna; Aboriginal poles in Canberra

Prisons to
PROSPERITY

The British colonization of Australia stemmed from the harsh 18th-century justice system that imposed two main punishments: execution or transportation to America. After American independence in 1776, a new dumping ground was sought. The eastern coast of Australia was chosen.

In January 1788, 1,030 convicts, together with about 445 government officials and a number of Royal Marines, landed at Port Jackson to found a new nation. These first arrivals had a hard time as they struggled to establish food crops, housing, and relations with the indigenous people. As free settlers arrived, exploration outside the Sydney area became necessary to cater for the demand for pastoral land that was to form the basis of the new colony's economy. Transportation continued until 1868 by which time an estimated 165,000 convicts had been sent to Australia.

Gold and Pastures
When gold was discovered in New South Wales and Victoria in the 1850s, the ensuing rush brought people from around the world and the city of Melbourne, particularly, boomed – ornate public buildings, botanical gardens, and fine houses were constructed – and the city became a

dynamic metropolis. In rural areas, farm workers joined the rush to the gold fields, and pastoralists found labour in short supply. Late in the 19th century the colonies of the nascent nation came together to plan a federation, and an 1899 referendum gave approval for the formation of a Commonwealth that was proclaimed soon after, in January 1901.

Nationhood

The new nation faced the 20th century as a European outpost. When war was declared in 1914, young men rushed to enlist for a conflict that had little bearing on Australia; more than 60,000 never returned. Again, in 1939, the country found itself in a war that began in Europe, and that reached its doorstep when the Japanese army advanced to the jungles of nearby New Guinea. Again, the trials of wartime meant common goals united the nation. After World War II, refugees from Europe were welcomed and a policy of encouraging migrants from many European nations provided the basis for the prosperity that continues to this day.

The 21st Century

Today, the population has grown to a diverse 22 million people, made up of descendents from the original inhabitants and people from some 200 countries and a variety of ethnicities. This influx of skilled workers has created a highly trained workforce and, along with close ties to Europe and Asia, Australia has harnessed the benefits of technology and e-commerce to ensure that the country is a competitive player in global business.

Traditional rural primrary production has been supplanted by coal, iron ore, oil and gas, and other mining industries as the basis of the new wealth. Increasing demand from Asian countries, especially China, has seen all parts of society become more prosperous. A vibrant tourist industry draws more than 6 million visitors each year.

An illustration of an early convict ship leaving England for Australia (left); a gold prospector in Queensland (middle); Australian soldiers in 1941, during World War II

BURKE AND WILLS

An Australian Tragedy

The year was 1860 and Australia was enjoying an Age of Optimism. The colony had become a place with a burgeoning population of free settlers attracted by vast tracts of superb pastoral land and the discovery of gold. This progress was the result of intrepid explorers who had opened up the interior of the continent.

On 20 August 1860, 15,000 Victorians assembled at Royal Park in Melbourne to watch the best-equipped expedition in the colony's history embark on the last, great exploration challenge: crossing the continent from south to north. The leader of the expedition was Robert O'Hara Burke – a police inspector on the goldfields with no experience in exploration or navigation.

In early October, Burke's expedition arrived at Menindee, the farthest northwestern settlement. Burke had replaced his second-in-command, with William John Wills, a 26-year-old surveyor and astronomer. After establishing a depot at Menindee, Burke set out on 19 October with seven men and 15 camels. A month later, the team crossed into Queensland and made camp at Coopers Creek. Here, beside a large coolibah tree, which still stands today, the party established Depot LXV.

Into the Unknown

With the temperature climbing, Burke was faced with a crucial decision: to wait out the summer in reasonable safety or make the 1,100km (685-mile) dash to the Gulf of Carpentaria. Aware that farther west John McDouall Stuart was attempting a south–north crossing from Adelaide, Burke decided to press on. He again divided his group, instructing William Brahe and three others to remain at Depot LXV, build a timber stockade called Fort Wills and wait for three months before returning to Menindee. To accompany him, Burke chose Wills, Charles Gray and John King.

The team struck out on 16 December. They trekked from waterhole to waterhole, traded with Aboriginal people for food, skirted the Stony Desert, crossed the Tropic of Capricorn, and passed close to the present-day sites of Mount Isa and Cloncurry. On 9 February, 1861, the explorers established Camp 119, just 50km (31 miles) from the Gulf. Heavy rain had fallen and the camels had become bogged down, so Burke and Wills set out on foot for the sea. They floundered through "soft and rotten" country and after two days were halted by mangrove swamps. The sea lay just beyond but without a boat the men were unable to reach their prize.

William John Wills (top left); the expedition departs by Samuel Thomas Gill (left);
The Return of Burke and Wills to Cooper's Creek, **by Nicholas Chevalier, 1868 (below)**

Burke and Wills in the early part of their expedition at Barnadown in 1860

The return journey was a race against time. Brahe was due to leave Depot LXV for Menindee soon. The party was beset by difficulties: storms rendered the ground too boggy for the camels; stifling humidity made walking difficult; Burke suffered dysentery. By late March, the four men were still about 500km (310 miles) north of Coopers Creek, supplies were exhausted, and they were forced to rely on camel meat. The conditions were too much for Gray, who became delirious and died. On 21 April, the remaining explorers reached Fort Wills only to find it deserted. A freshly blazed sign on the coolibah tree read: DIG 3 FT. N.W. APR. 21 1861. They uncovered a cache of provisions and a note from Brahe that said that he and the others had departed for Menindee just nine hours earlier.

Exhaustion

The men rested for two days, then followed Coopers Creek, hoping to reach a police outpost at Mount Hopeless, 240km (150 miles) away. They had buried a message beneath the coolibah tree. Inexplicably, the men neglected to add a new sign that told their rescuers to dig it up.

By 10 May Burke, Wills and King had come to the last waterhole on their intended route and had shot their last camel for food. Meanwhile, Brahe had returned to Coopers Creek and rode away after finding no new message. In late May, Wills alone headed back to the depot at Coopers Creek. He reached it on 30 May. Seeing no evidence that anyone had been at the camp, Wills buried his journals and a letter that gave the location of their camp and returned to his companions.

The three men grew weaker. By the end of June, Wills was unable to move and Burke and King tried to find the local Aboriginal tribe. After two days' walking back along the creek, Burke collapsed and died. King shot four birds, which he took back to Wills, only to find that he, too, had died.

Alone, King wandered until he encountered the Aboriginal tribe, who took pity on him. King lived with the tribe for two months until he was rescued and told the world of the fates of the legendary Burke and Wills.

EXPLORING AUSTRALIA'S
NATIONAL PARKS

Much of Australia's dramatic landscape is protected from development by more than 500 national parks. Australia is also home to 17 natural UNESCO World Heritage Sites.

Two or three hours by road from Hobart is Freycinet NP, which encompasses a peninsula of granite, bush and beaches. The highlight of the park's coastal scenery is Wine Glass Bay. A wild surf pounds against untouched beaches at Croajingolong NP, in eastern Victoria. The park covers 87,500ha (216,210 acres) of forest and heathland, and extends for 100km (62 miles) along a coastline so unspoiled that it has been dubbed the "wilderness coast".

Head inland to Australia's desert heart. Wide blue skies, red soil, orange rock and dry, golden spinifex grass characterize Karijini NP, a 630,000ha (1.5 million-acre) chunk of the Kimberley region. There is permanent water in a series of spectacular gorges in the park's north.

Wine Glass Bay lookout in the Freycinet National Park, Tasmania

Lord Howe Island (above); Purnululu NP (right)

At Nitmiluk NP, you can drift down Katherine River Gorge below cliffs of red-orange rock. Another river cruise operates on the Fitzroy River in Western Australia's Geikie Gorge NP.

In contrast to the arid interior are the lush rainforests of the eastern seaboard. Tropical rainforest dominates Eungella NP, 80km (50 miles) in Queensland. You may see platypuses in the waters of Broken River. World Heritage-listed Dorrigo NP is in New South Wales, in the highlands above Coffs Harbour. High rainfall feeds waterfalls and the subtropical vegetation. Well to the south of Dorrigo is the cool-climate rainforest of Tarra-Bulga NP, which features tree ferns 3m (10 feet) high and ancient myrtle beech trees.

Purnululu NP, Western Australia, features a rocky range called the Bungle Bungles, whose striking form has led to comparisons with Uluru. Another natural wonder lies in Bald Rock NP, on the New South Wales–Queensland border. Bald Rock is a single rounded piece of granite, some 750m (820 yards) long and 500m (550 yards) wide.

Australia's highest mountains are in Kosciuszko NP, in New South Wales. A major winter skiing area, the park is relatively quiet at other times when you can drive the scenic Alpine Way through the mountains. The twisted, stunted snow gum, a type of eucalypt, is characteristic of this park, as it is of Mount Buffalo NP in Victoria. Mount Buffalo's highland world also features groves of tall alpine ash trees and granite tors. Hartz Mountains NP, in Tasmania, encloses a glacier-sculpted landscape of peaks, lakes and cirques.

NATIONAL PARKS AUTHORITIES

Most of Australia's national parks are administered by State or Territory governments. The Federal government manages a handful of parks, including Kakadu and Uluṟu-Kata Tjuṯa.

- **Australia** Department of the Environment and Water Resources, tel: (02) 6274 1111; www.environment.gov.au/parks
- **Australian Capital Territory** Environment ACT, tel: (02) 6207 5111; www.tams.act.gov.au/live/environment
- **New South Wales** NSW National Parks & Wildlife Service, tel: 1300 361 967; www.nationalparks.nsw.gov.au
- **Northern Territory** Parks & Wildlife Service NT, tel: (08) 8999 5511; www.nt.gov.au/nreta/parks
- **Queensland** Environment and Resource Management, tel: 1300 130 372; www.derm.qld.gov.au/parks_and_forests
- **South Australia** Department For Environment and Heritage, tel: (08) 8204 1910; www.parks.sa.gov.au/parks
- **Tasmania** Parks & Wildlife Service, tel: 1300 135 513; www.parks.tas.gov.au
- **Victoria** Parks Victoria, tel: 13 19 63; www.parkweb.vic.gov.au
- **Western Australia** Department of Environment and Conservation, tel: (08) 6467 5000; www.naturebase.net

Snowy River in New South Wales

AUSTRALIA'S WILDLIFE:
more than just cuddly

There's a sudden rustle in the grass up ahead. A 2m (6.5ft) snake slithers across the trail, its black or brown scales blotched with orange and yellow warning spots that glimmer in the sun.

Bredl's carpet python (non-venomous)   Jungle carpet pythons are non-venomous

You are now sharing this pocket of the Australian bush with a taipan. Although the snake prefers evasion, if provoked it can hurl itself at its attacker, delivering deadly multiple bites with its 12mm (half-inch) fangs. The best course of action is to stand still and let it go on its way.

While the kangaroo and the koala are known internationally as furry emblems of Australia's fauna, not all the country's creatures look as cuddly. Some Australian species, like the taipan, are equipped with the world's deadliest toxins, while others boast impressive threat displays, grow to huge sizes, have unique breeding habits, or are examples of evolution in isolation.

As a proportion of total species, Australia is home to more venomous snakes than any other country. The deadliest of these is the inappropriately named fierce snake which, while it produces the most toxic venom of any snake in the world, is extremely timid. More aggressive is the death adder, which is reluctant to retreat if disturbed and will deliver a succession of toxic bites. The eastern brown snake, nervous and fast-moving, is found throughout most of eastern Australia. Known as *Pseudonaja*, which means "false cobra", the eastern brown flattens its neck and rears its head and the front third of its body from the ground in an S-shape when threatened.

Such threat displays by Australia's reptiles don't always indicate venomous intent. The frill-necked lizard, a shy tree-dweller that usually measures almost a metre from tip to tail, is renowned for standing on its hind legs, baring its impressive teeth and displaying an umbrella-like, translucent frill of skin that is up to four times its body diameter. As they

Frill-necked lizards are found in the north   **Funnel web spiders produce toxic venom**

have a nervous temperament, these lizards make poor zoo captives and are best observed in Australia's north, where they can often be seen racing beside the road on their hind legs, frills puffed, like mad Elizabethans.

Spiders Large and Small

A more dangerous threat display is that of the funnel web spider. Despite its small size, there are few more terrifying sights than this jet-black spider in attack mode with its front legs reared and curved fangs glistening with toxic venom. One of the world's most dangerous arachnids, the funnel web spider was responsible for 13 officially recorded deaths from 1927 until an anti-venom was discovered in 1981. The funnel web spider is so-named because of the shape of the web it builds around its burrows.

Forty species of the spider are found on Australia's east coast but the most common is the Sydney funnel web, whose habitat is smack-dab in the middle of the city. It is known for its aggressive behaviour and during the mating season males of the species leave their burrows and wander in search of a female – often turning up in suburban backyards and pools.

Unusual Species

Other Australian species, while not known for their bite, are known for their size, breeding habits or unique abilities. *Megascolides australis* – better known as the giant Gippsland earthworm – has been recorded at a length of 2.18m (7ft) when not extended and 3.96m (13ft) when extended. In Queensland, the southern gastric brooding frog is born as a live

A saltwater crocodile   **A black-footed rock wallaby**

froglet from the mouth of its mother, after hatching and metamorphosing in her stomach. This extremely rare frog is now feared extinct. Southern Queensland is also home to a living fossil – the Queensland lungfish, which, unchanged in 110 million years, has evolved in isolation and, equipped with both lungs and gills, can breathe on land or in the water.

Megafauna: The Ones That Got Away

Fossil records indicate that prehistoric Australia was home to a variety of big animals, known collectively as megafauna. Present-day Australia has no such large native animals. What prompted their extinction – climatic change or the arrival of Aboriginal people – has been debated for over a century. Visitors to Australia 100,000 years ago may have encountered:

Diprotodon – a large marsupial, related to the wombat, which was the size of a rhino; Wanabe – a giant snake that was nearly 1m (3ft) in diameter and grew up to 8m (26ft) long; Genyornis – a giant flightless bird that was twice the weight of an emu; and Megalania – a giant goanna that grew up to 7m (23ft) in length, twice the size of Indonesia's komodo dragon.

Still Out There?

Once plentiful, Tasmanian tigers, or thylacines, were hunted to extinction in the early 20th century, with the last of the species dying in captivity in 1936. Looking a bit like a dog with short legs and a kangaroo-like tail, Tasmanian tigers were large marsupials weighing up to 35kg (77 pounds) and measuring some 60cm (24in) at the shoulder. They

A captive emu, Airlie Beach   **A coarse-haired wombat in a meadow**

had light yellowish fur with dark stripes running across the back from the shoulders to the base of the tail and mighty jaws. Since 1936, more than 400 tiger sightings have been reported and the search continues…

Australia's Original Cartoon Creature

Which of Australia's unique species has been a Hollywood star? The koala or kangaroo would seem to be obvious contenders. But the marsupial with star quality is the Tasmanian devil. Warner Bros. cartoons depicted the devil as a feisty creature that spun on the spot, tornado-like. The real Tasmanian devil is a fierce carnivore, equipped with vice-like jaws – but it doesn't actually spin around. The devil was named by early European explorers who were spooked by its eerie growl.

A Great SPORTING Country

Australia has become one of the world's great sporting nations, where everyone from an early age is encouraged to "have a go" on land or on, and in, the sea – so much so that it is now an integral part of the Aussie psyche and all sports are played and supported with gusto.

Sport is an inherent part of Australia's national identity, built upon the achievements of sporting heroes like cricketer Don Bradman, swimmer Dawn Fraser, tennis player Rod Laver and athlete Cathy Freeman, and the gallery of Antipodean allstars is only going to get bigger.

World-Class Facilities and Athletes

The benign Australian climate provides the perfect environment in which to hone skills and physical fitness, coupled with the most amazing facilities throughout the country. Go to any high school in any state and you'll find athletics tracks, playing fields, racquet sports courts and team-game facilities of a fantastic standard as well as swimming pools fit for professionals – and many have the added bonus of acres of sandy beach and the warm seas. In every city and town you'll find parks and public courts and playing fields where kids can practise out of school and for amateur league teams to do battle on weekend afternoons. It is no wonder then that Australia, with its relatively small population yet huge

encouragement of any sporting potential, is now a tour de force on the world sporting stage. The 2000 Sydney Olympics proved Australia was ready to take on all-comers, and continues to do so in worldwide competitions.

Sport is not just for the elite in this country of outdoor lovers, but is embraced by all. It is epitomized by the 60,000 participants in the Sydney City to Surf fun run, just one of thousands of amateur events held each year.

Aussie Rules

However, the game that dominates is "Aussie Rules" or AFL, founded in Melbourne in the late 19th century. It is a game of hard knocks – a cross between rugby and football (soccer) – where all players have to be tough enough to endure hard contact, yet athletic enough to sprint the length of the pitch and kick the oval-shaped ball accurately while in full flight. The league culminates in a Grand Final held each September at the game's heartland, the Melbourne Cricket Ground. Rugby League and Rugby Union are the most popular codes in New South Wales and Queensland, while football (soccer) has a national league contest.

On Land and By Sea

Melbourne features highly in the sporting calendar, from the Australian Open tennis championship (January) and the Formula 1 Australian Grand Prix (March), to the nation's favourite horse race, the Melbourne Cup (November). Aussies really love Melbourne Cup Day and celebrate across the country.

The surrounding oceans create yet another fabulous sporting arena, providing challenging conditions to test surfers and sailors alike; the largest event is the Sydney to Hobart yacht race, beginning in Sydney Harbour on Boxing Day, while some of the world's best surfers ride the huge rollers each Easter at Bells Beach in Victoria.

From the top: A swimming race, Bondi beach; the Australian Grand Prix; an Aussie Rules football match; rafting at Penrith White Water Stadium

CELEBRATION
of a
NATION

Australians love a celebration and the roar of the crowd is a familiar sound – whether it's for football titans clashing for premiership honours, yachtsmen risking life and limb on the open seas, up-and-coming country music singers performing in the streets of Tamworth (NSW), or drag queens parading down Sydney's Oxford Street. "The bigger the crowd, the better the party" is the motto and visitors will find Aussies a welcoming bunch when it comes to celebrations.

ach year's festivities close – and kick off again a second later – with
ew Year's Eve. Every major Australian city holds boisterous celebrations,
vith revellers typically lining the streets of Melbourne and Sydney. A few
veeks later, on 26 January, Australians are back out in force to celebrate
ustralia Day, the anniversary of the landing of the First Fleet (➤ 12).

Passion for Racing

Nowhere in my travels have I encountered a festival of people that has
uch a magnificent appeal to the whole nation", wrote Mark Twain of
he Melbourne Cup horse race (➤ 110). More than a century later, his
escription holds true. The Cup brings Australia to a halt as thousands
ather at Flemington Racecourse – and millions more tune in their radios
r televisions – to cheer on horses that they have backed to win.

Racing is also the theme of the Alice Springs Camel Cup Carnival (July)
nd the hilarious Henley-on-Todd Regatta (September; ➤ 142), held in
he dry Todd River bed and contested by crews running in bottomless
boats". Darwin has its own "quirky" water event, the Beer Can Regatta
July or August), involving rafts made from beer and soft drink cans.

Outback Queensland's answer to the Melbourne Cup is the legendary
3irdsville Races. On the first weekend in September thousands of people
escend on the remote, dusty town of Birdsville (population 120) for the
aces, held on a dry claypan just outside town, and a "grand ball".

Clockwise from left: Fireworks over Sydney Harbour Bridge; Sydney Gay and Lesbian Mardi Gras; Henley-on-Todd Regatta; the Melbourne Cup horse race; a young Australian shows pride in his country on Australia Day

A YEAR'S WORTH

- **26 January:** Australia Day
- **January:** Tamworth Country Music Festival
- **February/March:** Gay and Lesbian Mardi Gras
- **March–September:** Football season (Aussie Rules)
- **First weekend in September:** Birdsville Races
- **September–October:** Floriade, Canberra
- **First Tuesday in November:** Melbourne Cup
- **26 December:** The Sydney to Hobart Yacht Race begins
- **31 December:** New Year's Eve celebrations

Festival Country

Also in the country – although not nearly as remote as Birdsville – is New South Wales' Tamworth Country Music Festival. Held in late January and attended by about 75,000 enthusiasts, the festival has more than 2,200 events that include all genres falling under the broad name of "country", from bush ballads and bush poetry to blue grass and country rock gospel.

Music and the arts are the focus of some of the nation's most renowned festivals. These include the January Sydney Festival, the January/February Perth International Arts Festival, the biennial Adelaide Festival of Arts and Adelaide Fringe Festival (February/ March), the Brisbane Festival (September) and Melbourne International Arts Festival (October).

Australia's bountiful produce is celebrated in food and wine festivals around the country. Some of the best known are the Barossa's Vintage Festival (Easter), the Hunter Valley Harvest Festival (April–June), Margaret River's Wine Festival (November), and the Hobart Summer Festival (late December–early January). Wine regions such as the Hunter, Barossa and Margaret River are also often associated with music – for example, the Hunter's famous Opera in the Vineyards event each October.

Other entertaining events include the Melbourne International Comedy Festival (March/April); Canberra's flower festival, Floriade (September/ October); Sydney's Royal Easter Show, a primarily agricultural event; and Brisbane's Royal Queensland Show in August. If you are in Alice Springs at the end of June, don't miss the eccentric Beanie Festival, when hand-made beanies (close-fitting knitted or crocheted hats) are on display. There are craft workshops and fun family events.

Party-time

Australia's biggest party, though, occurs in Sydney in February to March. The Sydney Gay and Lesbian Mardi Gras began in 1978 and was attended by 1,000 people. That year, marchers and police clashed violently. Today, the Mardi Gras has the blessing of the state government, the police and the community at large. Each year, more than 300,000 people cheer the floats and extravagantly costumed marchers.

Finding Your Feet

First Two Hours

Australia has a number of international gateways, with Sydney and Melbourne being the busiest. Taxis and buses are the main forms of transport to city centres.

Ground Transportation Fees (excluding tip)
$ under A$12 $$ A$12–A$20 $$$ A$20–A$28 $$$$ over A$28

Sydney
- **Sydney Airport** is 10km (6 miles) from the city centre.
- **Taxis** are the most direct mode of transport, but also the most expensive ($$$$, depending on traffic).
- Your next best option is the **Sydney Airporter** (www.kst.com.au), which operates a door-to-door service ($$) from the airport to your accommodation, Kings Cross and Darling Harbour areas. The bus departs about every 30 minutes.
- **Airport Link** ($$), the train service between the airport and city, provides the fastest option, taking 10–15 minutes to Central Station. The trains then continue around the City Circle line. Trains run daily every 10–15 minutes during airport operating hours and are often crowded during peak hours (☎ 13 15 00 within Australia; www.airportlink.com.au).

City Centre Visitor Information Centre
Sydney Visitor Centre, corner of Argyle and Playfair Streets, The Rocks ☎ (02) 9240 8788 or (1800) 067 676 (within Australia); www.sydneyvisitorcentre.com; open daily 9:30–5:30; closed Good Fri, 25 Dec.

Melbourne
- **Melbourne Airport** is 25km (15 miles) from the city centre.
- **Taxis** ($$$$) to the city centre are the most direct but most expensive bet.
- The best value is **Skybus Super Shuttle** ($$), which operates a shuttle bus service between the airport and Southern Cross Station in the city. Buses operate around the clock, departing every 10–15 minutes 6am–9pm and every 30 minutes at other times. Free minibus transfers are available to and from Southern Cross Station to Central Business District (CBD) hotels (☎ (03) 9600 1711; www.skybus.com.au).

City Centre Visitor Information Centre
Melbourne Visitor Centre, Federation Square, corner Swanston and Flinders streets (opposite Flinders Street Station) ☎ (03) 9658 9658; www.visitvictoria.com, www.thatsmelbourne.com.au; open daily 9–6; closed Good Fri, 25 Dec.

Brisbane
- **Brisbane Airport** is 13km (8 miles) from the city centre.
- **Taxis** ($$$$) to the city centre are direct but the most expensive option.
- The **Airtrain** ($$–$$$; ☎ (07) 3216 3308; www.airtrain.com.au) offers a fast, inexpensive service between the airport and Brisbane and the Gold Coast. Operating daily 5am–9pm, the Airtrain runs, on average, four times an hour to the Brisbane CBD and twice an hour to the Gold Coast.
- Also good value is the **Coachtrans shuttle bus** ($$) which departs for the city centre every 30 minutes between approximately 5:45am and 11:15pm (☎ (07) 3358 9700; www.coachtrans.com.au).

■ **Coachtrans** also operates a Gold Coast service ($$$$), ☎ (07) 3358 9700; www.coachtrans.co.au; 6:15am–11:15pm every 60 minutes.

City Centre Visitor Information Centre

Visitor Information Booth, Queen Street Mall ☎ (07) 3006 6290; www.visitbrisbane.com.au and www.queenslandholidays.com.au; open Mon–Thu 9–5:30, Fri 9–7, Sat 9–5, Sun and public holidays 9:30–4:30, Anzac Day 1–4; closed Good Fri, 25 Dec.

Cairns

■ **Cairns Airport** is 7km (4.5 miles) from the city centre.
■ The easiest option is to take a **taxi** to the city centre ($$).
■ The **Sun Palm Transport bus** is cheaper ($), meeting all flights and dropping you directly at your accommodation (www.sunpalmtransport.com).

City Centre Visitor Information Centre

Tourism Tropical North Queensland Gateway Discovery Centre, 51 The Esplanade ☎ (07) 4051 3588; www.tropicalaustralia.com.au and www.queenslandholidays.com.au; open daily 8:30–6:30, public holidays 10–6; closed Good Fri, 25 Dec.

Darwin

■ **Darwin Airport** is 12km (7.5 miles) from the city centre.
■ **Darwin Airport Shuttle service** ($; www.darwinairportshuttle.com.au) meets all flights and drops off at hotels.
■ **Taxis** to the city centre ($$$) are a more expensive option.

City Centre Visitor Information Centre

Tourism Top End Information Centre, Corner Knuckey and Mitchell streets ☎ (08) 8936 2499; www.tourismtopend.com.au and www.travelnt.com; open Mon–Fri 8:30–5, Sat 9–3, Sun 10–3; closed Good Fri, 25 Dec.

Adelaide

■ **Adelaide Airport** is 7km (4.5 miles) from the city centre.
■ **Skylink** operates a shuttle service ($; www.skylinkadelaide.com) to the city every 30–60 minutes from 6:15am to 9:40pm
■ **Taxis** to the city centre ($$$) are a more expensive mode of transport.

City Centre Visitor Information Centre

South Australian Visitor & Travel Centre, 18 King William Street ☎ (1300) 655 276; www.southaustralia.com; open Mon–Fri 8:30–5, Sat, Sun and public holidays 9–2; closed 25 Dec.

Perth

■ **Perth Airport** is 20km (12 miles) from the city centre.
■ **Perth Airport City Shuttle** and Airport Shuttle Fremantle run services to the city ($$) and Fremantle ($$$$), meeting all flights and dropping you at most city accommodation.
■ **Taxis** ($$$) are an expensive but more direct option.

City Centre Visitor Information Centre

Western Australian Visitor Centre, Forrest Place (corner Wellington Street) ☎ (08) 9483 1111 or (1800) 812 808; www.westernaustralia.com, www.wavisitorcentre.com; open May–Aug Mon–Thu 8:30–5:30, Fri 8:30–6, Sat 9:30–4:30, Sun 11–4:30; Sep–Apr Mon–Thu 8:30–6, Fri 8:30–7, Sat 9:30–4:30, Sun 11–4:30.

Getting Around

By far the best and most practical way to get around Australia is to fly. There is also a national rail network and an interstate coach network. Public transport systems in the state capital cities range from good to excellent. For more information visit www.australia.com (the Tourism Australia website).

Domestic Air Travel

■ The main **domestic airlines** are Qantas and Virgin Blue. Qantas, along with its subsidiaries Jetstar and QantasLink, has the more wide-ranging network of destinations throughout Australia. Virgin Blue, a no-frills airline, offers direct flights between most major destinations, such as Sydney–Darwin, Sydney–Melbourne and Sydney–Perth, as well as some tourist routes, such as Sydney–Whitsunday coast. Regional Express (Rex), smaller than the other two, links provincial centres and capital cities in New South Wales, Victoria, Tasmania and South Australia. A number of small operators cover resort areas, country towns, islands and remote Outback localities. All domestic flights in Australia are **non-smoking**.

■ Flying in Australia can be expensive, but with forward planning you should rarely have to pay full fare. **Many airlines offer discount deals**, but check with your travel agent about conditions regarding minimum travel, time restrictions and whether you need to purchase tickets before departure – many discounts are offered as part of an international package. Also, look for special online fares. Qantas, for example, offers discounted domestic travel if this is booked with an international ticket. Simply produce your international air ticket and proof of overseas residence when booking.

■ **Qantas** is an international and domestic carrier, with flights leaving from both the international and domestic terminals: many flights are at separate locations. Check you're in the right place if travelling with this airline: flights with flight numbers from QF001 to QF399 operate from international terminals; flight numbers QF400 and above operate from domestic terminals.

■ **Fly-drive deals** offered by the airlines and car-rental companies (➤ 34) are a good option. You can, for example, pick up a car in Sydney, drive to Melbourne, then fly to Adelaide where you pick up another car.

Reservations and information

■ **Qantas Airways** ☎ (02) 9691 3636 or 13 13 13 inside Australia; www.qantas.com.au
■ **Regional Express (Rex)** ☎ (02) 6393 5550 or 13 17 13 inside Australia; www.regionalexpress.com.au
■ **Virgin Blue** ☎ (07) 3295 2296 or 13 67 89 inside Australia; www.virginblue.com.au

Trains

■ Australia has a limited rail network that is neither cheap nor fast. It does, however, offer some **great train journeys**, notably the **Indian Pacific** (Sydney–Perth), which takes three days, and **the Ghan** (Adelaide–Darwin), which also takes three days, as well as regular services linking the cities from Cairns to Sydney, and on to Melbourne and Adelaide. Rail Australia handles enquiries and reservations for the major long-distance trains.

■ Most **long-distance trains** offer first-class, de luxe and economy compartments, sleeping berths and reclining seats, as well as dining and buffet cars.

■ **Reservations** are advisable on all long-distance trains, with bookings accepted up to nine months in advance on some services.

■ A number of **rail passes** offering unlimited economy travel for set periods are available to overseas visitors: these can be purchased either overseas or in Australia. The Austrail Flexipass is available for 15 or 22 days of travel, which can be taken any time over a six-month period. Other passes include the East Coast Discovery Pass, the Wanderer Rail Pass (Queensland services) and the Great Southern Railway Pass (all valid for six months), covering travel on the Indian Pacific and Ghan trains.

Reservations and information

■ **Rail Australia** ☎ (08) 8213 4441 (or 13 21 47 inside Australia for rail passes); www.railaustralia.com.au

Buses

■ Bus travel in Australia is the cheapest way to get around and a good way to see the landscape, though long stretches (more than a day) without a break can strain even the most relaxed traveller. That said, long-distance buses have **air conditioning**, videos, adjustable seats and on-board bathrooms. Unlike the railway system, they also offer **comprehensive route networks**. Greyhound Australia operates the largest mainland service, while Tasmanian Redline Coaches and TassieLink serve Tasmania.

■ **Greyhound Australia** has passes offering savings on extended travel.

■ A range of companies offer transport options at a local level, most in the form of **organized tours**. These provide a good alternative for those not wishing to rent a car and drive themselves to particular sights, for example, the Great Ocean Road (➤ 99). Check the relevant State tourist office for details of local operators (➤ 30).

Reservations and information

■ **Greyhound Australia** ☎ (07) 4690 9950 or (1300) 473 946 inside Australia; www.greyhound.com.au

■ **Tasmanian Redline Coaches** ☎ (1300) 360 000 or (03) 6336 1446; www.tasredline.com

■ **TassieLink** ☎ (1300) 300 520 or (03) 6230 8900; www.tigerline.com.au

Ferries

■ The only regular interstate ferry service is the *Spirit of Tasmania*. Two **passenger/vehicle ferries** bearing this name journey between Melbourne and Devonport, in Tasmania. Overnight services run from Melbourne daily. Additional daylight crossings take place in the summer peak season.

Reservations and information

■ *Spirit of Tasmania* ☎ (1800) 634 906 inside Australia; www.spiritoftasmania.com.au

Urban Transport

■ Most state capital cities have frequent **train** and/or **bus** services. Melbourne, and to a much lesser extent Sydney and Adelaide, also have **trams** (called light rail in Sydney). Sydney also has a **monorail** offering limited inner-city services, and, along with Perth and Brisbane, a regular local **ferry** service.

■ **Free inner-city services** include Melbourne's City Circle tram, Perth's Red, Blue and Yellow CATS (Central Area Transit buses) and Adelaide's City Loop and Bee Line buses.

■ **Smoking** is not permitted in public vehicles.

Public Transport Information

- **Sydney** ☎ 13 15 00 inside Australia; www.131500.info
- **Canberra** ☎ 13 17 10 inside the ACT; www.action.act.gov.au
- **Melbourne** ☎ 13 16 38 inside Australia; www.metlinkmelbourne.com.au
- **Brisbane** (including Gold Coast) ☎ 13 12 30 inside Queensland; www.translink.com.au
- **Darwin** ☎ (08) 8924 7666; www.nt.gov.au/transport/public
- **Adelaide** ☎ (1300) 3111 08 inside Australia or 1800 182 160 inside South Australia; www.adelaidemetro.com.au
- **Perth** ☎ (08) 9428 1900 or 13 62 13 inside Western Australia; www.transperth.wa.gov.au
- **Hobart** ☎ (03) 6233 4232 or 13 22 01 inside Tasmania; www.metrotas.com.au

Taxis

- Metered taxis operate in all major cities and towns. **Taxi ranks** can be found at transport terminals, large hotels and shopping centres, or you can hail one in the street. When the sign on the roof is lit up, the driver is seeking a passenger. There is a minimum "flagfall" charge, and a charge for the distance travelled. **Fares are displayed on the meter**; drivers do not expect to be tipped, but will accept gratuities.

Driving

Car Rental

- Public transport can be very limited outside Australia's urban areas and unless you join a tour, **renting a car** is often the only way you'll get to explore rural and remote areas and small towns in any depth.
- **Rental cars** are available nationwide. Vehicles can be rented at the airport on arrival, but it's advisable to book in advance, especially Dec–Jan.
- **Rates** vary according to operator, location, season, type of vehicle and rental period. You can pay anything from around $60 a day for a small car to $120 for a large model – online rates are the most competitive. Most rates include unlimited mileage in metropolitan areas.
- **Local** firms can be very good value, but check their terms carefully. Cars come with a full tank and you pay for the fuel used.
- The preferred **payment** method is credit card. Most firms will accept cash as final payment, but you may need credit card ID to qualify for rental.

Car Rental Companies

- **Avis** ☎ (02) 9353 9000 and (1300) 136 333 inside Australia; www.avis.com.au. **Budget** ☎ (02) 9353 9399 and (1300) 362 848 inside Australia; www.budget.com.au. **Hertz** ☎ (03) 9698 2555 and 13 30 39 inside Australia; www.hertz.com.au.

Insurance

- Compulsory **third-party insurance** and **collision-damage waiver** are standard inclusions in car rentals. Personal accident cover is also available.
- A premium may be charged for **drivers under 25** years of age.
- Car-rental companies will not offer insurance on **off-road driving**, which includes any non-bitumen or gravel roads.

Driving Laws

- Australians drive on the **left-hand side** of the road.
- The **maximum speed limit** on urban roads is 50–60kph (31–37mph) and 100–110kph (62–68mph) on country roads and highways, unless signs indicate otherwise.

- **Random breath testing** is carried out in all Australian States and Territories. The legal blood-alcohol level is a maximum 0.05 per cent.
- It is compulsory for drivers and passengers to wear **seatbelts** at all times.

Driving Licences
- If you're a bona fide tourist and your driving licence is in English, there is **no need for an additional permit** when driving in Australia. You must have your driving licence and passport with you at all times when driving. Those who do not have a licence in English must also carry a translation.

Fuel
- Fuel comes in **unleaded** and **diesel grades** and is sold by the litre. Filling stations are plentiful, except in some Outback areas, though trading hours vary. Most stations accept major debit and credit cards.

Breakdowns
- If your rental car breaks down, you should **contact the car-rental company** which will arrange to send road service or a replacement vehicle.

Motoring Clubs
- Bring your own **Automobile Association membership card** to take advantage of reciprocal rights with the affiliated automobile clubs in Australia.
- **NRMA** (NSW and ACT) ☎ 13 11 22 inside Australia; www.mynrma.com.au
- **Royal Automobile Club of Victoria** ☎ 13 72 28 inside Australia; www.racv.com.au
- **Royal Automobile Club of Queensland** ☎ 13 19 05 inside Australia; www.racq.com.au
- **Automobile Association of the Northern Territory** ☎ (08) 8924 5901; www.aant.com.au

Accommodation

Choosing where to stay in Australia is not simply about location and facilities, but also about convenience and price. Australia can be hot in mid-summer, so look for beachside locations, a breezy terrace, swimming pool and air conditioning. Equally, sitting with your feet up and enjoying the scenery is a popular pastime, so a room with a view is a priority.

The cities and countryside offer a wide range of **high-quality accommodation**, from budget hotels and small guest houses, to leading international hotels. Sydney and Melbourne are generally more expensive than the other cities. Most accommodation is contemporary – Australia has only a few buildings more than 150 years old – with much of it recently built or refurbished to capitalize on the country's popularity as a tourist destination. Australia's standard of living is high and so too is the standard of accommodation: rooms are generally more spacious than comparable venues in other cities, and on an international level offer excellent value for money. It is a sporting nation, so **leisure activities are offered as part of the service**. If a hotel does not itself provide swimming, a gym, tennis or golf, staff will be able to arrange such activities near by.

Ecotourism and environmentally sympathetic accommodation are important issues in Australia. **Luxurious wooden lodges** built on stilts with rainforest canopies are popular and are no more expensive than a city hotel.

Hotels

■ The cities offer many world-class **prestige hotels** with state-of-the-art facilities. Experienced international travellers will understand how one luxury international hotel is much the same as any other. It is the specific location that makes all the difference and several of Australia's top hotels have the edge over their rivals thanks not to their services but to their stunning views.

■ The situation is similar with **resorts** – once ensconced, you may find you could just as easily be in Fiji or Bali as on Queensland's Gold Coast. Resorts are designed primarily for people who want to stay in one location: they are generally luxurious and offer outstanding sporting and leisure facilities but are also, typically, large and somewhat impersonal.

■ **Boutique hotels**, premises that have only 10 to 20 rooms, typically individually decorated to a high standard, are a growing trend throughout the country. Some are moderately priced; however, others are at the upper end of the price range, offering personal attention and comfort. Often tastefully decorated, they can seem more luxurious than a prestige hotel, but with fewer extraneous facilities such as electrically operated curtains. They are a charming option worth investigating thoroughly.

Guest Houses

■ **Guest houses** similarly bridge the gap between hotels and bed-and-breakfast accommodation. They tend to have a small number of rooms but are usually not as luxurious as boutique hotels, and have fewer services.

■ Many guest houses will also **describe themselves as "B&Bs"** because bed-and-breakfast is what is included in the price. Widely available throughout the country, such accommodation may be in a five-bedroomed cottage in a mountain village, a renovated inner-city townhouse or part of an estate such as a winery.

Bed-and-Breakfast

■ Many venues offering bed-and-breakfast are, in fact, offering small **private cottages** or **apartments** that function like a miniature hotel, and the prices may therefore seem surprisingly high.

■ Places where guests stay in a room in a private house are distinguished by the term **"homestay B&B's"** and these are often quite luxurious, though in general this is quality budget accommodation.

■ **"Farmstay"** accommodation allows you to experience life on a working farm or cattle station; usually guests' sleeping quarters are separate from the owners' rooms, although shared meals and entertainment are considered part of the experience.

Motels

■ It is generally not possible to meander through the countryside stopping off at B&Bs discovered en route: roadside motels or motor lodges and pub accommodation have traditionally serviced such travels, and these places tend to be **functional** and basic rather than romantic. The holidaymaker deserves better, but the prolific number of motels can be useful when you are driving long distances, and they are economical.

■ There are several **motel chains**, as well as some independent companies, and they tend to be located along the main roads running into and out of towns.

■ **Pubs** or hotels offer simple and cheap accommodation that can prove equally useful when travelling but they can be very noisy, especially around closing time, and they are less likely to have in-room air conditioning.

Apartments

■ Serviced apartments are a great option for families and people who prefer to be self-sufficient and prepare their own meals. They offer privacy and can be like a home from home.

Camping

■ **Campsites** are an extremely popular form of budget accommodation with Australians. Most towns have a **caravan park** where you can pitch a tent or rent an on-site van (trailer house) or cabin, often without notice. Many of Australia's magnificent national parks offer camping, ranging from comprehensively serviced sites to basic bush camping.

Prices and Availability

■ Prices for overnight accommodation range from around A$50 for a motel room to more than A$500 per night. Always check whether the price being asked is per room or per person, as quotes will vary. Wherever possible, **book in advance**, particularly in the cities and on Queensland's Gold Coast and other resort areas. December and January are especially busy times, but Australia is an attractive destination even during the winter months.

Websites

■ **Tourism Australia's website** (www.australia.com) lists a reasonable selection of accommodation in various categories. Although you cannot book direct through this website, it does contain all the relevant information and contact details.

Booking Accommodation

■ Large travel companies have **accommodation websites** from which you can book as well as browse: the best is Hotel Club at www.hotelclub.com.
■ The **National Roads and Motorists Association** (NRMA; www.mynrma. com.au) produces booklets listing accommodation throughout Australia, available from NRMA offices.
■ Australia has a number of medium price **hotel/motel chains** offering central booking facilities. These include:
Best Western Hotels ☎ 13 17 79 within Australia or (02) 8913 3300; www.bestwestern.com.au
Choice Hotels ☎ (1300) 668 128 within Australia or (03) 9243 2400; www.choicehotels.com.au
Accor Hotels (Formule 1, Mercure and Ibis properties) ☎ (02) 8584 8666 or (1300) 656 565 (Ibis only); www.accorhotels.com.au
Country Comfort ☎ (1300) 272 132; www.countrycomforthotels.com.au
■ **Bed-and-breakfast bookings** can be made online through Bed and Breakfast Australia, www.bedandbreakfast.com.au or The Bed and Breakfast Book Online www.bbbook.com.au
■ **Farmstay bookings** can be made through Australian Farm Tourism ☎ www.australianbedandbreakfast.com.au
■ **Backpacking** is very popular in Australia. For information contact VIP Backpackers International ☎ (07) 3395 6111; www.vipbackpackers.com or Nomads World, ☎ (1800) 091 905; www.nomadsworld.com

---

ACCOMMODATION PRICES
Prices are for the least expensive double room in high season:
$ under A$150   **$$** A$150–A$280   **$$$** over A$280

Food and Drink

During the 1990s, Australia emerged on the international stage as one of the world's great gastronomic nations. A visit to a top Sydney or Melbourne restaurant is as prestigious among food critics and enthusiasts as dining in an elite establishment in New York, Paris or London. Yet in Australia good food is easily accessible and reasonably priced. You are as likely to enjoy an expertly cooked dish in a modern city cafe as in a formal restaurant.

Fine Dining

■ At the top end, **Australia has many fine dining establishments**, where much effort is put into crafting the dishes, ingredients may be expensive, the interior design chic and the service attentive. However, compared to similar places in other countries, these **venues tend to be very reasonably priced**. Expect to pay no more than A$100 for a three-course meal per head for the food. You will also find Australia's leading restaurants are more comfortable than comparable establishments elsewhere – the Australian attitude generally is to eschew anything elitist, and rigorous formality in restaurants is certainly on that list. Women should leave their evening dresses at home; men are rarely expected to wear jackets and often don't need to wear a tie. However, extreme air conditioning in top restaurants may encourage you bring an extra layer anyway.

Cafes, Bars and Bistros

■ The **modern cafe** is one of the things Australians do best so try to include at least one in your itinerary. Where once there were clear distinctions between bars and eating establishments (usually restaurants opening for lunch and dinner), the relaxation of liquor licensing laws has helped to create a new kind of establishment – a cross between a cafe, bar, bistro and brasserie. The defining feature is informality. Some are daytime haunts, serving excellent coffee and snacks, others offer full three-course meals. Most offer everything from early-morning breakfasts to after-dinner drinks. Many places are run by food enthusiasts, and some places, particularly in the cities, are **showcases for the latest in contemporary design**. Well-established formal restaurants sometimes add on a cafe-style section giving patrons a chance to taste the food of some of Australia's best chefs, without having to pay restaurant prices.

■ Generally, the bigger the city the better and the wider the choice. In most cities cafes can be found along the fringes of the CBD. **Well-known cafe strips** include Sydney's Oxford Street in Paddington and Victoria Street, Darlinghurst; Melbourne's Brunswick Street in Fitzroy and Fitzroy Street in St Kilda; Adelaide's Rundle Street; and Salamanca Place in Hobart. Country areas have also benefited from the trend towards the informal and the flexible, particularly wine-growing regions and areas near the major cities like the Great Ocean Road in Victoria and the Blue Mountains in New South Wales.

Ethnic Restaurants

■ Australia has **a variety of ethnic restaurants** ranging from informal to some of the most sophisticated eateries and many Australians are quite knowledgeable about the characteristics of the various cuisines. The dishes of China, Thailand, Japan and Vietnam are particularly popular but choose almost any nation in the world and you are likely to find a good restaurant specializing in its cuisine in the cities.

Pubs

■ Most **pubs** sell food though quality varies tremendously. Some have **"counter meals"**, where the meal is eaten in (or on) the main bar, others have separate dining areas. Pubs are often the best places to try **barbecued food**, apart from private homes. Some allow you to cook the food yourself on a large central grill, others ask you to choose your raw ingredients from a selection on display and then cook it for you. There is likely to be a **salad bar** to choose your accompaniments from, and around A$20 per head is a typical price.

Bring Your Own (BYO)

■ A Bring Your Own (known as BYO) alcohol policy is common among Australia's moderate and budget-priced restaurants. You take what you would like to drink to the restaurant, thereby saving the cost of the restaurant's mark-up, and the staff will serve it for you, usually charging a **"corkage fee"**. Some venues restrict the system to wine, others allow you to bring beer and other alcohol as well.

Australian Food

■ Australian chefs tend to feel uncomfortable when critics and guides attempt to label the type of food they produce unless the restaurant specializes in a particular cuisine. This is not preciousness, simply a reflection of the Australians' natural egalitarian approach: it's just food, after all, and why not have a menu that includes a plate of risotto or gnocchi alongside Southeast Asian noodles, a Lebanese mezze platter and gourmet hamburgers? This is a typically innovative **"Modern Australian"** menu. There may well be authentic Italian, Thai or Japanese dishes on the menu but the chef will often combine seemingly disparate ingredients from such countries on the same plate. The only rule that seems to apply to Australian cooking is that **if it tastes good, do it**.

■ Increasingly, Australian chefs and home cooks are incorporating **native bush ingredients** into their dishes, primarily indigenous herbs and spices and **popular meats such as kangaroo, emu and crocodile**. On the menus of most contemporary establishments you will see at least one bush food product, perhaps lemon myrtle used in a sauce for fish or chicken, or a dessert featuring wattleseed (acacia).

■ There are a few restaurants that **specialize in bush food** and a visit to one of these is a must, even if you only feel brave enough to try the local seafood or some macadamia nut ice cream.

Meal Times

■ Lunch is traditionally served from 12pm to 3pm, and dinner from 6pm to 9:30pm; however, in keeping with the relaxed lifestyle, **the majority of Australia's informal eating places are open all day**, seven days a week. Breakfast is also a key time for eating out, especially in the cities. A variety of delicious pancakes, fritters, toast, pastries, muffins, fruit and home-made cereals is typical, as well as traditional eggs and bacon. **Leisurely brunches are popular at weekends**, particularly near the water, so make the time for at least one good morning meal during your trip.

RESTAURANT PRICES
Prices per person for a meal, excluding drinks, tax and tip:
$ under A$20   **$$** A$20–A$30   **$$$** over A$30

Shopping

Whether you like browsing at local markets, luxurious department stores or trendy boutiques, you will find there are many satisfying ways to spend money in Australia, and when the exchange rate is favourable, even relatively high-priced items can seem like a bargain. The trick is to buy Australian-, Oriental- or Southeast Asian-made products; goods made in Europe or America – particularly high fashion – are often more expensive in Australia than elsewhere.

Arts and Crafts

- Australians are very patriotic and there is a flourishing industry for **contemporary Australiana**: cartoons depicting native animals, landmarks or beach life are printed on a seemingly endless supply of souvenirs. Ken Done's paintings and drawings have for many years led the market in this area, while landscape photographer Ken Duncan's stunning images are used on postcards, calendars and stationery.

- **Aboriginal art** is uniquely Australian and is available everywhere. You can buy original works from specialist city galleries and, in country areas, local community galleries. Ask for a certificate of authenticity. There are also a variety of designs available as souvenir goods, but be aware some souvenirs may exploit designs that are sacred to Aboriginal people.

- Lovers of **jewellery** will enjoy the extensive availability of **opals** – Australia produces nearly all the world's stock – South Sea pearls and diamonds. Duty-free shops are some of the best places to buy opal pieces as the variety tends to be good and overseas visitors receive the tax discount.

Clothes

- Australia is also the leader in **surfwear** and **accessories** with prestigious brands such as Billabong, Mambo, Quiksilver and Hot Tuna prized the world over. **Genuine Outback clothing** commands premium prices in Europe and America and, while it is cheaper in Australia, you may be a little disappointed that it is not much more so. The quality and durability of items such as Driza-Bone coats, Akubra hats, moleskin trousers, and RM Williams shirts, coats and boots are very high, and are priced accordingly.

Wine and Food

- **Australian wine** is known internationally for its excellent value for money and prices are even lower in Australia. This is an ideal opportunity to buy brands and vintages not often seen outside the country, as well as a chance to investigate Australia's expertise in producing **sweet and fortified wines**. Right behind the development of Australian wine is the market for **local foods**, including seafood, cheeses, olive products and meats.

Chain Stores

- When time for shopping is limited, be aware that **Australia has some excellent chain stores** that offer a good selection of all the above products, and many more. In the cities look for David Jones and Myer, both of which are competitively priced and offer good customer service.

Shopping Hours

- Shopping hours are generally from 9am to 5:30 or 6pm, with late-night shopping on Thursdays or Fridays until 9pm. In isolated rural areas shops may close at 1pm on Saturdays. **In the major cities and towns, some supermarkets are open 24 hours**, particularly in the run-up to holidays such as Easter and Christmas. The week between Christmas and New Year and the first few weeks of January are the best time for sales.

GST and Tourist Refund Scheme

■ The **Tourist Refund Scheme (TRS)** allows you to claim a refund on the Goods and Services Tax (10 per cent) and Wine Equalization Tax (14.5 per cent) that you pay on goods purchased in Australia. **The refund is paid on goods with a total minimum value of A$300**, bought from the same store no more than 30 days prior to departure. To claim a refund, you must **get a tax invoice** from the store where you bought the goods.

■ Contact **Customs** for further details ☎ (02) 6275 6666 or (1300) 363 263 when dialling from inside Australia; www.customs.gov.au

Entertainment

Australians love their "great outdoors" so much that even cultural and artistic activities – concerts, film, theatre, opera and so on – are frequently held in parks or at the beach. At festival and school holiday times, the entertainment may even be provided free.

Festivals and Shows

■ Many Australians are flamboyant and love **carnivals** and **festival parades**. Melbourne's **Moomba Waterfest** is Australia's largest outdoor event and includes internationally acclaimed outdoor performances, fireworks and a "river spectacular"; Sydney's **Gay and Lesbian Mardi Gras** is the largest event of its type in the world, running throughout February and culminating with a spectacular parade along Oxford Street. Other areas are so remote and facilities so few that to lift the monotony locals have come to specialize in wacky events; Alice Springs' **Henley-on-Todd Regatta**, where bottomless boats race along a dry river bed, is a good example, as is the area's annual carnival of camel racing, or Darwin's **Beer Can Regatta**.

■ **Agricultural shows** are key events in each region, and an excellent excuse to indulge in carnival rides, sideshows and games. Sydney's annual **Royal Easter Show** is one of the country's largest family events, attracting around a million people. The **wine regions** also like to have annual festivals to showcase their products, often enlisting the help of local restaurants and food producers to turn the event into a gourmet's delight. Others go a step further and organize music concerts or art exhibitions each year.

Daytime Activities

■ Daytime entertainment naturally focuses on enjoying the climate and countryside. Most cities have areas for **scenic walks** such as botanic gardens, national parks, river or coastal foreshore walks and wildlife parks; even gentle bushwalking is available in central locations. Most visitor information centres provide brochures and advice, or will put you in touch with local National Parks offices (► 19).

■ Alternatively, **harbour and river cruises** are widely available at the main foreshores and are a relaxing way to spend an hour or so. Dedicated operators will give a commentary, and snacks, meals or live entertainment are usually provided on board. If simply enjoying the sun and water is your priority, a cheaper alternative is to **take a round trip on a public transport ferry**. Visitor information centres and ticket booths based at the waterfronts are the best sources of specific details regarding sailing times, routes and prices.

Sporting Events

■ The summer, particularly December and January, is a key time for **international sporting events** such as cricket and tennis, while the winter months are dominated by Australian Rules, Rugby League and Rugby Union. There are so many events that tickets are rarely sold out in advance except for finals and a day at a sports ground is extremely enjoyable, even if you are not a great fan of the game involved. The catering facilities are good, and it provides an opportunity to meet the locals. **Horse-racing** is another popular day out in Australia and the major tracks offer extensive catering and other leisure facilities. Major racing carnivals are held in spring and autumn.

Films, Concerts and Plays

■ Famous for its sporting prowess, Australia has also produced **internationally renowned** opera singers, ballet dancers, actors and musicians.

■ **Australia's film industry** in particular is burgeoning and a few hours at the cinema is an inexpensive way to enjoy the country's cultural life.

■ There is a wide range of **theatre companies** offering excellent programmes from Shakespeare and popular musicals to contemporary experimental drama and unique indigenous works.

Eating Out

■ One of the most popular forms of entertainment is to **dine out, particularly alfresco**. Venues tend to combine eating and drinking and the distinctions between restaurants, bars, pubs and cafes have all but disintegrated. This is in part due to the licensing laws that discourage consumption of alcohol without food in many venues; Victoria's regulations have historically been different and so in Melbourne, for example, venues where you can drink without eating are more widely available.

■ Throughout Australia, **bars** tend to be associated specifically with the business or disco scenes; the increasing choice of trendy pubs is a more welcoming alternative and they often include live music late at night.

Casinos

■ **Most capital cities and many resorts have casinos**, which can be an exciting way to spend the evening if you have spent the day lying on the beach. Venues range from intimate and elegant to spectacular grandeur; despite the surface glamour, dress regulations rarely apply.

■ Along with international games such as **blackjack and roulette**, you will be able to play Australia's traditional favourite, **two-up**.

Making Reservations

■ The best events are extremely popular and likely to sell out in advance, so it is wise to consult a **major ticket-booking agency** as early as possible.

■ The key national agencies are Ticketek (☎ 13 28 49 within Australia; **http://premier.ticketek.com.au**) and Ticketmaster (☎ 13 61 00 within Australia; **www.ticketmaster.com.au**). These agencies will be able to advise on availability of theatre, concert and sporting events throughout the country and make your bookings for you.

ADMISSION CHARGES
The cost of admission for museums and other attractions mentioned in this guide is indicated by the following symbols:
Inexpensive under A$12   **Moderate** A$12–A$26   **Expensive** over A$26

Sydney

Getting Your Bearings

Exuberant and vital, Sydney is Australia's largest, oldest and best-known city. Set on the shores of a magnificent natural harbour and fringed by long golden beaches, Sydney basks under a mostly sunny, mild climate and beckons residents and visitors alike to an outdoor lifestyle.

Although its pace is faster than that of any other Australian city, by world standards Sydney is a relaxed metropolis whose inhabitants enjoy an enviably good life. Superb shopping, world-class museums, galleries, entertainment and excellent cuisine are as much a part of the Sydney experience as picnics and walks in its foreshore parks, swimming at its surf beaches and sailing or cruising around its harbour. Long known as the setting for two of Australia's most potent icons – the Opera House and the Harbour Bridge – Sydney firmly established its arrival on the world stage when it was chosen as the host for the 2000 Olympic Games. And though a modern and multicultural city, it hasn't forgotten its humble convict origins, which are most readily evoked in the historic Rocks area, just as its urge for imaginative reinvention is most vibrantly expressed in ultra-modern Darling Harbour, a former industrial and shipping centre turned entertainment, dining and shopping complex.

Previous page: The roof of Sydney Opera House

Below: A yacht passes Sydney Opera House

★ Don't Miss

At Your Leisure

In Three Days

If you're not quite sure where to begin your travels, this itinerary recommends a practical and enjoyable three days in Sydney, taking in some of the best places to see using the Getting Your Bearings map on the previous page. For more information see the main entries.

Day 1

Morning

Start the day at the **2 Sydney Opera House** (➤ 52–54) – Australia's most easily recognized building – and enjoy harbour views and fresh ocean breezes as you stroll around its distinctive exterior before taking a tour of the performance spaces. Then make your way past the cafes, restaurants and shops of the Opera Quays colonnades to Circular Quay (pictured left), with its lively mix of commuting crowds, sightseers and street musicians.

Catch a ferry for the 30-minute ride to the popular beachside suburb of Manly – one of the best ways to experience the spectacular beauty of **1 Sydney Harbour** (➤ 48–51). After arriving at Manly Wharf, take a stroll along The Corso – Manly's main pedestrian mall – and enjoy a quintessential Sydney experience: tucking into fish and chips (french fries) at Manly Fish Market and Cafe (➤ 66) on a bench overlooking Manly Beach.

Afternoon

Return to Circular Quay aboard the faster JetCat then stroll back around the covered walkway to Sydney Cove Oyster Bar (➤ 67), the perfect place to sip wine or beer outdoors as you drink in the harbour views and watch the comings and goings of ferries and other vessels.

Day 2

Morning

Spend the morning exploring
3 The Rocks (➤ 55–57) –
the heart of historic Sydney
and a tourist mecca. Sit
down to lunch at one of the
string of restaurants housed
in converted storehouses at
Campbells Cove.

Afternoon

Work off the meal (for obvious
reasons, alcohol free) with
a climb to the top of the
1 Harbour Bridge (left, ➤ 50)
or, for the less adventurous, a
walk across it. If you choose
the latter option, you can take a
ferry or train from Milsons Point
back to the city. Finish the day
with a meal at Rockpool (fish) (➤ 66) just a short stroll from the Opera
House, if you want to take in a performance.

Day 3

Devote the day to exploring **4 Darling Harbour** (below, ➤ 58–60), home
to three of Sydney's best attractions, the Sydney Aquarium, the National
Maritime Museum and the Powerhouse Museum, as well as a variety of
shops, cafes and restaurants. Stop for lunch at Cockle Bay Wharf (➤ 60),
then at day's end sample more of Sydney's fine cuisine at one of the many
cafes or restaurants in Darlinghurst, Potts Point or Kings Cross – the latter
renowned as the lively but somewhat seedy centre of Sydney nightlife.

❶ Sydney Harbour and Sydney Harbour Bridge

Sydney's reputation as one of the world's most beautiful cities owes much to the body of water that sweeps through its centre. Both major port and glittering playground, Port Jackson, as the harbour is officially known, is the city's focal point and its greatest asset.

Early recognition of Sydney's maritime potential came in 1770 when explorer James Cook (1728–79) sailed past in the *Endeavour* and noted "a bay or harbour in which there appeared to be good anchorage". Eighteen years later, on 26 January 1788, a fleet of British ships carrying convicts and officials entered what Governor Arthur Phillip described as the "finest harbour in the world" and landed in Sydney Cove, where the settlement of Sydney was founded. Although the Sydney Harbour of today is vastly different from that which greeted the occupants of the First Fleet, it has lost none of its ability to charm and excite.

With a shoreline stretching for 317km (197 miles), it encompasses sandstone headlands, quiet bays, inlets, sandy

An aerial view over Sydney

beaches, islands and waterside parks, offering an abundance of outdoor activities ranging from sailing, cruising and fishing to swimming, picnicking and walking.

On a sunny day there is no more uplifting sight than that of the harbour's cobalt waters dotted with ferries, yachts, cruisers, ocean liners and other vessels, while at night its still-busy waters take on a mysterious, more atmospheric beauty.

World-famous Landmarks

Tamarama is a suburb of Sydney

Presiding over all the activity, and an integral part of the harbour scene, are two of Australia's best-known landmarks: the **Sydney Opera House** (► 52–54) and the Sydney Harbour Bridge. Though you can enjoy excellent harbour views from both these structures, there really is only one way for the first-time visitor to fully appreciate the harbour's many delights: from the water. There are dozens of tour operators offering a variety of harbour trips, most departing from Circular Quay and Darling Harbour. You don't have to spend much to enjoy one of the best harbour trips going – the public ferry to Manly. This 30-minute ride takes you through the main reach of the harbour from Circular Quay, past the dramatic entrance guarded by North and South heads, to the beach suburb of Manly.

Leisure Activities

While busy throughout the week, the harbour really comes to life at weekends when hundreds of pleasure-craft ply the waters. It's also the venue for **boat race classics** such as the start of the Sydney to Hobart Yacht Race on Boxing Day (26 December) and the Ferrython and Tall Ships races in January. If you're visiting on a Sunday during spring or summer, you'll have the opportunity to watch the most spectacular of the harbour's racing yachts – the speedy and colourful 18-footers. Of course, you can view all these events from the shore, but it's much more fun to join a spectator ferry leaving from Double Bay (18-footers) or Circular Quay (others).

Harbourside walks are another great way to enjoy the water views and scenic foreshore and some of the best lie within Sydney Harbour National Park. Incorporating sections of the foreshore as well as five islands, the 393ha (970-acre) park features Aboriginal rock art, historic ports and gun emplacements, headlands with superb harbour or ocean views and secluded beaches. Most outstanding of the park's walks is the **Manly Scenic Walkway**, a 9.5km (6-mile; 3- or 4-hour) track from Manly Wharf to The Spit Bridge offering Aboriginal rock carvings, native coastal heath and pockets of subtropical rainforest. Easier on the legs and providing a memorable panorama is **North Head**, where three lookouts are connected by a short walking track. To get there, take bus No

135 from Manly Wharf. Most interesting of the islands is tiny **Fort Denison**. Once used as a penitentiary for convicts kept on minimum rations – hence its early nickname "Pinchgut" – it was fortified in the 1850s amid fears of foreign invasion and today you can take tours of the restored buildings.

The pick of the harbour's **sheltered beaches** also lie within the National Park's boundaries. Family-orientated Nielsen Park, in the eastern suburbs, has a clean beach, shaded lawns, pockets of bushland, an excellent kiosk and a protective shark net during the summer. If you want to cool down, it offers an alternative to the pounding surf of Sydney's ocean beaches.

The Bridge

For one of Sydney's peak experiences, however, you must visit the Harbour Bridge – opened in 1932 as the primary link between the south and north shores. Known to locals as "**The Coathanger**", this huge steel structure has impressive dimensions: its main span is 503m (1,650ft) long, the crown of the arch is 135m (443 feet) above sea level and the weight of steel in the arch span is 39,006 tonnes. The deck is 49m (160ft) wide, with eight road lanes, two railway tracks, a bicycle way and a footpath. The two granite-faced pylons

A view through the Harbour Bridge, framing Sydney Opera House

SYDNEY HARBOUR: INSIDE INFO

Top tips Vaucluse Point, at the eastern end of Nielsen Park, is **the perfect place to enjoy a picnic** as you watch the sun sink in a blaze of colour behind the city.
■ For a different perspective of the harbour, **climb the bridge at night** when the city lights are reflected in the water, transforming the view.

Hidden gem For an insight into Australia's immigration history, take a guided tour of the old **Q Station** (at North Head, tel: 1300 886 875; www.q-station.com.au) in Sydney Harbour National Park, which from 1832 to 1984 protected Sydney residents from the impacts of epidemic diseases. The **night-time paranormal tours** are especially atmospheric.

on either side of the main span are purely decorative: the arch itself rests on four giant steel pins at ground level.

By far the best and most exhilarating way to experience the bridge is with **BridgeClimb**. You don't need any special skills, just a sense of adventure and a pair of rubber-soled shoes. Clad in a grey "bridge suit" – intended to avoid distracting drivers below – and harness-linked to a static line, you'll be escorted in groups of 12 over the catwalk to the southeast pylon and then across the arch to the summit, which offers breathtaking, **360-degree views**.

The next best thing to climbing the bridge is to walk across it. Entrance to the walkway is via Cumberland Street in The Rocks or Milsons Point Station. The southeast pylon houses an exhibit on how the bridge was built; the 200-step climb to the top is worth it for the views.

TAKING A BREAK

For great fish and chips go to the Manly Fish Market and Café (➤ 66).

People on bridge tour

Sydney Harbour and Sydney Harbour Bridge
➕ 217 C5

Australian Travel Specialists (for private cruises and other tours)
✉ Opposite Wharf 6, Circular Quay ☎ (02) 9247 5151 🕐 Daily 8:30–6:30
✉ Shop 191 Harbourside, Darling Harbour ☎ (02) 9211 3192 or (1800) 355 537; www.atstravel.com.au 🕐 Daily 9–8 💲 Expensive

Sydney Ferries Information Centre
➕ 217 B4 ✉ Opposite Wharf 4, Circular Quay ☎ 13 15 00 (State Transit InfoLine); www.sydneyferries.info 🕐 Mon–Sat 7–6, Sun 8–6 💲 Ferry rides: inexpensive; ferry cruises: moderate

Sydney Harbour National Park Information Centre
➕ 217 B5 ✉ Cadmans Cottage, 110 George Street, The Rocks ☎ (02) 9247 5033; www.environment.nsw.gov.au 🕐 Mon–Fri 9:30–4:30, Sat–Sun 10–4:30; closed Good Fri, 25 Dec 🚉 Circular Quay 🚌 Sydney Explorer to Circular Quay, 431, 432, 433 🚢 Circular Quay 💲 Park: free; guided tours to Fort Denison: moderate

BridgeClimb
➕ 217 B5 ✉ 3 Cumberland Street, The Rocks ☎ (02) 8274 7777; www.bridgeclimb.com 🕐 Climbs (frequent intervals) last for 3.5 hours. Times vary; phone BridgeClimb for current times. Closed 30 Dec to mid-morning 1 Jan 🚉 Circular Quay 🚌 Sydney Explorer to Circular Quay, 431, 432, 433 🚢 Circular Quay 💲 Expensive

Pylon Lookout, Sydney Harbour Bridge
➕ 217 B5 ☎ (02) 9240 1100; www.pylonlookout.com.au 🕐 Daily 10–5; closed 25 Dec 💲 Walkway: free; Pylon Lookout: inexpensive 🚉 Circular Quay (southern side) 🚌 Sydney Explorer 🚉 Milsons Point (northern side) 🚢 Circular Quay

2 Sydney Opera House

With its gleaming sail-like roofs and magnificent harbourside position, the Sydney Opera House is an ethereal beauty and one of the world's most distinctive and unusual buildings. Its revolutionary design has long inspired controversy.

Today the building that sceptical Sydneysiders once nicknamed "The Hunchback of Bennelong Point" and "a pack of French nuns playing football" is hailed as an **architectural masterpiece** – it was added to the UNESCO World Heritage list in 2007. Beneath its "billowing sails" lies a complex of theatres and performance halls that stage everything from opera, dance, plays and concerts to films and rock concerts. To attend a performance here is a memorable experience.

Although now **one of the world's busiest performing arts centres**, the Opera House endured a long and difficult birth. Political scandal and technical problems dogged its construction, which began in 1959 after Danish architect

A stunning dusk view of the Opera House

Joern Utzon won an international design competition for the building. The scheduled opening date was set for Australia Day 1963 and to finance the project, which was estimated to cost A$7 million, the New South Wales Government began a public lottery. Then tragedy struck. The publicity surrounding the awarding of the first major lottery prize of £100,000 led to the kidnapping of the winner's eight-year-old son, Graeme Thorne, who was held to ransom and subsequently killed. Over the next few years Utzon's relationship with the constructing authority deteriorated and he resigned from the project in 1966. He never returned to Australia to see his building, which was completed in 1973 at a final cost of A$102 million and opened by Queen Elizabeth II in that same year.

The Exterior

There are many ways to experience the Opera House. The building's best feature is its exterior: simply strolling around the **outdoor terraces** is enough to savour its unique beauty and position, the breezy harbour views enlivened by a passing parade of yachts, ferries and ocean liners. It'll also give you a chance to get a close-up look at some of the 1,056,000 ceramic tiles that cover the "sails". On Sundays the forecourt erupts with colour and activity as the setting for a **market** selling quality Australian arts and crafts. One of the best places to sit and take it all in is the **Monumental Steps**, which rise in a grand sweep to the upper terraces. At night the

building is spotlit and a more magical setting for intermission drinks during evening shows is hard to imagine as the dark harbour waters glint with reflected city lights. The best views are to be had from the **northern foyers** (lobbies) of the Opera and Concert halls, and even if you're not able to take in a performance, you can still enjoy a drink with a view at one of the foyer (lobby) bars, which open one hour prior to performances and close after the last interval.

The Interior

Although not as spectacular as the building's exterior, the interior is still worth visiting and two guided tours are available. The hour-long **"Essential Tour"** includes the foyers (lobbies) and theatres and departs regularly throughout the day, while the early morning two-hour **"Backstage Tour"** takes you behind the scenes. The tours are led by expert guides, who provide interesting information about the building's history and architecture.

If you do want to see a show, be aware that popular operas, plays and musical performances sell out very quickly, despite the high prices, and the chances of getting a ticket are slender – though "restricted view" tickets for the opera are often available at a reduced price. For more relaxed entertainment, attend a performance in **The Studio**, an intimate contemporary venue that offers cabaret, comedy, music and innovative theatre.

If you've no particular preference for the type of performance you'd like to see, aim for the **Concert Hall** – the largest and most impressive of the venues.

On a tour of the interior

TAKING A BREAK

For a snack, drink or meal in the Modern Australian mode, plus great harbour views try the **Opera Bar** (➤ 66) on the Lower Concourse.

✚ 217 C5 ✉ Bennelong Point ☎ Tours and Performance Packages: (a variety of tour, performance and dining): (02) 9250 7250. Box office: (02) 9250 7777; www.sydneyoperahouse.com ⏰ Tours: daily backstage tour 7am; tour of the house daily 9–5; performances: most days; closed Good Fri, 25 Dec 💲 Essential tour: expensive; backstage tour: expensive; performances: moderate–expensive 🍴 Five restaurants and cafes ($–$$$) 🚇 Circular Quay 🚌 Sydney Explorer, any Circular Quay-bound bus ⛴ Circular Quay

3 The Rocks

The Rocks is Sydney's most historic and intriguing area, where the convicts and officers of the First Fleet established in 1788 what was then the farthest outpost of the British Empire. Named for the rocky outcrops that were once its dominant feature, The Rocks is a small collection of streets nestling beneath the southern end of the Harbour Bridge on the western side of Sydney Cove.

Today this **delightful tourist hub** full of converted warehouses, fine colonial buildings, cobbled streets, cafes, restaurants, shops and galleries is a world away from the squalor and overcrowding that characterized the site's early years. While it is the place in Sydney to find quality Australiana ranging from Akubra hats to Driza-Bone coats and opals, it also has its fair share of predictable souvenir merchandise. Its chief delight, however, lies in strolling the **picturesque streets and walkways**.

Background

In colonial times, The Rocks was a seamy neighbourhood inhabited by seamen, traders, prostitutes and criminals, and full of pubs, brothels and lodging houses. As the density of dwellings increased in the second half of the 19th century, the slum conditions worsened and by the 1880s and 1890s the area had become the notorious haunt of the "pushes" – gangs who mugged passers-by. The area's decline was hastened by **A sea-borne** bubonic plague in 1900, which resulted in the razing of entire **view of** streets. More demolition followed in the 1920s and early **Campbells** 1960s with the building of the Harbour Bridge and Cahill **Cove Historical** Expressway. But now the restored and renovated Rocks is **one District** **of Sydney's top attractions**.

A sea-borne view of Campbells Cove Historical District

Explore the City

The best place to start your visit is the **Sydney Visitor Centre**, located in The Rocks Centre at the corner of Argyle and Playfair streets. This information and booking agency offers many useful publications on Sydney and New South Wales, including a self-guiding Rocks tour brochure and map that will allow you to set off on a voyage of discovery of this historic area. Your next stop should be nearby Kendall Lane to visit **The Rocks Discovery Museum** (open 10–5 daily, free entry), housed in a restored 1850s sandstone warehouse and presenting the area's history.

From here head north along George Street to Hickson Road, stopping at the gallery of flamboyant Sydney artist Ken Done (in the historic Australasian Steam Navigation Co Building, 1884), and then continue down the Customs Officers Stairs to **Campbells Cove**. Here you will find a row of beautifully restored 19th-century sandstone storehouses, now housing fine restaurants.

Follow the boardwalk around to Dawes Point Park and make your way up the path beneath the bridge to George Street, site of a **lively weekend market** pitched at the tourist dollar, but still a good place to find quality Australian craftwork, unusual jewellery and antiques.

Historic streets

Continue along Gloucester Walk, and follow the map to **Susannah Place Museum** – an 1840s terrace (row house)-turned-museum offering a rare glimpse into the everyday lives of its occupants over 150 years – or take a shortcut down the steps to Argyle Street and the impressive **Argyle Cut**. Begun by convicts using only hand tools in 1843 and completed by paid labourers in 1859, the passage slices through solid stone to Millers Point, The Rocks' other, more residential, half.

Down the hill is the **Argyle Stores archway**, which leads to a cobbled courtyard and a complex of stylish shops and studios housed in a group of former warehouses. Return to the Visitor Centre building and head into Playfair Street and **The Rocks Square**, forming the main pedestrian area and with yet more stylish shops and eateries, as well as colourful street life. If you're in need of refreshment, wait until you reach nearby **Greenway Lane**, which leads to a delightful "inner sanctum" of cafes and courtyards. From here you can stroll down narrow Suez Canal, reputed to have been a

favourite haunt of the "pushes", into Nurses Walk, another
intriguing walkway. On rejoining George Street, cross the
road to look at **Cadmans Cottage** (1816) – one of the oldest
surviving buildings in Australia and now a Sydney Harbour
National Park information centre. By now, you'll no doubt be
ready for lunch so retrace your steps to Campbells Cove and
choose one of the restaurants you passed by earlier.

**Top left: The
Rocks area**

**A lively cafe in
The Rocks**

TAKING A BREAK

La Renaissance (27 Argyle Street, The Rocks) is a delightful
indoor and outdoor cafe offering a taste of France in Sydney.
It is renowned for its éclairs, croissants, brioches and other
treats.

The Rocks ⊞ 217 B5

Sydney Visitor Centre
⊞ 217 B5 ⊠ Corner of Argyle
and Playfair Streets ☎ (02)
9240 8788 or (1800) 067 676;
www.sydneyvisitorcentre.com.
au also www.therocks.com
⊙ Daily 9:30–5:30; closed
Good Fri, 25 Dec 🏷 Free
🍴 La Renaissance ($–$$)
🚇 Circular Quay 🚌 Sydney
Explorer, Nos 339, 343, 431,
432, 433 ⛴ Circular Quay

Susannah Place Museum
⊞ 217 B5 ⊠ 58–64
Gloucester Street ☎ (02)
9241 1893; www.hht.nsw.gov.
au ⊙ Mon–Fri 2–6, Sat–Sun
10–6; closed Good Fri, 25 Dec
🏷 Inexpensive

4 Darling Harbour

Its reputation may not precede it – like those two icons of Sydney tourism, the Harbour Bridge and the Opera House – but Darling Harbour has in recent times secured its place as one of the city's premier attractions.

Built around the calm waters of Cockle Bay, near the city centre, Darling Harbour offers two of the best, and most original, museums in the country as well as an aquarium, entertainment areas, gardens, parks, restaurants and cafes, a shopping centre and a convention and exhibition centre. Throughout the day and well into the night the complex pulses with people, live entertainment, buskers (street musicians) and various harbourside and water displays – though such festivity was not always the case.

Background
Cockle Bay was, at the beginning of the 20th century, a busy industrial centre and international shipping terminal. The advent of container shipping spelled the end of its commercial viability and for years the site lay idle, falling into ruin. Then in 1988, after a major facelift, Darling Harbour was opened. Although it failed to attract the thousands of tourists envisaged in the initial plan, the complex today has achieved its potential, boosted into prominence during the 2000 Olympics when it became the biggest Olympic site outside the main Games Stadium, at Homebush, in west Sydney.

Maritime Heritage
The 54ha (135-acre) site includes the large **Harbourside shopping centre** (good for souvenir shopping), and two star attractions just a short walk away – the Australian National Maritime Museum and innovative Sydney Aquarium.

Fountains at Darling Harbour

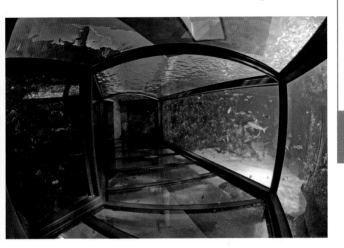

An insight into life under the sea at the Sydney Aquarium

Located at the western end of the historic Pyrmont Bridge, the **Australian National Maritime Museum** and nearby **Maritime Heritage Centre** explore Australia's relationship with the sea. It has a hands-on approach to maritime history and outside, moored at the docks, are various vessels including the replica of James Cook's HM *Bark Endeavour*, the submarine HMAS *Onslow* and an authentic warship, the destroyer, HMAS *Vampire*, which you can board to see how the crew lived.

Life in the Sea and on Land

At the eastern end of the Pyrmont Bridge is the **Sydney Aquarium**. It features more than 11,000 animals representing more than 650 species in a series of recreated marine environments. The highlight here is a "walk on the ocean floor", passing beneath two floating oceanaria with 140m (153 yards) of perspex underwater tunnels. From here, you can see schools of tropical fish, stingrays and the ever-popular sharks.

A visit to the neighbouring **Sydney Wildlife World** (open daily 9am–10pm; www.sydneywildlifeworld.com.au), featuring over 130 species of Australian creatures, including koalas, wallabies, reptiles and butterflies, is also worthwhile.

Surrounding the Bay

A short walk north of here brings you to **King Street Wharf**, a lively waterfront dining and entertainment complex, or you can head south to **Cockle Bay Wharf**, another happening place in which to eat quality food alfresco, while enjoying superb views of Darling Harbour.

A stroll around the end of the bay will bring you to the **LG IMAX Theatre** (www.imax.com.au), which serves up stunning documentaries on an eight-storey-high cinema screen. At night, you can sit on the steps in front of the building and enjoy the colourful spectacle of film and laser images projected on to giant waterscreens moored in the bay.

Just 10 minutes' walk from Darling Harbour proper is the fascinating **Powerhouse Museum**. A monumental structure, it explores almost every aspect of human creativity – with an emphasis on Australian innovation and achievement – from science and technology to social history, space exploration, decorative arts and design. The approach is hands-on with more than 250 interactive displays designed to entertain and educate. Don't miss the Boulton and Watt steam engine, the world's oldest surviving rotative engine, and the **Kings Cinema**, where you can watch silent films and early classics.

TAKING A BREAK

For some of Sydney's best Malaysian cuisine head for **Chinta Ria** at Darling Harbour's Cockle Bay Wharf.

🕇 217 A2

Sydney Visitor Centre, Darling Harbour
✉ 33 Wheat Road ☎ (02) 9240 8788 or 1800 067 676; www.sydneyvisitorcentre.com
🕐 Daily 9:30–5:30; closed Good Fri, 25 Dec
🖐 Free 🚇 Town Hall 🚌 Sydney Explorer
🚝 Monorail to Convention 🚢 Darling Harbour

Australian National Maritime Museum
🕇 217 A3 ✉ 2 Murray Street, Darling Harbour
☎ (02) 9298 3777; www.anmm.gov.au 🕐 Daily 9:30–5 (9:30–6 in Jan); closed 25 Dec 🖐 Free general admission; moderate–expensive for ships depending on number visited 🚇 Town Hall 🚌 Sydney Explorer, No 443 🚝 Light rail to Pyrmont Bay, monorail to Harbourside 🚢 Pyrmont Bay

Sydney Aquarium
🕇 217 A3 ✉ Aquarium Pier, Darling Harbour
☎ 13 33 86; www.sydneyaquarium.myfun.com.au 🕐 9am–10pm (last admission at 9)

🖐 Expensive 🚇 Town Hall 🚌 Sydney Explorer 🚝 Monorail to Darling Park 🚢 Darling Harbour

Cockle Bay Wharf
🕇 217 A2 🍴 Cafes, bars and restaurants ($–$$$)

Chinese Garden of Friendship
🕇 217 A2 ✉ Darling Harbour ☎ (02) 9240 8888; www.chinesegarden.com.au 🕐 Daily 9:30–5:30; closed Good Fri and 25 Dec
🖐 Inexpensive 🚇 Town Hall 🚌 Sydney Explorer 🚝 Light rail to Paddy's Markets, monorail to Chinatown 🚢 Darling Harbour

Powerhouse Museum
🕇 217 A1 ✉ 500 Harris Street, Ultimo
☎ (02) 9217 0111; www.powerhousemuseum.com 🕐 Daily 10–5; closed 25 Dec
🖐 Inexpensive 🚇 Town Hall or Central 🚌 Sydney Explorer 🚝 Light rail or monorail to Paddy's Markets 🚢 Darling Harbour

---

DARLING HARBOUR: INSIDE INFO

Top tips The easiest way to reach, and get around, the Darling Harbour area is the **Monorail**. There are two city centre stations on Pitt Street (near the Pitt Street Mall), and a further six stations surrounding Darling Harbour and Chinatown. Another option is the Metro Light Rail from Central Station. For details of both, see www.monorail.com.au

■ If you intend to visit Sydney Aquarium, Sydney Wildlife World and Sydney Tower, the **Sydney Attractions Pass** offers good value. Available from all three places, the pass represents a saving of over 15 per cent.

Hidden gem The **Chinese Garden of Friendship** is a tranquil haven where you can stop for a while and rest your feet. A bicentennial gift from Guangdong Province, the garden features lotus ponds, pavilions, waterfalls, winding pathways, beautiful trees and shrubs, and a tea house serving traditional Chinese tea and cakes. Near by is Sydney's colourful Chinatown precinct.

At Your Leisure

5 Taronga Zoo

The best place in Sydney to meet native Australian wildlife and view a large collection of exotic animals in near-natural enclosures is Taronga Zoo, which has a superb harbourside setting. For a stunning introductory overview, arrive by ferry and take the cable-car up the zoo's steep hill to the top entrance. Highlights include having your photograph taken with koalas, the Free Flight Bird Show, the entertaining seal shows and elephants in the Wild Asia exhibit.

🚆 217 off B5 ✉ Bradleys Head Road, Mosman ☎ (02) 9969 2777; www.zoo.nsw.gov.au ⏰ Daily 9–5 🚌 No 247 ⛴ Taronga Zoo Wharf 💰 Expensive ℹ A ZooPass, available from Circular Quay, includes a return ferry, cable-car or bus ride to the top entrance and zoo admission

6 Royal Botanic Gardens

A green haven in the heart of the city, the Royal Botanic Gardens occupy a superb harbourside position next to the Opera House and contain an outstanding collection of plants from Australia and overseas. Highlights include the Tropical Centre, with its striking glasshouses containing tropical ecosystems in miniature form, the Herb Garden and the Palm Grove, established in 1862 and today one

Giraffes feeding at Taronga Zoo, with the Opera House behind

of the world's finest collections of outdoor palm species. A stroll along the waterfront path offers one of the prettiest perspectives of the gardens, which are also historically significant, being the site of the fledgling colony's first farm – a visit to the display garden relating to this time is well worthwhile.

🚆 217 C4 ✉ Mrs Macquaries Road ☎ (02) 9231 8111; weekends: (02) 9231 8125; www.rbgsyd.nsw.gov.au ⏰ Gardens: daily 7–dusk. Tropical Centre: daily 10–4; closed Good Fri, 25 Dec 🚇 Circular Quay/Martin Place 🚌 Sydney Explorer ⛴ Circular Quay 💰 Gardens: free; Tropical Centre: inexpensive

The Royal Botanic Gardens

Sculpture in the grounds of the Art Gallery of New South Wales

7 Art Gallery of New South Wales

Housing some of the best art in Australia, the Art Gallery of New South Wales has superb collections of Australian, European, Asian and contemporary work as well as extensive holdings of photography, drawings, watercolours, artists' prints and sculptures. The cornerstone of the collection, however, is the Australian section, featuring works from the time of European settlement to the present day and including well-loved icons such as Tom Roberts' *The Golden Fleece – Shearing at Newstead* (1894). Another compelling exhibition is the Yiribana Gallery, which contains the country's most extensive permanent display of Aboriginal and Torres Strait Islander art. The artworks here range from traditional bark paintings and painted poles to the watercolours of Albert Namatjira and striking contemporary works by famous Aboriginal artists such as Emily Kame Kngwarreye.

🚹 217 C3 ✉ Art Gallery Road, The Domain ☎ (02) 9225 1744 or (02) 9225 1790 (recorded information line); www.artgallery.nsw.gov.au ⏰ Thu–Tue 10–5, Wed 10–9; closed Good Fri, 25 Dec 🚆 St James/Martin Place 🚌 Sydney Explorer, No 441 💲 Free (charges for some special exhibitions)

8 Sydney Tower

For a breathtaking, 360-degree view of Sydney, take a trip up the 304.8m (1,000ft) Sydney Tower, Australia's tallest building. The best time to visit is at sunset, though the glittering night-time panorama is spectacular too. On clear days you can see as far west as the Blue Mountains, 70km (44 miles) away. Admission includes a visit to the Observation Deck as well as the OzTrek virtual ride around Australia's landmarks. The tower also offers revolving restaurants and the Skywalk experience (www.skywalk.com.au), which takes the fearless on to a high open-air platform.

🚹 217 B3 ✉ 100 Market Street ☎ (02) 9333 9222; www.sydneytower.com.au ⏰ Daily 9am–10:30pm; closed 25 Dec 🚆 St James 🚌 Any Circular Quay-bound bus 💲 Moderate (Skywalk expensive)

Head to the top of Sydney Tower for panoramic views

9 Australian Museum

One of the world's top natural history museums, the Australian Museum features all the specimens and artefacts you'd expect to find in such a venerable institution along with interactive displays for kids.

Not to be missed are the Indigenous Australians and Dinosaurs exhibits. A quirky highlight of the Skeletons display is a human skeleton pedalling a bicycle, and you don't have to be a geologist to enjoy the Albert Chapman Mineral Collection, renowned worldwide for its diversity and crystal perfection.

➕ 217 C2 ✉ 6 College Street ☎ (02) 9320 6000; www.austmus.gov.au ⏰ Daily 9:30–5; closed 25 Dec 🚇 Museum/St James 🚌 Sydney Explorer, Nos 311, 324, 325, 327, 389 💲 Inexpensive

10 Paddington

This district of Victorian-era terraced houses, with their decorative wrought iron, straddles the eastern suburb thoroughfare of Oxford Street. This road is lined with speciality shops selling fashion, homewares, books and gifts. There are numerous excellent cafes and restaurants, and arthouse cinemas. The Saturday Paddington Markets (open 10–4) is one of Sydney's best.

➕ 217 off A2 ✉ Paddington ☎ www.paddingtonmarkets.com.au ⏰ Market: Sat 10–4 🚌 378, 380, 382 💲 Free; bus inexpensive

Bondi, Sydney's famous beach, which teems with people in summer. There are cafes and shops in the area

FIVE GREAT SYDNEY BEACHES
- Nielsen Park for sheltered harbour swimming and picnics
- Bronte for family-orientated fun and unpretentious cafes
- Tamarama for social cachet
- Bondi for the crowds, sand, surf and trendy cafes and restaurants
- Manly for its exuberant atmosphere and excellent fish and chips

11 Bondi

Famous for its surf life-savers and its boomerang stretch of golden sand, Bondi is hallowed ground to Australians and tourists alike. It is not, however, the best place to go for a quiet swim or sunbathing session. Although the beach is an egalitarian affair, shared by families, backpackers, "body beautifuls" and surfers, it does get overcrowded in summer. Bondi's other attractions include Campbell Parade's cosmopolitan cafes, restaurants, pubs and shops, the Marine Discovery Centre in the Pavilion, Sunday markets and a golf course. For a seaside experience without tourist hype, visit nearby Bronte, a family-orientated beach with great cafes and a shady park. You can walk to Bronte in 20 to 30 minutes along a clifftop track from the southern end of Bondi Beach.

➕ 217 off C1 ✉ Bondi Beach ☎ Bondi Pavilion: (02) 8362 3400; www.bondivillage.com ⏰ 24 hours daily 🚇 Bondi Junction, then bus Nos 380, 382 🚌 Bondi Explorer, Nos 333, 380, 389 💲 Free

Where to... Stay

Prices
Prices are for the least expensive double room in high season:
$ under A$150 $$ A$150–A$280 $$$ over A$280

Aarons Hotel $

This offers incredible value in the heart of the dining and entertainment district, with a restaurant, guest laundry and 24-hour reception with a tour desk. It is handy for Chinatown and Darling Harbour, plus rail and bus public transport.

➕ 217 B1 ⊠ 37 Ultimo Road, Sydney ☎ (02) 9281 555; www.aaronshotel.com.au

Bondi Beach House $–$$$

Just 100m (110 yards) from famous Bondi beach, this is a good-value accommodation option. There are single and double rooms with shared bathrooms, and three suites, which have their own facilities. The elegantly decorated guesthouse also has fully equipped kitchens and a large sun deck with barbecues.

➕ Off map ⊠ 28 Sir Thomas Mitchell Road, Bondi Beach ☎ (02) 9300 0369; www.bondibeachhouse.com.au

Cambridge Hotel $$

This friendly hotel, just a short walk from trendy Oxford Street and the CBD, represents good value for money. There is a pool and spa and high-speed WiFi is available. Its restaurant, Cafe 212, serves breakfast and dinner daily.

➕ 217 C1 ⊠ 212 Riley Street, Surry Hills ☎ (02) 9212 1111; www.cambridgehotel.com.au

Four Points by Sheraton $$–$$$

This is Australia's largest hotel, with 630 rooms and suites, most with balconies and harbour views. Decorated in stylish, modern tones, the hotel is convenient for Sydney's shopping, tourist attractions and nightlife. It also has all the other facilities you'd expect in a major international hotel.

➕ 217 A3 ⊠ 161 Sussex Street, Darling Harbour ☎ (02) 9290 4000; www.fourpoints.com/sydney

Harbourside Apartments $$–$$$

Just a seven-minute ferry ride from Circular Quay, McMahons Point on the lower north shore has outstanding views. The Harbourside Apartments are right near the water and make a tremendous home away from home for those interested in self-catering accommodation. Studios, one-bedroom and two-bedroom apartments are available, all fully serviced and very comfortable. There is also a restaurant on site.

➕ 217 off B5 ⊠ 2A Henry Lawson Avenue, McMahons Point ☎ (02) 9963 4300; www.harboursideapartments.com.au

Park Hyatt Sydney $$$

The hotel is in probably the best location in Sydney, opposite the Opera House. It is worth staying here for the location alone, but this is also one of the city's most luxurious hotels, with state-of-the-art facilities including high-speed internet access, marble baths, 24-hour butler service, a rooftop pool, a spa and fitness centre.

➕ 217 B5 ⊠ 7 Hickson Road, The Rocks ☎ (02) 9241 1234; www.sydney.park.hyatt.com

Shangri-La Hotel $$$

This modern hotel, housed in a city high-rise, is elegantly

Where to...
Eat and Drink

Prices
Prices per person for a meal, excluding drinks, tax and tip:
$ under A$20 $$ A$20–A$30 $$$ over A$30

Bayswater Brasserie $$–$$$

This long-running restaurant is one of the best options in the Kings Cross nightlife area. Serving Modern Australian food, and with a groovy bar, the always-buzzing Bayswater Brasserie offers a good range of vegetarian, meat and seafood dishes at reasonable prices – as well as some tempting desserts.

217 off C2 ☒ 32 Bayswater Road, Kings Cross ☎ (02) 9357 2171; www.bayswaterbrasserie.com.au
🕓 Fri 12–3, daily 6pm–10

bills $–$$

A favourite Sydney spot for relaxed brunching and lunching, the airy bills cafe, one of Bill Granger's eateries, features a large communal pine table piled with newspapers and style magazines to browse through while you sip a cappuccino or latte. The blackboard menu features light contemporary dishes such as fritters, salads and chunky cakes – ricotta pancakes with banana and honeycomb butter is the house speciality. You'll want to return, but more importantly, you won't want to leave. The same great food is also available at "bills 2" ($$–$$$), an offshoot in nearby Surry Hills.

217 off C2 ☒ 433 Liverpool Street, Darlinghurst ☎ (02) 9360 9631; www.bills.com.au 🕓 Mon–Sat 7:30am–3, Sun 8:30–3 Ⓟ Also: bills Surry Hills ☒ 359 Crown Street, Surry Hills ☎ (02) 9360 4762 🕓 Daily 7am–10pm

Golden Century $–$$$

The endless surge and bustle of this 600-seat Chinese seafood restaurant is reminiscent of Hong Kong. Live fish, crabs and lobsters can be selected from tanks for cooking Cantonese style. The menu also offers steamed, paper-thin abalone and scallops in garlic sauce. Residents of Chinatown drop in for an evening dish of Chinese rice porridge.

217 B2 ☒ 393 Sussex Street ☎ (02) 9212 3901; www.goldencentury.com.au 🕓 Daily noon–4am

Kingsleys Steak & Crabhouse $$–$$$

In a great location on a beautifully renovated old wharf near Kings

furnished, has superb facilities, and some of the best uninterrupted harbour views in Sydney. The Blu Horizon Bar on the top floor offers such a fantastic view that as well as the hotel's own guests, Sydneysiders and people from other hotels come here for cocktails. More superb views can be had from the hotel's Altitude restaurant. Guests have access to the hotel's spa and health club and shops.

217 B4 ☒ 176 Cumberland Street, The Rocks ☎ (02) 9250 6000; www.shangri-la.com/sydney/

Vulcan Hotel $–$$

This heritage-listed former pub was refurbished in the late 1990s to provide quality accommodation at an affordable price. Within easy walking distance of Darling Harbour and central shopping areas, the Vulcan has a garden cafe, leafy courtyard with barbecue and a friendly atmosphere.

217 A1 ☒ 500 Wattle Street, Ultimo ☎ (02) 9211 3283; www.vulcanhotel.com.au

Cross, this is one of the best places to sample great steak. The menu offers more than 20 steak options, and oyster, prawn, crab, fish and lamb dishes are also available. Kingsley's boasts a very good wine list (particularly reds), a bar area and outdoor harbourside seating.

217 off C2 ✉ **6 Cowper Wharf Road, Woolloomooloo** ☎ **(1300) 546 475; www.kingsleys.com.au** ⏱ **Daily 12–10**

The Malaya $$

This excellent Malaysian restaurant, located in the Darling Harbour area and with great water views, is particularly famous for its delicious laksas (spicy vegetable, chicken or seafood soup with rice noodles). For more than 40 years, however, The Malaya has also served up fine curries, Chinese, Indonesian and Singaporean dishes. The extensive menu includes set meals.

217 A3 ✉ **39 Lime Street, King Street Wharf** ☎ **(02) 9279 1170; www.themalaya.com.au** ⏱ **Mon–Sat 12–2:30, Sun 6–8:30, Mon 6–9, Tue–Sat 6–10**

Manly Fish Market and Cafe $–$$

Manly is famous for its fish and chips, and this cafe is one of the best. Dine in, or get a take-out from the fish market next door and enjoy your meal on the beach.

217 off B5 ✉ **25 South Steyne, Manly** ☎ **(02) 9976 3777; www.manlyfishmarketandcafe.com.au** ⏱ **Daily 12–9**

Opera Bar $$

If your dining fantasy is to sit with a cold drink by the Opera House watching boats float down the harbour, Opera Bar is for you. Tables are by the water and look out over the Harbour Bridge and Circular Quay. Go for coffee or a full meal. Mediterranean and Asian touches feature alongside steak and seafood. On a sunny day the easy-going attitude, live entertainment and locale are hard to beat.

217 C5 ✉ **Lower Concourse, Sydney Opera House, Bennelong Point** ☎ **(02) 9247 1666; www.operabar.com.au** ⏱ **Daily 11:30–late**

Rockpool $$–$$$

Charismatic owner Neil Perry is one of Australia's most high-profile chefs, renowned for his innovative fusion cooking, using only the best produce. Diners here are offered a four-course meal that includes a wide choice of signature seafood delicacies. Alternatively, the eight-course grand tasting menu (with wines to match) can be ordered if you've booked for a whole table of diners.

217 B4 ✉ **107 George Street, The Rocks** ☎ **(02) 9252 1888; www.rockpool.com** ⏱ **Tue–Sun from 6pm**

Sailors Thai and Sailors Thai Canteen $–$$$

Conveniently situated in The Rocks, Sailors Thai derives its name from its location in the atmospheric old Sailors' Home built in 1864. Choose to eat in the ground-floor canteen for a casual meal of such dishes as squid salad with chilli and lime dressing, and crisp and salty pork belly, or, for privacy and

a charming view, head to one of the rear balcony seats. Downstairs is a formal restaurant where you can feast on exquisite dishes rarely seen even in Thailand.

217 B5 ✉ **106 George Street, The Rocks** ☎ **(02) 9251 2466; www.sailorsthai.com.au** ⏱ **Canteen: Mon–Sat 12–10; restaurant: Mon–Fri 12–2:30, Mon–Sat 6–10**

Sean's Panaroma $$–$$$

A few steps away from the fast food outlets on Campbell Parade, but still within sight and sound of famous Bondi Beach, is this casual restaurant with a regularly changing Modern Australian menu, that might include dishes such as seared South Australian scallops, Barossa chicken paté or braised snapper fillet. There are also delicious pasta dishes and satisfying desserts. The wine list is succinct and edgy with BYO permitted.

217 off C1 ✉ **270 Campbell Parade, Bondi Beach** ☎ **(02) 9365 4924; www.seanspanaroma.com.au** ⏱ **Fri–Sun lunch from noon, Wed–Sat dinner from 6**

The Summit $$–$$$

Sydney's famous revolving restaurant offers extraordinary 360-degree views of the cityscape. Sleek, retro-style decor complements a Modern Australian menu (the signature dish is twice-cooked pork belly), with cocktails and an extensive wine list, accompanied by a tinkling piano to complete the setting. This is a truly unique venue for a leisurely lunch, cocktails and a snack in the Orbit Lounge, or a memorable evening among the stars and city lights.

🚹 217 B4 ⊠ Level 47, Australia Square, 264 George Street ☎ (02) 9247 9777; www.summitrestaurant.com.au ☺ Mon–Fri 12–3, daily from 6pm

Sydney Cove Oyster Bar $$–$$$

This waterside venue is situated on the foreshore of Sydney Cove and most of the tables are outside, offering fabulous views of the Harbour Bridge and the Opera House. The tiny kitchen specializes in quality seafood such as fresh Sydney rock oysters and a mouth-watering selection of prawns, crab, lobster and fish, plus cheeses and salads. They are open for traditional breakfasts, and offer a wide range of teas, juices and coffee. Champagne breakfasts start at 10am.

🚹 217 C4 ⊠ 1 East Circular Quay ☎ (02) 9247 2937; www.sydneycoveoysterbar.com ☺ Daily 8am–late

Tetsuya's $$$

The unique cuisine is based on a combination of Japanese and French food cooked to perfection. The set-price 10-course degustation menu, which typically includes the finest beef and seafood you are likely to eat, might include confit of Petuna ocean trout, or wagyu beef with lime and wasabi. The service is the epitome of professionalism and, although a visit here is a special occasion, feel free to dress casually. Booking is essential.

🚹 217 B2 ⊠ 529 Kent Street ☎ (02) 9267 2900; www.tetsuyas.com ☺ Lunch Sat from 12, dinner Tue–Sat from 6

Where to... Shop

PITT STREET MALL

The city centre's main shopping district is centred on Pitt Street Mall. It contains several large shopping centres, the Myer department store, boutiques and the historic Strand Arcade. This beautifully refurbished building is worth visiting for its architecture and decor as much as for the stylish speciality shops.

GEORGE STREET

George Street is home to the vast Queen Victoria Building, a magnificent 1890s sandstone building with five levels of shops, boutiques and cafes. Nearby is the gigantic Dymocks bookshop (No 424), good for books about Australia and, across the road, R M Williams (No 389), a good retailer of quality country and Outback clothing.

THE ROCKS

On George Street, towards the harbour, is The Rocks, an excellent source of Australian and Aboriginal contemporary arts and crafts, costume and precious jewellery and art, in original form, as prints and art, and splashed across mugs and T-shirts.

On the walk from Queen Victoria Building to The Rocks you will also find a concentration of duty-free stores and, at the weekend, The Rocks outdoor market offers homewares, antiques, gifts, and arts and crafts.

Where to...
Be Entertained

CINEMAS

A small **art-house cineplex** is located in the Opera Quays building near the Opera House, but most of the city's cinemas are in George Street. Sydney has two summertime outdoor cinemas, one harbourside in the Royal Botanic Gardens, the other in Centennial Park in the eastern suburbs.

CONCERTS AND THEATRE

Sydney's **Opera House** is a working performance venue. For information and bookings call the box office (tel: (02) 9250 7777). The companies that perform there include the Sydney Symphony Orchestra, Opera Australia, the Australian Ballet and the Sydney

Dance Company. Outdoor arts events include Shakespeare by the Sea, Symphony in the Park and Opera in the Domain. The **Wharf Theatre** (tel: (02) 9250 1777) is home to the Sydney Theatre Company, which also stages plays at the Opera House's Drama Theatre.

CASINOS AND NIGHTCLUBS

Star City entertainment complex and casino in Pyrmont (tel: (02) 9777 9000; www.starcity.com.au) offers evening entertainment including stage and cabaret acts. Several large hotels have nightclubs.

FESTIVALS

January is devoted to the **Sydney Festival**, with free events and

OXFORD STREET AREA

Street fashion and trendy household goods are best sourced on Paddington's Oxford Street. This popular area offers stylish brand names such as **Scanlan & Theodore**, **Morrissey** and **Collette Dinnigan**, as well as **Akira** and **Lisa Ho** (both in nearby Woollahra) and **Country Road**. On Saturdays there is also the hip **Paddington Market**, for clothes, jewellery and interior decor items.

BARGAIN SHOPPING

For quality discount shopping, take the ferry from Circular Quay to **Birkenhead Point** shopping centre. This complex offers clothing and accessory brands. **Paddy's Markets** in Haymarket lures bargain hunters; the discounted sheepskins and crafts are interesting. Food lovers should head to Pyrmont to visit the **Sydney Fish Market**, the country's largest, open daily from 7am.

Australia Day activities. Darling Harbour stages arts events, including a jazz festival in June. The Writer's Festival is in May and the famous **Gay and Lesbian Mardi Gras** runs from February to March.

SPORT

Sydney hosts regular sporting events. Cricket and Australian Rules football are played at **Sydney Cricket Ground** (SCG), at Moore Park. Rugby League matches are held at **Aussie Stadium**, near SCG, and at **Telstra Stadium**, Homebush Bay. The main racecourses are **Royal Randwick** (tel: (02) 9663 8400) and **Rosehill Gardens** (tel: (02) 9930 4000).

The Sydney Morning Herald and *The Daily Telegraph* are key sources information; also useful is the free *What's On In Sydney*, available widely; and http://sydney.citysearch.com.au

New South Wales and Canberra

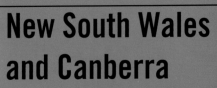

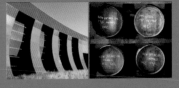

Getting Your Bearings

Claimed for Great Britain and named by explorer
James Cook (1728–79) in 1770, New South Wales is
Australia's premier State in every sense. Site of the
first European settlement, it is today the most
populous State in Australia and home
to Sydney, the country's largest and
most vibrant city.

While this historic and beautiful State
capital is especially popular with
holidaymakers, the rest of New
South Wales offers a huge variety
of landscapes and experiences.
You can swim at sweeping
surf beaches, explore the
Outback's far horizons, tour
the scenic high country
of New England, or try
winter skiing or summer
bushwalking in the
continent's highest
land – the Snowy
Mountains.

You don't have to
go to extreme lengths
or faraway places to
experience some of the
State's best attractions.
Just two hours' drive
north of Sydney lies the
Hunter Valley, cradle of the
Australian wine industry
and a bastion of fine food
and good hospitality, while
west of the city lie the Blue
Mountains, whose deep forested
gorges, escarpments and plunging
waterfalls have cast a spell on visitors
since colonial times.

The focal point of the State's south is
the Australian Capital Territory, created
early in the 20th century to become the
site of the new national capital, Canberra.

Gulgong

Wellington

Lake
Burrendong

Macquarie

32

90 Molong

Parkes

Orange

Forbes

32

Canowindra

24

24

Lake
Wyangala

Cowra

41

Temora

81

Young

Croo

94

Lachlan

Cootamundra

Goulburn

41

31

23

20

Yass

Lake
Georg

Tumut

Canberra

Queanbeya

18

ACT

Nat

Namadgi
National
Park

Cabramurra

Tantangara
Res

Kosciuszko
National Park

Lake
Eucumbene

23

Snowy
Mountains

Cooma

2228

Wadbilliga
National Park

Mount
Kosciuszko

Nimmitabel

18

Snowy

Bega

Bombala

South East Forests
National Park

Ede

Genoa

Divid

Great

Page 60: Hawkesbury River in New South Wales

**Opposite: Garema Place in Canberra's Central
Business District (CBD)**

Walcha

Apsley

15

34

Tamworth

37

MacDonald

Werrikimbe
National Park

Hastings

34

Quirindi

Wauchope

15

Taree

Scone

Barrington Tops
National Park

Gloucester

Tuncurry

84

Forster

Muswellbrook

Wallis
Lake

Wollemi
National
Park

Singleton

Myall Lakes
National Park

15

Hunter

**Hunter
Valley** 3

Maitland

Yengo
National
Park

Cessnock

Newcastle

Dharug
National
Park

Lake
Macquarie

Blue
Mountains

Gosford

Toukley

Windsor

**Hawkesbury River
(Riverboat)** 9

Norman Lindsay
Gallery & Museum

gra Boyd
ial Park

SYDNEY

Botany Bay

ake
urragorang

50 km

0

30 miles

Wollongong

Shellharbour

48

Berry

Nowra

Ulladulla

ans Bay

★ Don't Miss

1 Canberra ➤ 74
2 Blue Mountains ➤ 77
3 Hunter Valley ➤ 80

At Your Leisure

4 Questacon – The National
   Science and Technology
   Centre ➤ 82
5 Australian Institute of Sport
   (AIS) ➤ 82
6 Yarralumla Diplomatic
   Estate Tour ➤ 82
7 Jenolan Caves ➤ 82
8 Norman Lindsay Gallery
   & Museum ➤ 83
9 Hawkesbury River, Riverboat
   Postman cruise ➤ 83

In Four Days

If you're not quite sure where to begin your travels, this itinerary
recommends a practical and enjoyable four days exploring
New South Wales and Canberra, taking in some of the best places
to see using the Getting Your Bearings map on the previous page.
For more information see the main entries.

Day 1

Set out early from Sydney for the 70–120km (43–75-mile) drive along
the Western Motorway (M4) to the **2 Blue Mountains** (➤ 77–79), an area
renowned for its spectacular scenery of precipitous cliffs rising from
densely forested valleys. Spend the morning exploring some of the
region's prettiest villages, taking in the views and breathing the eucalyptus-
scented air at panoramic lookouts, and enjoying rides on the Scenic
Skyway, Scenic Railway or Scenic cableway. For lunch, try Katoomba's
(above) Paragon Restaurant (➤ 86). Return to Sydney via the scenic Bells
Line of Road, stopping on the way to meander through the Mount Tomah
Botanic Garden.

Day 2

Take a 45-minute flight to **1 Canberra** (High Court, top right, ➤ 74–76), at
the foot of the Great Dividing Range, and pick up a rental car at the airport
for a leisurely two-day tour of Australia's verdant "bush capital". Visit the
most outstanding of its national museums, galleries and institutions and
sample its cafes and restaurants. Finish the day with a meal in Manuka,
where you'll find an abundance of excellent eateries.

Day 3

Morning

Begin the day with a drive to Black Mountain Tower, atop Black Mountain, for a magnificent 360-degree view of the city and surrounds. Then descend to the lower slopes for a wander through the Australian National Botanic Gardens, where you can experience the great diversity, colour and often spectacular beauty of Australia's native plants.

Afternoon

After lunch at one of Canberra's many restaurants, spend the afternoon at the Australian War Memorial, a national icon of remembrance and one of the world's great war museums, before flying back to Sydney.

Day 4

Spend a peaceful day exploring the **3 Hunter Valley** (➤ 80–81), one of Australia's premier wine-growing districts (below), just a two-hour drive from Sydney along the Pacific Highway and the F3 Freeway. Enjoy the scenic, rolling hill country of the valley's central Polkobin area as you tour the region, tasting its signature Shiraz and Semillon as well as other varieties at the cellar doors. At lunchtime, sample gourmet fare at one of its best restaurants, perhaps Terroir restaurant on Broke Road.

Canberra

Often described as a city scattered through a park, Canberra is spacious, gracious and abundantly green. A planned city unlike any other in Australia, the nation's capital combines grandeur with liveability.

Canberra's imposing modern architecture, monuments, broad avenues and leafy suburbs are set amid a pleasant environment of gardens and swathes of native bushland that merge seamlessly with the surrounding hills, mountains and valleys. That said, it does have a staid atmosphere and a reputation as the province of politicians and public servants.

Unlike Australia's other cities, most of which developed from convict origins in the 18th and 19th centuries, Canberra is relatively young – less than a century old. It wasn't until 1901 that unification of the colonies – or Federation – occurred and then the search began for a national capital. In 1908 a site was chosen – roughly midway between arch rivals Sydney and Melbourne, which were both vying for the honour.

The view of Canberra from the National Museum of Australia's outdoor area

A New City
The Commonwealth Government took possession of the 2,358sq km (920 square-mile) district in 1911, the same

year that an international competition was launched to design the new city. It was won by American architect Walter Burley Griffin (1876–1937), whose brilliant design called for a parliamentary triangle of sweeping avenues in which major national buildings would be built around the glittering centrepiece of an artificial lake. Radial roads extending from this central area would connect with suburban centres.

To appreciate the imagination of his design, and for an excellent orientation of the city's major features, start at the National Capital Exhibition, on the northern shore of Lake Burley Griffin. When you've got your bearings, cross the Commonwealth Avenue Bridge to the A\$1.1 billion **Parliament House**, opened in 1988 and renowned for its impressive modern architecture. Highlights include watching parliament in session from the public gallery, the view from the grassed-over roof, the lobby with its 48 marble-clad pillars designed to be evocative of a eucalyptus forest and the Great Hall, which houses one of the largest tapestries in the world. You're free to roam the public areas, but the guided tour is recommended.

National Museums

By way of contrast visit the **Old Parliament House**, at the foot of Capital Hill. Built in 1927 as the provisional home for Australia's Federal Government, it was used for an astounding 61 years. Now the **Museum of Australian Democracy**, this is where you can learn about the nation's democratic history. From here, it's a short walk or drive to the **National Gallery of Australia**, which contains more than 100,000 works of art. Not to be missed are its core collection of Australian art, the Aboriginal Memorial on the entrance level, American artist Jackson Pollock's *Blue Poles* and the sculpture garden.

The nearby **National Museum of Australia**, built to celebrate the centenary in 2001 of Federation, employs a fresh approach to Australian history, culture and the environment, blending exhibits, technology, interactive media, live performances and hands-on activities. Here you'll find the personal stories of ordinary and extraordinary Australians alongside symbols of the nation such as adventurer Francis Birtles' car, given to the Federal Government in 1929 after his epic England–Australia drive. Highlights include the world's largest collection of bark paintings and a huge three-dimensional map of Australia displaying the language group boundaries of Aboriginals and Torres Straight Islanders, exploration routes and population demographics – and how these have all changed over time.

The courtyard at the National Museum of Australia

Complete your tour of the museums with the unforgettable experience of a visit to the **Australian War Memorial**, which commemorates the sacrifice of Australian

---

CANBERRA: INSIDE INFO

Top tips Driving in Canberra can be challenging owing to its unique layout of **concentric circular streets**. It's worth having a good look at a map before you set off. There is, however, generally plenty of parking at the main sights.

■ If you are in Canberra on a Sunday, don't miss the **Old Bus Depot Markets** (Wentworth Avenue, Kingston; www.obdm.com.au). Open from 10 to 4, this multi-award winning attraction offers quality crafts and foodstuffs and a tempting international food court.

---

people who have served in war. As well as a moving memorial, this is one of the world's great war museums, it houses a massive collection of weapons, vehicles, uniforms, medals, rare battlefield relics, photographs, letters and works of art by some of Australia's most notable painters.

Views and Gardens

For a panoramic view of the city and surrounds, head up to the 195m (640ft) **Black Mountain Tower**, then descend to the lower slopes for a wander through the **Australian National Botanic Gardens**. Its array of more than 6,000 species represents about one-third of all known Australian flowering plants, conifers and ferns, making it the largest collection of native flora in the country.

TAKING A BREAK

Overlooking a picturesque courtyard in Old Parliament House, **Café in the House** (➤ 85) serves tasty modern international food in an elegant setting.

Canberra 🚹 215 E3

Canberra and Region Visitors Centre
🚹 216 off B6 ✉ 330 Northbourne Avenue, Dickson ☎ (02) 6205 0044 or (1300) 554 114; www.visitcanberra.com.au 🕐 Mon–Fri 9–5, Sat–Sun 9–4; closed 25 Dec

Parliament House
🚹 216 B4 ✉ Capital Hill ☎ (02) 6277 5399; www.aph.gov.au 🕐 Daily 9–5; closed 25 Dec 🎟 Free. Guided 20- or 45-min tours 🚌 31, 34, 39

Museum of Australian Democracy
🚹 216 B4 ✉ King George Terrace, Parkes ☎ (02) 6270 8222; www.moadoph.gov.au 🕐 Daily 9–5; closed 25 Dec 🎟 Inexpensive 🚌 31, 34, 36, 39

Black Mountain Tower
🚹 216 A6 ✉ Black Mountain Drive, Acton ☎ (02) 6219 6111 and (1800) 806 718 🕐 Daily 9am–10pm 🎟 Inexpensive

National Gallery of Australia
🚹 216 C5 ✉ Parkes Place, Parkes ☎ (02) 6240 6411; www.nga.gov.au 🕐 Daily 10–5; closed 25 Dec 🎟 Free (charge for exhibitions) 🚌 30, 34

National Museum of Australia
🚹 216 B5 ✉ Acton Peninsula ☎ (02) 6208 5000; www.nma.gov.au 🕐 Daily 9–5; closed 25 Dec 🎟 Free (not exhibitions) 🚌 34

Australian National Botanic Gardens
🚹 216 A6 ✉ Clunies Ross Street, Acton ☎ (02) 6250 9450; www.anbg.gov.au/anbg/ 🕐 Jan Mon–Fri 8:30–6, Sat–Sun 8:30–8; Feb–Dec daily 8:30–5; closed 25 Dec 🎟 Free 🚌 No 34 to University (then 10-min walk) No 81 on weekends

Australian War Memorial
🚹 216 A6 ✉ Treloar Crescent, Campbell ☎ (02) 6243 4211; www.awm.gov.au 🕐 Daily 10–5; closed 25 Dec 🎟 Free (donation) 🚌 Nos 33 and 40

② Blue Mountains

Idyllic and serene, breathtaking and spectacular, the Blue Mountains inspire superlatives. Encompassing the raw beauty of sandstone cliffs and forested gorges, as well as the cultured elegance of the historic towns and villages that dot its ridges, the Blue Mountains have long been a favourite retreat.

The Three Sisters rock formation in the Blue Mountains

A playground for outdoor enthusiasts, with bushwalking, birding, rock climbing, horseback riding and mountain biking among the most popular activities, the region is also renowned for its **scenic drives**. While its highlights can easily be enjoyed in a full-day trip, there are any number of luxury resorts, grand old-style hotels and charming B&Bs to tempt those with time to linger.

Named for the **distinctive blue haze** that hangs over the valleys – caused by scattered rays of light coming in contact with fine dust particles and droplets of oil dispersed from the eucalyptus trees – the World Heritage-listed Blue Mountains are in fact not mountains at all, but a dissected, sandstone plateau.

Background

To early settlers, this spur of the Great Dividing Range presented a seemingly impenetrable barrier to the fertile pasture land beyond. It was not until 1813, when explorers Blaxland, Wentworth and Lawson made their historic crossing over the divide, that Australia's agricultural potential was realized, though the plateau itself remained an untapped resource for another 50 years. Then, with the building of a railway line, Sydney's fashionable set discovered the region as a resort, building elegant homes and hotels to escape the stifling summer heat on the coast. Nowadays, the mountains are just two hours from the city by road or rail, with travellers following much the same route as the pioneering explorers of old.

Tour the Area

On reaching the mountains proper, make your first stop the Visitor Information Centre at Glenbrook, where you'll find useful maps and brochures, and no doubt notice the crisper character of the air. From Glenbrook the route passes through pleasant scenery and a string of towns of varying degrees of leafy charm to **Wentworth Falls**, where the region's major attractions begin to emerge. A small, peaceful village with a big, old pub – The Grand View – Wentworth Falls is worth a stop for a view of the falls after which it is named. Plunging 300m (985ft) to the valley floor, the falls are best viewed from above, at Falls Reserve, just beyond the township, which is also the starting point for several walks.

Sylvia Falls in the Valley of the Waters, Blue Mountains National Park

Leura, 6km (4 miles) to the west, is perhaps the prettiest of the Blue Mountains' 26 towns and villages, and is filled with cafes, craft shops and historic homes and gardens that recall the elegance of life in the 1920s. From here, you can follow the signposted, 8km (5-mile) **Cliff Drive**, a famously scenic route. The road runs along the edge of the escarpment to Katoomba, the mountains' largest town, and offers stunning views over the Jamison and Megalong valleys. Be sure to stop at the intersection with Echo Point Road, a short walk from the **Echo Point Lookout** and an unforgettable view of the mountains' most recognizable landmark, the **Three Sisters rock formation**.

BLUE MOUNTAINS: INSIDE INFO

Top tips The best time to take a ride on any of **Scenic World's** attractions is before 11am or after 2pm; during the middle part of the day coaches arrive from Sydney and the queues can be long.
- The **Three Sisters are floodlit at night**, with spectacular effect, and are well worth an evening visit if you stay overnight.

Hidden gem The picturesque village of Mount Wilson, 8km (5 miles) north of Bells Line of Road, is famous for its **superb gardens**, many of which are open for inspection during spring and autumn, and the Cathedral of Ferns, a stretch of road flanked by rainforest thick with tree ferns. "Withycombe", a gracious house here, was once the summer residence of the family of Nobel-prize-winning author, Patrick White.

More Attractions

Just around the corner from Echo Point is **Scenic World**, comprising the Scenic Skyway, Scenic Railway and Scenic Cableway. The **Skyway** is a cable-car that runs 270m (886ft) above the valley floor, offering startling bird's-eye views. The **Scenic Railway**, built in 1879 to service a coal mine in the Jamison Valley, is said to be the world's steepest incline railway, descending 415m (1,360ft) at a maximum gradient of 52 degrees. The aerial tramway, the **Scenic Cableway**, drops steeply over the edge of a 100m (330ft) cliff, travelling 545m (1,788ft) to the valley floor.

After these thrills, head into **Katoomba** for lunch. Although some of the town's Victorian charm has been lost to overt tourism, aspects of its former gracious self still exist, most particularly at the art deco Paragon Restaurant (➤ 86).

From Katoomba, rejoin the highway for the 10km (6-mile) drive west to the Blackheath and nearby **Govetts Leap**, with superb views and the **National Parks Heritage Centre**. From Blackheath it's a short drive to Mount Victoria. Turn right at the Mount Victoria Hotel into Darling Causeway to link up with the Bells Line of Road for the trip back to Sydney.

This alternative route takes you through a remote and peaceful part of the Blue Mountains, providing a contrast to the holiday bustle on the other side of the Grose Valley. Along the way you can visit **Mount Tomah Botanic Garden**, a cool-climate annexe of Sydney's Royal Botanic Gardens. Beyond Mount Tomah, the thick forests give way to a landscape of gentle rolling foothills dotted with small farms, providing a suitably scenic end to your tour of the mountains.

TAKING A BREAK

Blackheath's **Victory Theatre** (tel: (02) 4787 6002) has both an antiques centre and an excellent cafe.

✚ 215 E3

Information Centres

✉ Great Western Highway, Glenbrook; Echo Point, Katoomba ☎ (1300) 653 408; www.visitbluemountains.com.au 🕐 Glenbrook: daily 9–4:30; Echo Point: daily 9–5; both closed 25 Dec 🍴 Paragon Restaurant ($; ➤ 86) 🚉 From Sydney 💷 Free

Scenic World

✉ 1 Violet Street, Katoomba ☎ (02) 4782 2699; www.scenicworld.com.au 🕐 Daily 9–5, last rides at 4:50 🚉 From Sydney 💷 Moderate–expensive depending on the number of riders

National Parks Heritage Centre

✉ Govetts Leap Road, Blackheath ☎ (02) 4787 8877; www.nationalparks.nsw.gov.au 🕐 Daily 9–4:30; closed 25 Dec 🚉 From Sydney 💷 Free

Mount Tomah Botanic Garden

✉ Bells Line of Road, Mount Tomah ☎ (02) 4567 2154; www.rbgsyd.nsw.gov.au 🕐 Oct–Feb 10–5; Mar–Sep daily 10–4; closed 25 Dec 💷 Inexpensive

3 Hunter Valley

Many of Australia's best-known wines come from the Hunter Valley, the oldest commercial grape-growing area in the country. Where there is wine, there are often music, festivals, great restaurants, boutique hotels and peaceful scenery, all of which the Hunter has in abundance.

The valley is also one of the country's richest farming areas, as well as one of its most productive sources of coal. Old coal towns, many displaying a wonderful collection of heritage buildings, are as much a part of the scene as the rows of vines, paddocks of cattle, fields of grain and vegetable patches.

First Vineyard

A Scottish viticulturalist, James Busby (1801–71), is credited as the founder of the Hunter Valley wine industry, which was established largely to provide a less socially destructive alternative to the rum that had become a de facto currency of the then colony of New South Wales. In May 1824 Busby was granted 2,000 acres (809ha) of land on the Hunter River and five years later he produced red wine from the vines he planted there. By 1850 a fledgling industry was born with about 200ha (495 acres) under vines. Nowadays, the Hunter Valley is home to more than 120 wineries and wine outlets, the majority of which are in the **Pokolbin area** of the Lower Hunter, close to the town of Cessnock. At Pokolbin, the **Wine Country Visitor's Centre** is an excellent source of free maps and advice on wineries, events and other attractions.

Winery Visits

To get an idea of the full range of the Hunter's wineries aim to visit one of the modern "big company" style establishments, a more traditional family concern and one or two of the small boutique wineries, which specialize in producing

The verdant Hunter Valley

small quantities of high-quality wine. Recommendations include: **Lindemans Wines**, now more than 160 years old; **McWilliams Mount Pleasant Estate**, which produces the Elizabeth Semillon, Australia's most awarded white wine; **Tyrrell's Vineyards**, a family concern where you can walk among 100-year-old vats; **Allandale Winery**, a small operation offering premium-quality varietal wines and views to Brokenback Mountain; and **Petersons Wines**, a small family winery producing award-winning wines since 1981.

While Shiraz and Semillon are considered the Hunter's classic wines, there are many other varietals, and the **Hunter Valley Wine Society**, which offers a taste of many of the region's top wines, is well worth a visit. The society shares the same building as the Wine Country Visitors' Centre, Pokolbin.

Half the fun of wine-country touring is the way you go about it. Driving gives you a chance to explore at your own pace – though you'll have to watch your alcohol intake. However, there are also buses, horse-and-carriage rides, hot-air ballooning and even skydiving on offer. A popular option is to rent a bicycle from **Hunter Valley Cycling**.

TAKING A BREAK

Treat yourself to lunch at **Muse** at the Hungerford Hill winery on Broke Road (tel: 02 4998 7666).

🖪 215 E3

Wine Country Visitor's Centre
✉ 455 Wine Country Drive, Pokolbin
☎ (02) 4990 0900; www.winecountry.com.au 🕐 Mon–Sat 9–5:30, Sun and public holidays 9–4 (later in summer); closed 25 Dec 🎟 Free
🚌 Rover Coaches from Sydney
🚌 Maitland, then bus to Cessnock

Hunter Valley Cycling
✉ Pokolbin ☎ (0418) 281 480; www.huntervalleycycling.com.au
🕐 Daily 9–5 🎟 Expensive

Hunter Valley Wine Society
✉ 455 Wine Country Drive, Pokolbin
☎ (02) 4990 8206; 🕐 Mon–Sat 9–5, Sun and public holidays 9–4; closed 25 Dec

---

HUNTER VALLEY: INSIDE INFO

Top tips Try to **tour the wineries during the week**; the Hunter Valley is a popular weekend destination for Sydneysiders, at which time both the number of visitors and the accommodation prices increase.

■ As a rule children and wine tours don't mix, but if you have kids and need entertainment, head to **Hunter Valley Gardens** (www.hvg.com.au), in Broke Road, Pokolbin, where you'll find not only wine-tasting and dining, but entertainment such as aqua golf, picnic grounds, display gardens and children's playgrounds.

■ With four excellent courses, the Hunter Valley is also a golfer's paradise.

Hidden gem Tucked away in the scenic Mount View area, at the southern tip of Pokolbin, is the **Briar Ridge Vineyard** (on Mount View Road), a charming boutique winery producing "distinctively Hunter" wines.

■ The region's most interesting historical attraction is **Wollombi**, a picturesque village with sandstone buildings, 29km (18 miles) southwest of Cessnock.

At Your Leisure

4 Questacon – The National Science and Technology Centre

Questacon's purpose is to make science and technology fun for everyone, and this interactive display certainly delivers. Set up in 1988, the centre has seven huge galleries to explore, containing more than 200 exhibits. Here, you can experience a virtual roller coaster, a simulated earthquake and a lightning display. You can also see a tornado in action, and learn how to balance a ball in mid-air. As well as encouraging people to interact with the exhibits and involve their hands, bodies and minds, Questacon also promotes understanding with special science shows, and volunteer "explainers" on hand to answer any questions.

🔲 216 B5 ✉ King Edward Terrace, Parkes, Canberra ☎ (02) 6270 2800; www.questacon.edu.au 🕐 Daily 9–5; closed 25 Dec 🎟 Moderate 🚌 No 34

5 Australian Institute of Sport (AIS)

A passion for sport is not a pre-requisite of this tour of the AIS – the training centre for elite Australian athletes; a curious nature and a love of minor celebrity is enough. The 90-minute tour includes a trip through the gymnasium and swimming pool, sometimes when the athletes are training, and also a rare chance to see how you would measure up as an elite athlete through hands-on interactive sports technology. There are also exhibits of Australian sporting legends, including a cricket bat used by Sir Donald Bradman (1908–2001), and clothing, Olympic medals and other memorabilia belonging to stars such as athletes Cathy Freeman and Betty Cuthbert, swimmer Ian Thorpe, tennis players Rod Laver, Evonne Goolagong and Margaret Court, and basketballer Lauren Jackson.

🔲 216 off B6 ✉ Leverrier Street, Bruce, Canberra ☎ (02) 6214 1010; www.ausport. gov.au/tours 🕐 Mon–Fri 8:30–5, Sat–Sun and public holidays 10–4; closed 25 Dec. Tours: 10, 11:30, 1 and 2:30 daily 🎟 Moderate 🚌 No 80

6 Yarralumla Diplomatic Estate Tour

Some of the most surprising architecture in Canberra can be found in the suburb of Yarralumla, which is not only home to The Lodge – the official residence of the Australian prime minister – but also to more than 80 diplomatic missions. The best way to view them is to take the Yarralumla Diplomatic Estate Tour, a self-drive, clearly signposted tour shown on a special map and guide, which is available from the **Visitors' Centre**.

The United States Embassy, on Moonah Place, was built in 1943 in the tradition of American Colonialism and was the first diplomatic mission to develop a home-grown style. Since then, fellow embassies have followed the US lead and now the suburb is crowded with unique dwellings such as the Indian Embassy, with its white temple and moats, and the Papua New Guinea Embassy, which adopted a traditional Spirit House approach, complete with totem poles.

Canberra and Region Visitors' Centre
🔲 216 off B6 ✉ 330 Northbourne Avenue, Dickson ☎ (02) 6205 0044; www.visitcanberra.com.au 🕐 Mon–Fri 9–5, Sat–Sun and public holidays 9–4; closed 25 Dec

7 Jenolan Caves

Part of the Blue Mountains World Heritage Area, magical Jenolan Caves are a renowned series of limestone caverns with incredibly varied and colourful formations. Located 194km (120 miles) west of Sydney, the region was long visited by Aboriginal people before European "discovery" in the 1830s. The caves may be the world's oldest (possibly 340 million years old) and 11 are open to the public, with regular tours of various lengths and difficulty. Guided adventure caving is available, as are evening "ghost tours". The caves are also used for concerts, and the area has some great bushwalks.

If you have the time, an overnight stay at heritage-listed Jenolan Caves House is highly recommended.

🚹 215 E3 ☒ Jenolan Caves Road, Jenolan Caves ☎ (02) 6359 3911 or (1300) 763 311; www.jenolancaves.org.au ⏰ Tours: daily 9:30–5:30, generally every 30 minutes (booking advisable) 💷 Moderate–expensive, depending on number of caves visited 🚉 Katoomba, from where buses run tours to caves

8 Norman Lindsay Gallery & Museum

Painter, sculpture and author, Norman Lindsay was one of Australia's most recognized, and controversial, artists. Renowned for his voluptuous nudes and risqué novels, he was also the author of the children's classic *The Magic Pudding*. Born in 1879, Lindsay lived in his Faulconbridge mountain retreat from 1913 until his death in 1969. It was here that he produced an enormous amount of work, much of which reflects his rejection of the moral and sexual restraints of the era.

Today, his home is a gallery and museum devoted to his life and work, with exhibits of his paintings, cartoons, illustrations and sculptures.

🚹 215 E3 ☒ 14 Norman Lindsay Crescent, Faulconbridge ☎ (02) 4751 1067; www.normanlindsay.com.au ⏰ Daily 10–4; closed 25 Dec 💷 Inexpensive 🚉 Faulconbridge and Springwood

9 Hawkesbury River, Riverboat Postman cruise

Often overlooked by people visiting Sydney, the Hawkesbury River, just north of the city, is none the less remarkable for its sparkling waterways and surrounding farmland, set against the backdrop of a national park.

A river cruise is the best way to explore this area. Of the several cruises available, perhaps the most unusual is the Riverboat Postman – Australia's only surviving riverboat mail-run. Since 1910, the riverboat has carried mail and essentials to the few hundred residents who choose to live along the waterways, cut off from roads, trains and often communication. Along the way the skipper provides rich nuggets of the river's history, while you sit back and watch the spectacular scenery. Lunch is available on board.

🚹 215 E3 ☒ Hawkesbury River Ferries, Brooklyn Public Wharf, Brooklyn ☎ (02) 9985 7566 ⏰ Mon–Fri: mail boat departs wharf at 9:30, returns 1:15 💷 Expensive 🚉 Hawkesbury River

Boats moored on the Hawkesbury River

FOR KIDS
- Blue Mountains: Scenic World, Jenolan Caves
- Canberra: Australian National Botanic Gardens, Australian War Memorial, Questacon – The National Science and Technology Centre
- Hawkesbury River, Riverboat Postman cruise

Where to... Stay

Prices
Prices are for the least expensive double room in high season:
$ under A$150 $$ A$150–A$280 $$$ over A$280

CANBERRA

Hyatt Hotel Canberra $$–$$$

This luxury hotel is in a charming position close to Lake Burley Griffin, yet it is only five minutes' walk from the city centre. Rooms are spacious and there is a cafe, bar, tea-lounge and health club.

🏠 216 B2 ⬛ Commonwealth Avenue, Yarralumla ☎ (02) 6270 1234; www.canberra.park.hyatt.com

Olims Hotel Canberra $–$$

Near the Australian War Memorial, Olims opened in 1927. The rooms and suites are built around a central, landscaped courtyard with fountain, lawns and gardens. There is a restaurant, cocktail bar, and a bistro for informal eating.

🏠 216 C3 ⬛ Corner Ainslie and Limestone Avenues, Braddon ☎ (02) 6243 0000; www.olimshotel.com

BLUE MOUNTAINS

The Carrington $–$$$

Generations of British royalty have favoured this grand old hotel. The hotel offers all today's mod cons and is only minutes from the Three Sisters rock formation and local shops. Rooms are priced to suit all pockets.

🏠 215 E3 ⬛ 15–47 Katoomba Street, Katoomba ☎ (02) 4782 1111; www.thecarrington.com.au

Kubba Roonga Guesthouse $$

Built in 1915, this heritage guesthouse offers old-world ambience and charm with seven guest rooms. There are two cosy lounge areas with fires, a dining room and delightful gardens. The rates include a cooked breakfast.

🏠 215 E3 ⬛ 9 Brentwood Avenue, Blackheath ☎ (02) 4787 5224; www.kubbaroongaguesthouse.com

Lilianfels Blue Mountains Resort and Spa $$$

This luxurious hotel started life in 1889 as the palatial summer retreat of a New South Wales politician. Set in an English-style garden, it looks over the rugged cliffs and wild forests of the Jamison Valley. Guests can laze on the shady verandah, relax in a spa retreat, or work out in the gym or swimming-pool. The hotel's restaurant, Darley's (▶ 85), is renowned for its Modern Australian cooking.

🏠 215 E3 ⬛ Lilianfels Avenue, Echo Point, Katoomba ☎ (02) 4780 1200; www.lilianfels.com.au

HUNTER VALLEY

Peppers Guest House Hunter Valley $$–$$$

You will not forget a stay at Peppers. This luxurious 48-room hotel combines many contradictory styles: colonial yet contemporary; elegant yet cosy; glamorous and yet relaxing. There are charming views out over the hills, wide verandahs, a conservatory swimming pool, and Chez Pok (▶ 86), one of the Hunter's most awarded restaurants. Another attraction here is the day spa, where massages, facials and body treatments, such as Hawaiian hot stone therapy, are on offer.

🏠 215 E3 ⬛ Ekerts Road, Pokolbin ☎ (02) 4993 8999; www.peppers.com.au

Where to...
Eat and Drink

Prices
Prices per person for a meal, excluding drinks, tax and tip:
$ under A$20 $$ A$20–A$30 $$$ over A$30

CANBERRA

Café in the House $-$$

This is a cafe-style, casual dining venue within the Museum of Australian Democracy, which also houses the National Portrait Gallery. Visitors and local business folk order from a wide selection encompassing sandwiches and cakes to prime steaks. The Kitchen Cabinet, in the cafe, offers good regional produce to shoppers.

➕ 216 B2 ⊠ Museum of Australian Democracy, King George Terrace, Parkes, Canberra ☎ (02) 6270 8156; www.oph.gov.au ⓒ Daily 9–5 and dinner Fri

The Chairman and Yip $$

The inspiration driving Canberra's favourite modern Asian restaurant is essentially Cantonese, but Thai, Japanese and other influences enliven the various menus. The stir-fried tiger prawns with chilli and plum jam and the slow-roasted duck breast with coconut are popular. There are European desserts and a solid Australian wine list. At lunchtime, only set menus are available.

➕ 216 B3 ⊠ 108 Bunda Street, Canberra City ☎ (02) 6248 7109; www.thechairmanandyip.com ⓒ Tue–Fri 12–2, Mon–Sat 6–10:30

Courgette $$$

Courgette is one of Canberra's top restaurants; the cuisine is Modern Australian with European influences. Chef James Mussillon turns out stunning seafood dishes, including Yamba king prawn with preserved lemon, smoked ocean trout, and leek tart. The wine list includes aged Australian varieties.

➕ 216 B3 ⊠ 54 Marcus Clarke Street, Canberra ☎ (02) 6247 4042; www.courgette.com.au ⓒ Mon–Fri 12–3, 6–11, Sat 6–11

Fekerie's Ethiopian Cuisine $-$$

The northern suburb of Dickson is renowned for its Asian food, but this excellent African restaurant is well worth sampling. There are some great curries and a good choice of vegetarian dishes, with unusual accompaniments such as Ethiopian cottage cheese and bread.

➕ 216 off B3 ⊠ 74/2 Cape Street, Dickson ☎ (02) 6262 5799; www.fekeries.com.au ⓒ Tue–Fri 12–2, Tue–Sun 6–10

Ottoman Cuisine $$-$$$

This is one of the capital city's best restaurants and certainly the best Turkish venue in the country. The main menu includes lamb wrapped in eggplant slices, chargrilled king prawns marinated with cumin, and crispy confit of duck leg. Extremely popular with locals, the buzz and service make this a fun night out.

➕ 216 B1 ⊠ Corner of Blackall and Broughton streets, Barton ☎ (02) 6273 6111; www.ottomancuisine.com.au ⓒ Tue–Fri 12–2:30, Tue–Sat 6–10

BLUE MOUNTAINS

Darley's $$$

This highly regarded restaurant is part of Lilianfels, a country hotel that dates from the 1880s (▲ 84). Darley's has an elegant atmosphere, with wood panelling, fireplaces and comfortable chairs. The cooking is Modern Australian, and renowned chef Hugh Whitehouse focuses on slow-cooked dishes that use the finest local and organic produce.

The menu is imaginative and might include quail tortellini, or rare roasted duck breast with red Persian lentils and figs.

215 E3 ✉ **Lilianfels Avenue, Echo Point, Katoomba** ☎ **(02) 4780 1200; www.lilianfels.com.au** ◷ **Dinner Mon–Sat from 6:30**

Mount Tomah Botanic Garden Restaurant $–$$$

Far more than just a typical gardens cafe (although snacks and coffee are available), this is a fine restaurant that offers a cosmopolitan Modern Australian-restaurant menu, which may include excellent gourmet dishes such as red-wine marinated steak or baked figs stuffed with goat's cheese. The views are spectacular, too.

215 E3 ✉ **Mount Tomah Botanic Garden, Bells Line of Road, Mount Tomah** ☎ **(02) 4567 2060; www.rbgsyd.nsw.gov.au** ◷ **Daily 10–4 in summer; 10–3 in winter**

Paragon Restaurant $

A typical old-fashioned Australian milk bar built in 1916 which boasts an art deco interior listed by the National Trust, the Paragon is as much a tourist attraction as the Three Sisters. Traditional breakfasts are served all day long, as well as the delicious "Devonshire" teas so popular in the Blue Mountains. Also on the menu are warming soups, pasta, home-made bread and pies, steak and chops.

215 E3 ✉ **65 Katoomba Street, Katoomba** ☎ **(02) 4782 2928** ◷ **Daily 10–5**

Vulcan's $$

Nestled in the mountain township of Blackheath, Vulcan's has earned itself a fine reputation among food lovers who come for the robust country dishes slow-cooked in the old bakery oven, and for the proficient and stylish atmosphere. Vegetarian options are available. Be sure to book ahead.

215 E3 ✉ **33 Govetts Leap Road, Blackheath** ☎ **(02) 4787 6899** ◷ **Fri–Sun 12–2:30, 6–9**

HUNTER VALLEY

Bluetongue Brewery Cafe $–$$

In a region of renowned (but expensive) restaurants this reasonably priced cafe is a good option. Attached to a boutique brewery, it has indoor and outdoor dining, delicious, good-value meals, fine beers, cocktails and a fun atmosphere. Try the unique Beer Tasting Paddle to learn about their unique brews.

215 E3 ✉ **Hunter Resort, Hermitage Road, Pokolbin** ☎ **(02) 4998 7777; www.hunterresort.com.au** ◷ **Lunch daily 12–5**

Chez Pok $$–$$$

Exciting Modern Australian cooking is the order of the day at Peppers Guest House restaurant, which has stylish old-world charm. If the weather is not too hot, ask for a table on the terrace to enjoy views over the gently rolling hills; alternatively there is an enclosed verandah and pretty main dining room. Most of the produce is local and the wine list specializes in Hunter reds. This is not just for lunch or dinner: you're welcome for breakfast and morning or afternoon tea too.

215 E3 ✉ **Peppers Guest House (▶ 84) Hunter Valley, Ekerts Road, Pokolbin** ☎ **(02) 4993 8899** ◷ **Daily breakfast (7–10), lunch (12–2), afternoon tea, dinner (7–9)**

SOUTHERN HIGHLANDS

Hordern's $$$

The restaurant in stately Milton Park Country House Hotel offers refined dining in an elegant country setting, with magnificent views of the garden. The modern European menu might include dishes such as fresh goat's curd on toasted walnut bread or crisp-skinned ocean trout with asparagus and red peppers. The wine list is mainly Australian, with a selection of vintage reds.

215 E3 ✉ **Horderns Road, Bowral** ☎ **(02) 4861 1522; www.milton-park.com.au** ◷ **Daily 7:30–9**

Where to...
Shop

CANBERRA

The Australian Capital Territory's best speciality stores are in the villages dotted around the city.

It is well worth a short trip to visit **Bungendore Wood Works Gallery** on the Kings Highway at Bungendore (tel: (02) 6238 1682). More than 200 of the country's foremost woodwork designers display their craft, from small objects to large art and furniture. **Civic** is the city's main business and retail district, and there are also large shopping malls in **Woden**, **Tuggeranong** and **Belconnen**. For something more personal, try the vibrant inner-city shopping centres at **Kingston** and **Manuka**. Or, if you are shopping for a picnic, you can't beat Canberra's fresh food markets at **Fyshwick**.

Just 15 minutes' drive from the CBD is **Gold Creek Village** (corner of Gold Creek Road and O'Hanlon Place, Barton Highway), a self-contained shopping, dining and recreation precinct, with a reptile centre, and a collection of old buildings housing gift and souvenir shops, arts and crafts galleries, produce stores and clothing outlets.

BLUE MOUNTAINS

Most villages in the Blue Mountains have a browse-worthy arts and crafts and antiques shop, as well as shops selling local food products, second-hand clothes and books.

The **National Trust Norman Lindsay Gallery and Museum** is located at 14 Norman Lindsay Crescent in Faulconbridge. Original prints, watercolours and etchings are on display, and you can buy reproductions and books on Lindsay's work.

Wentworth Falls has speciality shops and galleries, including the **Falls Gallery** (161 Falls Road), with its changing exhibitions of works on paper and ceramics by emerging and well-established artists. Nearby **Leura** offers exclusive speciality shopping and the popular Leura Candy Store (Shop 6, Leura Strand Arcade), with more than 2,000 unique and unusual candies, chocolates, and fudges.

In the main town of **Katoomba**, Katoomba Fine Art (98 Lurline Street) represents well-known Blue Mountains artists.

At **Blackheath**, you'll find quality, handcrafted jewellery from Australian, European and other artists at Jewel Blue Mountains Gallery (40 Govetts Leap Road). The Victory Theatre Antique Centre (17–19 Govetts Leap Road) represents 30 dealers, with a wide range of furniture, jewellery, fine porcelain, works of art, Australiana, silver, rugs, books, records, and unusual and collectable items.

The artist-owned **Gallery Blackheath** (44 Govetts Leap Road) exhibits a wide range of works of local artists, plus works in all mediums by award-winning resident artists.

HUNTER VALLEY

The main shopping areas are **Cessnock**, catering for wine growers and tourists alike, and **Hunter Valley Gardens** (Broke Road, Pokolbin) with its lovely gardens and a village of shops, restaurants and cafes. Here are the Hunter Valley Chocolate Company, Village Books, British Lolly Shop, Ken Duncan Panographs, and The Waiter's Friend.

For many visitors to the Hunter Valley, however, wine is likely to be the major purchase. Just about all wineries in the district offer cellar-door tastings and sales. Purchase a minimum of a case and most wineries will organize freight home.

Where to...
Be Entertained

CANBERRA

In February, the **National Multicultural Festival** attracts performers from all over the world, plus live music, circus-style acts and exhibitions, food and wine stalls, and street parties. **The Royal Canberra Show** in February offers agricultural displays, a parade, fireworks and music, and, in March, the **Celebrate Canberra Festival** is a major event. During the **Floriade** flower festival every September/ October, parks and gardens feature lavish plantings of bulbs.

In April, you can explore more than 30 cellar doors in the local region, during the **Canberra District Wine Harvest Festival**, an annual event that offers tours, wine-making demonstrations, wine tastings and delicious food. **Canberra International Music Festival**, each May, takes place in memorable venues, including the city's unique embassy buildings. Enjoy concerts by international and Australian artists plus lectures and other musical events.

A theatre scene flourishes around the **Canberra Theatre Centre** in Civic Square, and the **Australian National University** has regular music performances. There is a boutique casino on Binara Street in Civic, which has entertainment and an excellent restaurant.

BLUE MOUNTAINS

In March, the annual **Festival of Folk, Roots and Blues** attracts some of Australia's and the world's best acoustic performers to several Blue Mountains venues.

The district's biggest festival is the June to August **Yulefest**, during which the local hotels and restaurants offer traditional winter-Christmas trappings. At this time, the Blue Mountain's biggest annual event, the **Winter Magic Festival** sees Katoomba's streets taken over by local musicians, mask-makers, dancers, gymnasts, clowns, drummers, choirs and poets. The festival includes the popular ArtStreet, with exhibitions of local art in shop windows and along the arcades and main streets of the mountain communities. The equally popular **Katoomba Short Film Festival** also takes place at this time.

From September to November, the **Spring Garden Festival** attracts visitors to enjoy the many lavish public and private gardens.

The Leura Gardens Festival, held in October, is a highly successful fund-raiser for the local hospital.

HUNTER VALLEY

The Hunter's popular events include the **Harvest Festival** in April/June, **Lovedale Long Lunch** in May and **Broke Village Fair** in September.

In April, the **Hunter Valley Steamfest** includes train rides, market stalls, family activities and train-themed movies. The rural town of **Dungog** hosts a film festival in May, showcasing the best Australian cinema.

The area is also famous for its music festivals such as October's **Jazz in the Vines** (at Tyrrell's Vineyards) and **Opera in the Vineyards** (Wyndham Estate), and **Bimbadgen Blues** at Bimbadgen Estate (September).

For details contact visitor centres: Canberra: tel: (1300) 554 114; Blue Mountains: (1300) 653 408 (in Australia); Hunter Valley: (02) 4990 0900.

Victoria

Getting Your Bearings

Victoria is the smallest mainland state, but within its 227,600sq km (87,880 square miles) lies a treasure trove of scenic landscapes, from magnificent alpine country and historic goldfields areas, to rich grazing land, densely forested wilderness, desert and a spectacular coastline.

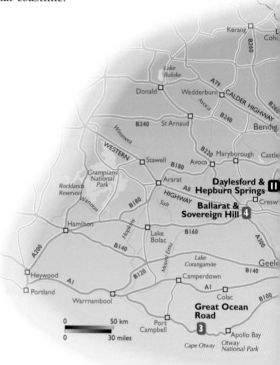

Victoria was also the site of Australia's wealthiest gold rush, which began in 1851, the same year that the fledgling colony gained independence from New South Wales. Reminders of this frantic boom period, which sparked a population explosion and shaped Victoria's history, are most evident in the grand architecture of the state's capital, Melbourne, and in the gold towns of Bendigo and Ballarat, the latter home to a superb re-created 19th-century gold-mining township. With its compact size and extensive network of sealed roads, Victoria is ideal for exploration by car and though Melbourne rightly commands attention with its stylish shops, cultural festivals, major sporting events, theatres and restaurants, there

★ Don't Miss

At Your Leisure

Page 89:
The Great
Ocean Road,
near Lorne

is much to see within two or three hours of the city. Not-to-be-missed excursions include Ballarat, the Great Ocean Road – one of the world's great scenic drives – and Phillip Island for its internationally renowned nightly Penguin Parade. But don't forget to pack a variety of clothing – while generally enjoying a temperate climate, Victoria is notorious for its volatile weather, particularly along the coastal regions, where temperatures can alter by 17°C (30°F) in just a few hours.

In Five Days

If you're not quite sure where to begin your travels, this itinerary recommends a practical and enjoyable five days exploring Victoria, taking in some of the best places to see using the Getting Your Bearings map on the previous page. For more information see the main entries.

Day 1

Start your tour with two days in ❶ Melbourne (above, ➤ 94–96) and spend one day discovering why it's regarded as the cultural capital of Australia. Ride the signature trams and stroll the tree-lined boulevards as you explore the real Melbourne, a place of cultural diversity, restaurants by the thousand, stylish shops, sporting passion, magnificent parks and gardens, and fickle weather.

Day 2

Morning
Walk through the beautiful grounds of the Royal Botanic Gardens – one of the great gardens of the world – then take a guided tour of the city's cathedral of sport, the Melbourne Cricket Ground.

Afternoon
After lunch, set off for ❷ Phillip Island (➤ 97–98), just under two hours' drive from Melbourne. Famous for its nightly Penguin Parade – where hundreds of little penguins waddle from the sea to their burrows – the island is also home to Australia's largest fur seal colony and an ideal place to get a close-up view of koalas.

Day 3

Drive to **4** **Ballarat** (➤ 102–103), just over an hour from Melbourne along the Western Freeway, and experience life in the gold-rush era at its major attraction, **4** **Sovereign Hill** (left), a fascinating recreation of a mid-19th-century gold-mining township.

Day 4

Morning

Set off early for an exhilarating two-day journey along the **3** **Great Ocean Road** (➤ 99–101), one of the world's most spectacular coastal routes. Stretching for a distance of 300km (185 miles) along the State's southwest coast, it offers forests and mountains on one side, sheer cliffs and ocean on the other and a string of beaches and charming seaside settlements in between.

Afternoon

Reach the Twelve Apostles (below) – an amazing collection of rock formations – late in the afternoon, then spend the night at Port Campbell, an ideal base for exploring Port Campbell National Park.

Day 5

Continue to Warrnambool then return to Melbourne along the Princes Highway via Camperdown and Colac (worth a stop for a look at the abundant bird life on lakes Colac and Corangamite) – a pleasant inland route that passes through some of Victoria's prime sheep- and cattle-grazing country.

❶ Melbourne

Exuding elegance and culture, Melbourne has a combined passion for food, wine, the arts and sport that distinguishes it from all other Australian cities.

A traditionally conservative city, its grand Victorian-era buildings, tree-lined boulevards and gracious parks and gardens were financed by wealth from Australia's biggest and most prolonged gold rush which started in 1851 and continued into the early years of the 20th century. Melbourne's cultural diversity, however, springs largely from the boom in immigration that followed World War II. Its towering skyscrapers are a more recent phenomenon and, for the most part, blend in with the Melbourne of earlier times. Lacking the obvious physical attractions of its flashy northern cousin, Sydney, and with a climate notorious for its fickle "four seasons in one day" character, Melbourne offers its treasures discreetly. Half the fun of getting to know this most European of Australian cities comes from riding the trams that lend such character to its city streets.

Central Area

A great way to start your exploration is at the boisterous **Queen Victoria Market**, opened in 1878 and very much a Melbourne institution. It is *the* shopping experience, with more than 1,000 stalls offering everything from clothing and jewellery to antiques and fresh produce in an enjoyably chaotic atmosphere. Then, by way of contrast, make your way to the **National Gallery of Victoria: International** (NGVI) on St Kilda Road. This vast building houses the state's collection of non-Australian art, including European paintings, Asian sculptures, and Egyptian, pre-Columbian, Greek and Roman works. The NGVI also has expansive exhibition space, and hosts regular touring exhibitions. A ten-minute walk towards the city over the Princes Bridge brings you to Federation Square (the location of the visitor centre) and its futuristic-looking buildings, one of which houses the **Ian Potter Centre: NGV Australia** – the National Gallery of Victoria's Australian art collection, one of the country's finest.

Top: The city skyline, seen from Southgate

Above: Melbourne Central Complex incorporates the historic Shot Tower under a glass cone

While in the central city area, take the opportunity to explore a couple of its best-known streets and arcades. Vibrant Swanston Street features shops, arcades, alfresco cafes, major civic buildings and inspiring architecture. The ritzy east ("Paris") end of Collins Street is a more decorous affair, crammed with expensive boutiques, galleries and speciality shops. Melbourne's grandest arcade – the Block – is a treasure trove of Victorian-era architecture and elegant shops, while its oldest, the 1869 Royal Arcade, entertains visitors with effigies of biblical Gog and Magog striking the hours on an elaborate clock. A short walk through here from Little Collins

Street will bring you into Bourke Street Mall where you can catch a tram bound for St Kilda, the city's most popular seaside suburb.

St Kilda

The best of St Kilda is free: a stroll along the beachfront and pier. On Sundays, crowds of Melburnians come to relax, exercise or browse at the arts-and-crafts market on the Upper Esplanade. Sunday crowds also pack the footpaths of Acland Street, renowned for its continental cake shops, delicatessens and cafes. St Kilda's other main street, Fitzroy, was once renowned as Melbourne's sleazy red-light district, but nowadays the strip's trendy cafes are the hangout of a stylish crowd who come to see and be seen. While St Kilda may be considered Melbourne's playground, its cultural heart lies on the south bank of the Yarra River. If you're looking for high-quality theatrical or cultural events, you'll find them in abundance at **The Arts Centre**, which includes the Hamer (concert) Hall, the Theatres Building and the Performing Arts Collection museum. Reserve the early evening for a trip to **Eureka Skydeck 88**, which occupies the 88th floor of one of the city's tallest buildings and offers 360-degree views.

Parks and Cricket

Change the pace, and focus, of your visit and enjoy the beautiful landscapes of the **Royal Botanic Gardens Melbourne**, which rate as Australia's best. The park's many European deciduous trees are at their most spectacular in autumn. Then, sports buff or no, head for the **Melbourne Cricket Ground** (MCG) to view the temple in which Melbourne sporting fanatics worship. The main stadium for the 1956 Olympic Games and the 2006 Commonwealth

MELBOURNE: INSIDE INFO

Top tip Melbourne has two free transport services. The burgundy City Circle trams (www.metlinkmelbourne.com.au) run in both directions every 12 mins 10am–6pm (not Good Friday or 25 December), and the Melbourne City Tourist Shuttle bus (www.thatsmelbourne.com.au) operates every 15–20 mins 9:30am–4:30pm.

In more depth Take a cruise on the Yarra River, departing from Southgate. Melbourne River Cruises (tel: (03) 8610 2600; www.melbcruises.com.au), for example, offer relaxing trips that take in several sights.

Hidden gem See how Melbourne's wealthy lived over a century ago at the Rippon Lea Estate, at 192 Hotham Street, in the suburb of Elsternwick (tel: (03) 9523 6095; www.ripponleaestate.com.au).

Games, the MCG seats 100,000 people and is regarded as the sporting heart of the State, if not the nation, playing host to international cricket matches in summer and Australian Rules Football in winter. Regular guided tours include sporting museums and a walk on the hallowed turf.

TAKING A BREAK

For a dose of old-world elegance laced with tea (or coffee) and delicious cakes, take time out in the Block Arcade's **Hopetoun Tea Rooms** ($; ➤ 107).

✚ 215 D2

Queen Victoria Market
✚ 216 A3 ✉ Corner Queen and Elizabeth streets ☎ (03) 9320 5822; www.qvm.com.au 🕐 Tue and Thu 6–2, Fri 6–5, Sat 6–3, Sun 9–4; closed 1 Jan, Good Fri, Anzac Day, Melbourne Cup Day, 25 and 26 Dec 🚶 Free 🚇 Flagstaff and Melbourne Central (Elizabeth Street exit) 🚊 Trams 19, 57, 59; buses 220, 232

Eureka Skydeck 88
✚ 216 B1 ✉ 1 Riverside Quay, Southbank ☎ (03) 9693 8888; www.eurekaskydeck.com.au 🕐 Daily 10am–late 💲 Moderate 🚊 Tram 56; buses Queen and Flinders streets routes

National Gallery of Victoria
✚ 216 B1 ✉ Ian Potter Centre: cnr Russell Street/Federation Square (✚ 216 C2). NGV International: 180 St Kilda Road ☎ (03) 8620 2222; www.ngv.vic.gov.au 🕐 Tue–Sun

10–5; closed Good Fri, 25 Dec 🚶 Free 🚇 Flinders Street 🚊 Trams City Circle, 1, 3, 5, 6, 8, 16, 22, 25, 48, 64, 67, 70, 72, 75

St Kilda
✚ 216 off C1 ☎ www.melbourne.com.au 🚊 Trams 12, 15, 16, 96, 112; buses 246, 606

Royal Botanic Gardens Melbourne
✚ 216 off C1 ✉ Birdwood Avenue, South Yarra ☎ (03) 9252 2429; www.rbg.vic.gov.au 🕐 Daily 7:30–sunset 🚶 Free 🚊 Trams 3, 5, 8, 16, 64, 67

Melbourne Cricket Ground
✚ 216 off C1 ✉ Jolimont Terrace, Yarra Park ☎ Tours: (03) 9657 8879; General: (03) 9657 8879; www.mcg.org.au 🕐 Daily, 1-hour guided tours 10–3, except on event days; closed Good Fri, 25 Dec 💲 Moderate 🚊 Trams 48, 70, 75 🚉 Jolimont

② Phillip Island

Phillip Island is best known for its nightly Penguin Parade at Summerland Beach. Here, at sunset every day of the year, hundreds of little penguins – at 30–35cm (12–14 inches) tall, the world's smallest – emerge from the sea and waddle up the beach to their burrows in the dunes.

A variety of experiences is available. You can join the hordes on the **main observation stand**, or choose from more personalized options, including an **exclusive viewing platform** or elevated tower, complete with a personal ranger. Many thousands of people turn up to watch this magical procession, so arrive at least an hour before sunset. Bookings are recommended (essential for the exclusive viewing options). The penguins emerge from the water and waddle up the beach over a period of about an hour. At the parade's end watch the penguins' antics in and around the burrows from elevated boardwalks, then learn more about them at the display in the **Visitor Centre**.

Little penguins on the shore of Phillip Island

In the hours leading up to the parade, you'll have ample opportunity to explore other island attractions, which include spectacular coastal scenery, pleasant beaches, sleepy

townships and abundant wildlife. A good place to start is the **Koala Conservation Centre**, where elevated boardwalks put you close to the koalas in their tree-top homes.

Another very worthwhile attraction is the nearby **Nobbies Centre** overlooking rugged Seal Rocks, home to abundant birdlife and Australia's largest colony of fur seals. The Centre (free entry) offers interactive displays and ranger-led walks, and the area has clifftop boardwalks from which to view the wildlife.

TAKING A BREAK

The **cafe** at the Penguin Parade offers a range of light meals, snacks and cakes. Visitors in the winter months will welcome the cafe's mugs of hot soup before the parade begins.

Phillip Island's rugged Cape Wollamai

✚ 215 D2

Phillip Island Information Centre
✉ 895 Phillip Island Tourist Road, Newhaven ☎ (03) 5956 7447 and (1300) 366 422; www.visitphillipisland.com 🕔 Daily 9–5; 25 Dec 2–5
🚌 V/Line bus to and from Melbourne stops at the main town of Cowes, or join a tour from Melbourne; there is no public transport around the island
⛴ Cowes from Stony Point

Penguin Parade
✉ Summerland Beach ☎ (03) 5951 2820; www.penguins.org.au 🕔 Visitor Centre: daily 10–parade's end 💲 Moderate–expensive

Nobbies Centre
✉ Ventnor Road, Summerland ☎ (03) 5951 2820; www.penguins.org.au
🕔 Check website 💲 Free

Koala Conservation Centre
✉ Fiveways on the Phillip Island Tourist Road ☎ (03) 5952 1610; www.penguins.org.au 🕔 Daily 10–5:30 💲 Inexpensive

3 Great Ocean Road

There are few driving experiences in the world to match that offered by the Great Ocean Road. Twisting and turning along the dramatic, windswept coastline of Victoria's southwest, it passes through charming seaside villages and dense forests, offering a drive of uninterrupted scenic splendour for around 300km (185 miles).

Built between 1919 and 1932, the road was both an employment scheme for soldiers returning from the battlefields of World War I and a memorial to those who didn't return.

The Great Ocean Road proper begins in **Torquay**, a seaside town 95km (60 miles) southwest of Melbourne and a mecca for surfing enthusiasts the world over. Not far from here is the world-famous **Bells Beach** where some of the biggest waves in Australia come crashing down on a picture-perfect curve of sand. Even if surfing is beyond your capabilities, you'll be impressed by those who can and a visit here will whet your appetite for the rest of the drive. The first leg of the Great Ocean Road follows the coastline between Torquay and Apollo Bay, passing through the holiday towns of Anglesea – well known for the kangaroos that graze on its golf course – and Lorne. Both nestle at the base of the **Otway Ranges**, a natural treasure trove of towering eucalyptus trees, temperate rainforest, cliffs and waterfalls. If you're in the mood to stop this early in the trip, **Lorne** is the place to do it. A popular weekend destination for upwardly mobile Melburnians, it offers a range of excellent cafes and surprisingly good boutiques stocked with the latest designer wear. Just a short, well-signposted drive from town, you can take a pleasant walk

Loch Ard Gorge in Port Campbell National Park is the site of a famous shipwreck

through bushland to the cascading Erskine Falls – one of the area's popular attractions and well worth a visit.

An elevated view over the Great Ocean Road at Lorne

Superb Scenery

From Lorne, the drive to Apollo Bay offers a feast of ocean and mountain scenery as it follows a narrow, twisting section of the Great Ocean Road; take time to stop at some of the numerous lookouts, especially **Cape Patton**, to savour the panoramic views. After Apollo Bay – a holiday and fishing village set on a wide crescent-shaped beach – the road leaves the coast and winds through the lush slopes of the Otways. This is rainforest country, filled with mighty trees, birds, wild flowers and native animals. Much of this region is protected in **Great Otway National Park,** which includes Melba Gully and its 35-minute Madsens Track Nature Walk, which winds through rainforest and takes you to the base of the Big Tree, a towering eucalypt, around 300 years old.

Take a 15-minute detour east at Lavers Hill to **The Otway Fly Tree Top Walk,** a 600m (655-yard) elevated walkway that takes you high among the trees and provides wonderful views of this magnificent temperate rainforest.

The road rejoins the coast at Port Campbell National Park, the route's wildest and most awe-inspiring coastal sight. Part of the **"Shipwreck Coast"** that claimed more than 80 vessels in the days when sailing ships were the main form of ocean-going transport, this narrow park is best known for its natural rock sculptures, carved from the soft limestone cliffs by the

constant pounding of waves. The most admired of these are the **Twelve Apostles**, a succession of limestone pillars rising to 50m (165ft) from the ocean. They are at their most spectacular at sunset. Not far from here is **Loch Ard Gorge**, named after a legendary shipwreck along this coast. It was here in 1878 that an apprentice ship's officer and an Irish immigrant woman, both 18, were washed ashore after the *Loch Ard* foundered on rocks. They were the only survivors from around 50 people on board.

More scenic points dot the road on the way into **Port Campbell**, a fishing village built on a spectacular gorge. This quiet town has a good range of accommodation and restaurants and is the ideal base for exploring the area. There's a small beach for summer swimming, the region is renowned for its fishing and surfing, and diving and boat tours are available.

West for Whales

If you continue west, you'll reach the whale-watching centre of Warrnambool – and the end of your journey along the Great Ocean Road. On the way you'll pass other formations including London Bridge, which lost one of its arches in 1990, and the beautiful Bay of Islands before the final stretch through dairy country. **Flagstaff Hill Maritime Village**, a recreated 19th-century port at Warrnambool, is worth a visit before you head back to Melbourne along Princes Highway.

TAKING A BREAK

Lively, Kosta's in Lorne (➤ 108), offers Modern Australian food with a Greek twist.

➕ 214 C2

Geelong and the Great Ocean Road Visitor Information Centre
➕ 214 C2 ✉ Stead Park, Princes Highway, Corio ☎ (03) 5275 5797 and (1800) 620 888; www.greatoceanroad.org 🍴 Kosta's ($$) 🚌 V/Line bus to Apollo Bay, with a Friday-only continuation to Port Campbell and Warrnambool, or coach tour from Melbourne, but driving is the best option

The Otway Fly Tree Top Walk
➕ 214 C2 ✉ 360 Phillips Track, Weeaproinah ☎ (03) 5235 9200; www.otwayfly.com 🕐 Daily 9–5

Flagstaff Hill Maritime Village
➕ 214 C2 ✉ Merri Street, Warrnambool ☎ (03) 5559 4600; www.flagstaffhill.com 🕐 Daily 9–5 🎟 Moderate

GREAT OCEAN ROAD: INSIDE INFO

Top tip The Great Ocean Road is exposed to chill winds that sometimes blow from the Antarctic, **so be prepared with warm clothing.**

Hidden gem The Port Campbell Visitor Information Centre on Morris Street (tel: (1300) 137 255) contains the **Shipwreck Museum**, featuring interesting displays on the *Loch Ard* and other aspects of the region's maritime history.

4 Ballarat and Sovereign Hill

Filled with reminders of the prosperous gold-rush era, Ballarat is a provincial city of considerable history and charm. The alluvial gold that was discovered near here in 1851 proved to be the tip of a golden iceberg containing fantastically rich quartz reefs that were not exhausted until 1918, by which time Ballarat had contributed more than a quarter of Victoria's total wealth of gold.

You need only look at the flamboyant buildings, statues, elaborate gardens and grand streetscapes to see evidence of the city's gold-rush origins, but for a real taste of this exciting era, make your first stop Sovereign Hill, on the city's outskirts.

Sovereign Hill

Here is a recreated gold-mining township of the 1850s where people dressed in period costume ply the trades of the time and horses haul carriages and carts and provide power for the early mining machinery on the **Red Hill Gully Diggings**. After trying your luck panning for gold amid the tents and mud-and-bark huts of the diggings, head up to Main Street for a taste of town life.

A tour of the **Gold Mine** is essential. Tours (40 minutes; bookings essential) take you underground into a 600m-long (650-yard) tunnel and reveal the conditions under which the miners worked. Another highlight is the **Gold Pour**, where A$50,000 worth of real gold are smelted and poured.

Sovereign Hill's gold processing plant

BALLARAT AND SOVEREIGN HILL: INSIDE INFO

Top tips For just over A$42 you can get a **Ballarat Eureka Pass**, which gives two days' unlimited admission to Sovereign Hill, the Gold Museum and the Eureka Centre. The Ballarat Fine Art Gallery is free. The pass is available from any of these attractions as well as the Ballarat Visitor Information Centre.

■ An interesting Sovereign Hill experience is the **Red Hill Mine tour.** You find your own way through narrow tunnels, with sound-and-light effects that tell the story of deep lead alluvial mining in the 1850s and the discovery of the 69kg (152lb) "Welcome Nugget", the world's second largest gold nugget.

In more depth A 90-minute sound-and-light show, *Blood on the Southern Cross*, takes place nightly across the panorama of Sovereign Hill, dramatizing the battle of the Eureka Stockade. Booking essential (tel (03) 5337 1199).

The **Gold Museum** opposite Sovereign Hill houses nuggets, alluvial deposits and coins. It focuses on the history and uses of gold as well as featuring interesting temporary exhibitions. Entry is included in your Sovereign Hill ticket.

Ballarat
On your way into Ballarat's central business district, take a short detour to the **Eureka Centre**, on the site of the Eureka Rebellion. Dynamic displays tell the brief and bloody story of this rebellion by the miners against an unjust and corrupt goldfields administration in 1854 – an event that many say heralded the birth of true democracy in Australia.

In downtown Ballarat, stroll along Lydiard Street to see one of the country's most impressive, intact Victorian-era streetscapes. Two buildings are worth attention: **Ballarat Fine Art Gallery**, housing one of the most comprehensive regional collections of Australian art, and **Her Majesty's Theatre** (1875), Australia's oldest surviving, purpose-built theatre.

TAKING A BREAK
Sovereign Hill's Main Street **New York Bakery** serves coffee, teas and lunches or try modern Australian cuisine at **Tozers Restaurant** in the Ansonia on Lydiard hotel ➤ 107).

✚ 214 C2

Visitor Information Centre and Eureka Centre
✉ Eureka Street, Sovereign Hill ☎ (03) 5320 5758 or 1800 446 633; www.visitballarat.com.au. Eureka Centre: (03) 5333 1854 🕐 Daily 9–5. Eureka Centre daily 9–4:30 💷 Inexpensive 🚉 Ballarat Railway Station 🚌 No 8

Sovereign Hill
✉ Bradshaw Street ☎ (03) 5337 1100; www.sovereignhill.com.au
🕐 Apr–Sep 10–5, Oct–Mar 9–5:30; closed 25 Dec 💷 Expensive 🚌 No 9

Gold Museum
✉ Corner of Grant and Bradshaw streets ☎ (03) 5337 1107 🕐 Daily 9:30–5:20; closed 25 Dec 💷 Inexpensive

At Your Leisure

5 Cafe Life

For a quintessential Melbourne experience and a chance to savour the city's multicultural make-up, immerse yourself in the inner suburb cafe life. It's at its vibrant best in Brunswick Street, Fitzroy, where alternative funk meets urban cool. All things Italian, including great coffee, are celebrated in Lygon Street, Carlton, while the city centre's famous narrow laneways are also packed with atmospheric cafes. In St Kilda's former red-light district, Fitzroy Street, cafe life takes on a terminally cool air, and in fashionable Chapel Street, South Yarra, it finds its most lively expression in a youthful crowd sporting the latest fashions.

216 C3 ⊠ Fitzroy (Brunswick Street)
216 B3 ⊠ Carlton (Lygon Street)
216 off C1 ⊠ St Kilda (Fitzroy Street)
216 off C1 ⊠ South Yarra (Chapel Street)
🍴 Cafes, restaurants and bars ($–$$$)

6 Old Melbourne Gaol

Gloomy, sinister and reputedly haunted, Old Melbourne Gaol none the less provides a fascinating insight into 19th-century prison life. Built in stages from 1841 to 1864, the bluestone gaol was the scene of 136 hangings, including that of the notorious bushranger Ned Kelly, whose death mask and gun are on display. Other compelling exhibits include the histories and grim death masks of other noted prisoners and a lashing triangle and cat-o'-nine-tails. Eerie candlelight night tours can also be taken.

216 B3 ⊠ Russell Street ☎ (03) 9663 7228; www.oldmelbournegaol.com.au 🕐 Daily 9:30–5 (plus some evenings, call for details); closed Good Fri, 25 Dec 🚇 Melbourne Central 🚋 City Circle Tram; buses 200, 201, 203, 207, 251 ⑪ Moderate (expensive for night tours)

7 The Hotel Windsor

Having afternoon tea at Australia's grandest Victorian-era hotel is a Melbourne tradition and a wickedly indulgent affair. Luxuriate in the opulent surroundings and treat yourself to a traditional selection of sandwiches, scones, cakes, tarts and desserts – all washed down with plenty of tea or coffee.

216 C2 ⊠ 111 Spring Street ☎ (03) 9633 6000; www.thehotelwindsor.com.au 🕐 Daily 3:30–5:30 (reservations essential) ⑪ Expensive 🚇 Parliament 🚋 City Circle tram

8 Carlton Gardens

Just north of the city centre, Carlton Gardens offers several attractions, including the ultra-modern Melbourne Museum with its displays on Aboriginal culture, Australian icons such as the racehorse Phar Lap, and a living rainforest. The area also has an IMAX theatre and formal gardens, and the magnificent World Heritage listed Royal Exhibition Building (1879), tours of which depart from the museum.

216 C3 ⊠ Nicholson Street, Carlton ☎ (03) 8341 7777 (or 13 1102 within Victoria); www.melbourne.museum.vic.gov. au 🕐 Museum: daily 10–5; Royal Exhibition Building: tours daily at 2pm (bookings essential); both closed Good Fri, 25 Dec ⑪ Inexpensive 🚋 Trams: City Circle, 86, 96

Inside Old Melbourne Gaol

Neatly ordered Yarra Valley vineyards

9 Yarra Valley

Some of Australia's best wineries are found in the beautiful Yarra Valley, at the foot of the Great Dividing Range. Just an hour's drive from Melbourne, this region is noted for its Pinot Noirs, Chardonnays, Cabernet Sauvignons and *méthode champenoise* wines. Most of its 70-plus wineries are open daily for wine tastings. Be sure to visit **Domaine Chandon**, which offers brilliant views over the valley from its wine tasting room. Take time to appreciate other valley attractions such as **Healesville Sanctuary** (www.zoo.org.au), one of the best places to see Australian wildlife in captivity, and enjoy the scenic drives and bushwalks threading their way through the surrounding mountain forests.

215 D2

Yarra Valley Visitor Information Centre
The Old Court House, Harker Street, Healesville (03) 5962 2600; www.visityarravalley.com.au Daily 9–5; closed 25 Dec Lilydale, then bus to Healesville

10 Mornington Peninsula

Rich in natural beauty, the Mornington Peninsula – a boot-shaped promontory between Port Phillip and Western Port bays, an hour's drive from Melbourne – has long been one of the city's most popular weekend retreats. Port Phillip Bay offers sheltered beaches, such as Safety Beach at Dromana, ideal for swimming, while the rugged coast facing Bass Strait, protected within Mornington Peninsula National Park, is more suited to visitors who prefer surfing and scenic walks. Other prime attractions include seal- and dolphin-watching cruises, golf courses, 50 wineries, restaurants and Arthurs Seat, a granite outcrop offering breathtaking views.

215 D2

Peninsula Visitor Information Centre
359B Point Nepean Road, Dromana (03) 5987 3078 and (1800) 804 009; www.visitmorningtonpeninsula.org/ Daily 9–5; closed Good Fri, 25 Dec Frankston Sorrento, Stony Point

11 Daylesford and Hepburn Springs

Victoria's scenic spa country, centred on the twin towns of Daylesford and Hepburn Springs and only a 90-minute drive from Melbourne, contains the largest concentration of natural mineral springs in Australia. People have been "taking the waters" here since the 1870s. You will find a variety of restorative treatments on offer but, when the pampering palls, diversion is easily found in the towns' numerous galleries, antiques shops, gardens, cafes and restaurants.

214 C2

Daylesford Regional Visitor Information Centre
96 Vincent Street (03) 5321 6123; www.visitdaylesford.com Daily 9–5; closed 25 Dec Trains run between Melbourne and Woodend, then buses to Daylesford

FOR KIDS
- Melbourne: St Kilda, Eureka Skydeck 88, Royal Botanic Gardens, Old Melbourne Gaol
- Phillip Island
- Sovereign Hill
- Healesville Sanctuary

Where to...
Stay

Prices
Prices are for the least expensive double room in high season:
$ under A$150 $$ A$150–A$280 $$$ over A$280

MELBOURNE

Georgian Court $-$$
An inexpensive bed-and-breakfast in one of Melbourne's most historic and elegant suburbs, the Georgian Court lies within walking distance of the main tourist attractions and shops.

✚ 218 off C2 ⊠ 21–25 George Street, East Melbourne ☎ (03) 9419 6353; www.georgiancourt.com.au

Magnolia Court Boutique Hotel $-$$
In a leafy, tranquil area, this boutique hotel is constructed from three distinct buildings. It is a chic choice and rooms and suites are priced to suit a variety of pockets.

✚ 218 off C2 ⊠ 101 Powlett Street, East Melbourne ☎ (03) 9419 4222; www.magnolia-court.com.au

The Windsor $$$
Australia's grandest Victorian hotel has elegantly appointed rooms and spacious, ornamented public areas. Opposite Parliament House and overlooking Fitzroy and Treasury gardens, the Windsor is within a few minutes' walk of Melbourne's best shopping, restaurants and bars.

A highlight here for non-residents as well as guests is afternoon tea served in the restaurant (▶ 104).

✚ 218 C2 ⊠ 111 Spring St ☎ (03) 9633 6000; www.thewindsor.com.au

St Kilda Road Parkview Hotel $$
This good-value hotel is on St Kilda Road, south of the city centre and not far from Southbank, the Royal Botanic Gardens, Arts Centre and many other attractions. Facilities include a gym, bar and restaurant.

✚ 218 C1 ⊠ 562 St Kilda Road ☎ (03) 9529 8888; www.viewhotels.com.au

PHILLIP ISLAND/MORNINGTON PENINSULA

Abaleigh on Lovers Walk $$
This is a real island experience: a romantic bed-and-breakfast on the beach at Cowes, a five-minute stroll along the sand from the main street. Chose between a two-storey apartment, a studio room, or a waterfront cottage. All rooms are private and fully self-contained, with large living areas and courtyards. Breakfast provisions are included, and there are nearby gym, golf and tennis facilities.

✚ 215 D2 ⊠ 6 Roy Court, Cowes, Phillip Island ☎ (03) 5952 5649; www.abaleigh.com

Peppers Moonah Links Resort $$-$$$
Part of the luxurious Peppers chain, this state-of-the-art, 96-room resort boasts some of Australia's best golf facilities, including two 18-hole championship courses. Constructed with natural timbers and featuring clean modern lines, Peppers Moonah Links is a stylish and relaxing base from which to explore the Peninsula. Rooms and suites are available and the facilities include fine dining at Pebbles Restaurant, a day spa and gym, tennis, croquet and cycling.

✚ 215 D2 ⊠ Peter Thomson Drive, Fingal ☎ (1300) 987 600; www.peppers.com.au/moonah

Where to...
Eat and Drink

GREAT OCEAN ROAD

Cumberland Lorne Resort $$–$$$

In addition to its penthouse suites and one- or two-bedroom apartments, this excellent seaside resort offers a day spa, swimming pool, gym, squash and tennis courts, restaurant, kids' club for the over-5s and many other recreational facilities.

🚩 214 C2 ⊠ 150 Mountjoy Parade, Lorne
☎ (03) 5289 4444; www.cumberland.com.au

Johanna Seaside Cottages $$

Located near Lavers Hill, and with beach access and ocean views, this collection of self-contained cottages nestled amid sand dunes is an idyllic Great Ocean Road base.

🚩 214 C2 ⊠ 395 Red Johanna Road, Johanna Beach ☎ (03) 5237 4242;
www.johannaseaside.com.au

Merrijig Inn $–$$

Overlooking the river and the wharf, this inn has a pretty cottage garden, attic bedrooms, and quaint sitting areas. The bar here has been a refuge for seafarers for more than 160 years.

🚩 214 C2 ⊠ 1 Campbell Street, Port Fairy
☎ (03) 5568 2324; www.merrijiginn.com

BALLARAT

Ansonia on Lydiard $$

Polished wood floors, quality bed-linens and Shaker beds are among the fine details here. The Ansonia has a glass atrium roof running the length of the premises. Facilities include a library, guest lounge and a very good restaurant.

🚩 214 C2 ⊠ 32 Lydiard Street South, Ballarat ☎ (03) 5332 4678;
www.theansoniaonlydiard.com.au

Sovereign Hill Lodge $–$$

Overlooking Sovereign Hill, this venue has something to suit all budgets, from suites with Jacuzzis to regular rooms and dormitories.

🚩 214 C3 ⊠ Magpie Street, Ballarat
☎ (03) 5337 1159; www.sovereignhill.com.au

MELBOURNE

Attica $$$

One of Melbourne's best restaurants, the decor here is warm and luxurious, with velvet drapery and sound-muting panels. Specialities include marron tail with sea vegetables, poached quince with stinging nettle sorbet, and sweet crabmeat with barberries. The wine list is extensive.

🚩 218 off C1 ⊠ 74 Glen Eira Road, Ripponlea ☎ (03) 9530 0111;
www.attica.com.au ⏰ Tue–Sat 6pm–10pm;
Fri–Sat noon–2pm; Sat 8am–10.30am

Hopetoun Tea Rooms $

An original etched mirror covers an entire wall of this Victorian tea room situated in a Heritage conservation building, the famous Block Arcade. The tea rooms have refreshed exhausted shoppers for more than a century and afternoon teas are the main culinary feature: savoury pinwheel sandwiches and a large selection of delicious cakes accompanied by a refreshing cup of tea or coffee.

🚩 218 B2 ⊠ Shops 1 & 2 Block Arcade, 282 Collins Street, Melbourne ☎ (03) 9650 2777 ⏰ Mon–Fri 9–4, Sat 10–3

Pearl $$$

Chef Geoff Lindsay produces intrinsically Australian dishes with international flavours using top-quality, fresh ingredients. Selections include roast lamb cutlets with pomegranate, red duck curry with crispy fried egg, stir-fry of minced quail with water chestnuts, and tartare of Moondarra beef. The wine list is exceptional.

☩ 218 off C2 ⊠ 631–633 Church Street (corner of Howard Street), Richmond ☎ (03) 9421 4599; www.pearlrestaurant. com.au 🕔 Daily 12–11

Richmond Hill Café & Larder $–$$

Housed in a Victorian building in the lively inner suburb of Richmond, this casual café and cheese shop has a marvellous atmosphere and offers top-quality food at reasonable prices. Go for breakfast, brunch, lunch or try one of the famous cheese platters – dishes are seasonal and Mediterranean or French-inspired, featuring

☩ 218 off C2 ⊠ 48–50 Bridge Road, Richmond ☎ (03) 9421 2808 🕔 Daily 8:30–5

The Stokehouse $$–$$$

On St Kilda's waterfront and with views across Port Phillip Bay, the very popular Stokehouse offers two options. Fine dining is available upstairs, while the downstairs section is an informal bistro with outdoor seating – both sections of the restaurant have great food.

☩ 218 off C1 ⊠ 30 Jacka Boulevard, St Kilda ☎ (03) 9525 5555; www.stokehouse. com.au 🕔 Daily 12–2, 6–10

PHILLIP ISLAND/ MORNINGTON PENINSULA

The Baths $–$$

Located on the beach at Sorrento, on the Mornington Peninsula, this airy restaurant occupies the site of the old sea baths, once frequented for their health-giving properties. Nowadays, the Modern Australian cuisine is the drawcard, featuring innovative seafood, meat and chicken dishes and a range of tempting desserts. There is also an inexpensive "Fish and Chippery".

☩ 215 D2 ⊠ 3278 Point Nepean Road, Sorrento ☎ (03) 5984 1500; www.thebaths.com.au 🕔 Daily 8:30am–11pm

The Foreshore Bar and Restaurant $$–$$$

With great ocean views, outdoor seating and a bar area, this is one of the best restaurants on Phillip Island. The menu includes snacks, soups, salads, pies, seafood such as oysters, mussels and barramundi, and the island's own beef and lamb.

☩ 215 D2 ⊠ 11 Beach Road, Rhyll, Phillip Island ☎ (03) 5956 9520; www.theforeshore.com.au 🕔 Daily 12–2:30, 6–8:30

Hotel $–$$

All-day dining is available at this café/restaurant/bar opposite the Cowes jetty. From hearty breakfasts and light meals such as sandwiches and focaccias, to mains like fish and chips or porterhouse steak, Hotel offers very good value.

☩ 215 D2 ⊠ 11–13 The Esplanade, Cowes, Phillip Island ☎ (03) 5952 2600; www.hotelphillipisland.com 🕔 Breakfast, lunch and dinner daily

GREAT OCEAN ROAD

Chris's Beacon Point Restaurant & Villas $$–$$$

Chef-owner Chris Talihmanidis hails from Greece and makes regular trips back there to source ideas for this well-reputed modern Greek venue with superb ocean views. Local crayfish and other seafood feature on the menu along with wines from nearby producers.

☩ 214 C2 ⊠ 280 Skenes Creek Road, Skenes Creek, near Apollo Bay ☎ (03) 5237 6411; www.chriss.com.au 🕔 Daily 8:30am–10:30pm

Kosta's $$–$$$

With sea-facing windows and white walls decorated with local

Where to...
Shop

Melbourne is Australia's style capital and a shoppers' paradise. At its heart are **Collins Street**, a lengthy strip of designer fashion names, and the **Bourke Street Mall** area, where you'll find a collection of Australia's mid-priced quality brands. Here, too, is the **GPO shopping centre** – a sophisticated fashion, food and general shopping precinct.

The key department stores, **Myer** and **David Jones**, are here too. The adjacent Little Collins Street, known as Men's Alley, offers a good selection of mid-priced casual boutiques.

At the city's northern edge, **Melbourne Central** (300 Lonsdale Street) has more than 300 stores, a cinema complex and many bars and restaurants. Nearby, the glamorous QV development (Albert Coates Lane, off Lonsdale Street) offers a range of exclusive boutiques.

The city centre has a notable collection of book shops, including **Hill of Content** (tel: (03) 9662 9472) for its general range, and the sizeable **Foreign Language Bookshop** (tel: (03) 9654 2883).

Flinders Lane is the centre of the city's art world. Here you can peruse the **Flinders Lane Gallery** (tel: (03) 9654 3332) and **Gallery Gabrielle Pizzi** (tel: (03) 9654 2944). A large number of art dealers may also be found in Gertrude Street, Fitzroy, in nearby Brunswick Street and around Richmond and South Yarra.

Don't forget **Queen Victoria Market** (▶ 94), where you can shop or take a guided walking tour.

MELBOURNE CITY CENTRE

---

art, Kosta's is one of Lorne's most popular restaurants. The menu, Modern Australian with Greek influences, changes seasonally.

➕ 214 C2 ⊠ 48 Mountjoy Parade, Lorne ☎ (03) 5289 1883 ⓦ Wed–Sun 6–10, lunch in summer only

Pippies by the Bay $$

Modern Australian cuisine is the speciality of Pippies, part of the Flagstaff Hill Maritime Village and one of the Great Ocean Road's finest restaurants. Choose from a range of seafood, or meat or vegetarian dishes created from the best local produce. Get a table that overlooks Flagstaff Hill and Lady Bay.

➕ 214 C2 ⊠ Flagstaff Hill, 91 Merri Street, Warrnambool ☎ (03) 5561 2188; www.flagstaffhill.com ⓦ Tue–Fri 10am–late, Sat 9am–late, Sun 9–5

BALLARAT

The Boatshed Restaurant $–$$

This stylish but casual venue offers an uninterrupted vista of Lake Wendouree and View Point. The international menu incorporates a variety of modern favourites, from pasta, curries and vegetable platters to fish and chips. Stop for breakfast, lunch, a cocktail, or coffee and cakes.

➕ 214 C2 ⊠ Wendouree Parade, Ballarat ☎ (03) 5333 5533; www.boatshed-restaurant.com ⓦ Daily 7am–late

L'Espresso $–$$

This sophisticated Italian-style cafe, combined with a music store, in the heart of Victoria's most historic gold town, is a pleasant surprise for travellers. Quality pasta and risottos satisfy lunchtime appetites. Leave room for the home-made desserts, which might include hazelnut ice-cream and pear and chocolate tart. Every Thursday to Saturday, the cafe is transformed into a cosy restaurant.

➕ 214 C2 ⊠ 417 Sturt Street, Ballarat ☎ (03) 5333 1789; www.ballarat.net.au/lespresso/ ⓦ Daily 7–6; Fri from 6:30pm

Where to...
Be Entertained

INNER SUBURBS

Chapel Street (www.chapelstreet.com.au) in **South Yarra and Prahran** is the place for fashion names such as Collette Dinnigan (tel: (03) 9827 2111) and Scanlan & Theodore (tel: (03) 9824 1800). In **Toorak Village** are names such as MaxMara (tel: (03) 9824 1511). Husk (tel: (03) 9827 2700), on Malvern Road, offers stylish casuals as well as household goods.

Take a tram ride to **Richmond** for discount shopping: Bridge Road (www.bridgerd.com.au) has factory outlets as well as boutiques offering discounted prestige labels.

OUT OF TOWN

The **Ballarat** region is renowned for its art galleries, antiques, alpaca and woollen products at the historic Creswick Woollen Mills, and for several markets. These include the weekly "Trash and Treasure" markets.

MUSIC AND DRAMA

The centre of Melbourne's concert and theatre scene is the east end of the city, near the State Parliament House. The main venues are the **Princess Theatre** (163 Spring Street, tel: (03) 9299 9800), **Her Majesty's Theatre** (corner of Exhibition and Little Bourke streets, tel: (03) 8643 3300) and **The Comedy Theatre** (corner of Exhibition and Lonsdale streets, tel: (03) 9299 9800).

The **Sidney Myer Music Bowl** (Linlithgow Avenue, tel: (03) 9281 8000), a Greek-style amphitheatre set in gardens, is a premier concert venue and features rock events and classical music. **The Arts Centre** (100 St Kilda Road, tel: (03) 9281 8000; www.theartscentre.com.au) contains venues for theatre, opera, ballet and classical music.

In addition the city is home to several **festivals**: the Melbourne International Arts Festival in October, the International Comedy Festival in March/April, and the Melbourne Food and Wine Festival in February/March.

SPORTING ACTIVITIES

Melbourne is a great city for sporting enthusiasts. The **Australian Open Tennis** championships are in January, and the **Formula One Grand Prix** world championship event is held annually in March. The October/ November **Spring Racing Carnival** includes the internationally renowned **Melbourne Cup** on the first Tuesday of November. The **Australian Rules Football** season runs throughout the winter months culminating in the **Grand Final** at the MCG in September.

NIGHTLIFE

The **Crown Entertainment Complex** (tel: (03) 9292 8888; www.crowncasino.com.au) on the banks of the Yarra River is well worth a visit. Open 24 hours a day, it boasts 13 cinemas, a theatre, 40 restaurants, bars and a nightclub, shopping and more than 300 gaming tables.

OUTSIDE MELBOURNE

Ballarat hosts a **Begonia Festival** in March at the botanical gardens. Along the Great Ocean Road, key events are **Port Fairy Folk Festival** (March) and **Bells Beach** surfing classic (Easter).

Queensland

Getting Your Bearings

Big, sunny, laid-back and outgoing, Queensland is Australia's holiday country. The second largest state after Western Australia, it is a region of tremendous contrasts: behind the sparkling Pacific coastline with its palm-fringed beaches and rolling surf lies a hinterland of lushly forested plateaux and ranges, and fertile farming lands that gradually give way to the vast and colourful Outback.

Established as a self-governing colony in 1859, Queensland has long been sustained by agriculture and mining, but tourism has taken the lead as its major money earner. Climate is a big part of the attraction – much of the Sunshine State is virtually winterless – though the Tropical North's hot and humid wet season (peaking in January to March) can be draining.

Its subtropical capital Brisbane, in the southeast, was founded as a penal settlement in 1824, but is today the most relaxed of Australian cities and a gateway to the non-stop entertainment and sweeping beaches of the glitzy, if sometimes brash, Gold Coast and its cool green hinterland. In the Tropical North, the vibrant city of Cairns is the perfect base for forays into World Heritage rainforests and to the incomparable Great Barrier Reef with its idyllic islands, crystal-clear blue waters, stunning coral and huge variety of marine life.

★ Don't Miss

At Your Leisure

Page 111: Port Douglas beach

Opposite: Surfers Paradise on the Gold Coast

Cooktown

Tropical North Queensland **3**

8 **Tjapukai Aboriginal Cultural Park**

Cairns

7

Atherton Tableland

Innisfail

Hinchinbrook Island National Park

6 **Undara Lava Tubes**

Ingham

Townsville

Great Barrier Reef **2**

Great Basalt National Park

Ayr

Bowen

Hook Island National Park

Charters Towers

Airlie Beach

Whitsunday Islands National Park

Eungella National Park

Mackay

Clermont

Military Training Area

Goodedulla National Park

Great Keppel Island

Emerald

Rockhampton

Curtis Island

Gladstone

Biloela

Great Sandy National Park

Expedition National Park

Bundaberg

Monto

Hervey Bay

Maryborough

5 **Fraser Island**

Murgon

Gympie

Miles

Caloundra

Moreton Island

Dalby

Toowoomba

BRISBANE

Gold Coast Theme Parks **4**

Warwick

Gold Coast & Hinterland **1**

200 km

100 miles

Below: The train from Cairns to Kuranda

In Five Days

If you're not quite sure where to begin your travels, this itinerary recommends a practical and enjoyable five days exploring Queensland, taking in some of the best places to see using the Getting Your Bearings map on the previous page. For more information see the main entries.

Day 1

Head out from Queensland's modern capital, Brisbane, for the 70km (44-mile) drive south along the Pacific Motorway and Gold Coast Highway to one of Australia's best-known holiday playgrounds – the big, brash **❶ Gold Coast** (left; ➤ 116–118), where high-rise development rims superb surfing beaches. Enjoy a day of sand, surf and shopping in Surfers Paradise then, when the sun goes down, turn your attention to wining and dining (➤ 130–131) and, if you're in the mood, the glitz and glamour of Gold Coast nightlife (➤ 129–130 for accommodation).

Day 2

Leaving the hustle and bustle of the Gold Coast, venture into the cool, green **❶ Hinterland** (➤ 116–118) for a scenic day trip to the Green Mountains (O'Reilly's Plateau) section of the World Heritage-listed Lamington National Park. Just 90 minutes' drive from the Gold Coast, the park offers a wealth of subtropical rainforest, majestic mountain scenery and vivid bird life. Return to your accommodation on the Gold Coast for the night.

Day 3

Morning
Drive back early to Brisbane and, leaving the car at the airport, take a 2.25-hour flight to Cairns, an excellent base from which to explore the **❷ Great Barrier Reef** (➤ 119–123).

Afternoon

On arriving in Cairns, spend the rest of the day exploring this modern coastal city, the tourist heart of **3 Tropical North Queensland** (➤ 124–126). Cairns is bounded by the Great Barrier Reef to the east, rainforest-covered hills to the west (above) and palm-fringed beaches to the north and south.

Day 4

Rise early and hop aboard a boat departing from Cairns' Trinity Wharf area and spend a day viewing the brilliantly coloured corals, fish and other fascinating marine life of Australia's top tourist attraction, the World Heritage-listed **2 Great Barrier Reef** (➤ 119–123). After returning to Cairns at day's end, head for a well-earned feed in one of the best seafood restaurants: try Barnacle Bill's on The Esplanade (➤ 131).

Day 5

Morning

Set off early for a scenic drive north of Cairns along the coast-hugging Captain Cook Highway to the World Heritage rainforest of Daintree National Park. Take a cruise on the Daintree River, where you can observe a wealth of Wet Tropics wildlife.

Afternoon

Walk through the ancient rainforest and swim in the crystal-clear waters of Mossman Gorge, then explore the delightful resort village of Port Douglas (left) before returning to Cairns.

◨ Gold Coast and Hinterland

Known as much for its bustling, glittering, brash exuberance as its stunning surf beaches, the Gold Coast is one of Australia's most popular holiday destinations.

With around 300 days of sunshine each year, warm temperatures and 70km (44 miles) of golden beaches stretching from South Stradbroke Island in the north to Coolangatta in the south, this highly developed coastal strip offers swimming, surfing and a host of watersports – as well as restaurants, shops, nightlife and non-stop entertainment (see Gold Coast Theme Parks, ➤ 127). Its overt commercialism may not be to everyone's liking – inducements to spend a fortune are endemic – and it's not the place to come to for peace and quiet, but if you're looking for a holiday with plenty of zest, you won't be disappointed.

Surfers Paradise
Though a popular holiday spot since late in the 19th century, the Gold Coast really began to take off in the 1950s when developers woke up to the area's potential and built the first multi-storeyed beachfront apartments at Surfers Paradise.

Now with a towering skyline, excellent shops, restaurants and a multitude of nightlife options, the town is the place to begin your exploration.

The area around **Cavill Avenue**, its main thoroughfare, is a hive of activity from early morning to late at night, with free street entertainment and shops and indoor and outdoor eateries.

Above: Surfing on the Gold Coast

Below: Highrise apartments at Surfers Paradise

When you've had enough of people-watching and shopping, head for the beach and some surf action.

The wide beach at **Surfers Paradise** has all the essentials – surf, golden sand and clear blue water – but it's also one of the busiest and its fringe of high-rise buildings can cast shadows in the afternoon. If you're happy to stay where the action is (including, for the energetic, free beach-volleyball), spread your towel down here, but to enjoy the prettiest and most peaceful of the Gold Coast's beaches, head south to **Rainbow Bay** at Coolangatta. Curving between two rocky points, this small beach is perfect for swimming, sunbathing and surfing.

Currumbin Wildlife Sanctuary

When you've absorbed enough sun and beach culture, call into Currumbin Wildlife Sanctuary (www.currumbin-sanctuary. org.au), 18km (11 miles) south of Surfers Paradise. This large bushland reserve, featuring animals unique to Australia, is the pick of the region's wildlife parks. A highlight here is the **rainbow lorikeet feeding**, which takes place twice daily. To catch the afternoon session, be sure to arrive by 4pm.

Dining Options

When thoughts turn to food, it's worth knowing that the Gold Coast claims more restaurants per square kilometre than any other place in Australia. The variety of styles and the range of prices cater to all tastes, but if it's fine dining you're after, head to Tedder Avenue at Main Beach and its chic outdoor eateries and bars. For more **good dining and late-evening entertainment** head to Conrad Jupiters Casino at nearby Broadbeach where you can also catch a Las Vegas-style show, while **Orchid Avenue** in Surfers Paradise is the main nightclub and bar strip.

Hinterland

Exchange the gold and blue of the coast for the green of the mountainous hinterland and head west on a scenic drive through Nerang and Canungra to the UNESCO World Heritage-listed **Lamington National Park**. Protecting the largest area of undisturbed subtropical rainforest remaining in southeast Queensland, this park lies on an ancient volcanic landscape known as the Scenic Rim. Its most magnificent forests lie in the Green Mountains section, reached via a winding road that ends at the long-established **O'Reilly's Rainforest Retreat**.

GOLD COAST AND HINTERLAND: INSIDE INFO

Top tips The Gold Coast's beaches are patrolled year-round by professional lifeguards backed up by volunteer Surf Life Saving Association members and are perfectly safe if you follow a few simple rules signalled by coloured flags. **Always swim between the red-and-yellow flags** where the water is under constant surveillance. Red flags mean don't swim, conditions are dangerous, yellow means proceed with caution (strong swimmers only) and green indicates that conditions have become safe again.

■ Dawn and dusk are the best times for fishing in the Gold Coast's inland waterways. The break-walls of the Seaway Entrance and Wave Break Island, inside the Broadwater entrance, offer **excellent shore-based fishing**. Outside the wall is the Sand Pumping Jetty, a safe place for surf fishing, while the tourist strip around Surfers Paradise has good beach fishing, especially in the winter.

As well as offering easy access to forests, creeks and waterfalls, **Green Mountains** is renowned for its bird life. You need go no farther than the picnic grounds or guest house, where crimson rosellas eat seed from your hand, to spot the vivid black-and-gold regent bower bird, while at the perimeter of the forest, pied currawongs, king parrots, satin bower birds and brush-turkeys are readily seen. But the highlight of this area is the **Tree Top Walk**. Swinging 16m (52ft) above the ground, this suspended boardwalk offers close-up views of the rainforest canopy and a 30m (100ft) lookout with spectacular views over the western ranges. When you return to earth, take a walk along one of the many excellent ground-level tracks. The pick of the short walks are the **Rainforest Return**, a 1.3km (0.75-mile) return walk along part of the Border Track that emerges near the guest house, and the 3.4km (2-mile) return walk to Python Rock, which leads to a lookout giving excellent views of a plunging waterfall.

TAKING A BREAK

At **O'Reilly's Rainforest Retreat** (tel: (07) 5544 0644), choose between the inexpensive Mountain Cafe with its casual atmosphere or the guest house dining room, which offers moderately priced three- or four-course meals.

Toolona Creek,
Lamington
National Park

➕ 215 F5

Gold Coast Information and Booking Centre
✉ Cavill Avenue, Surfers Paradise ☎ (07) 5538 4419; www.verygc.com
🕐 Mon–Sat 8:30–5, Sun and public holidays 8:30–4 🚌 Coachtrans from Brisbane 🚉 Helensvale, Nerang and Robina stations (from Brisbane), then Surfside bus to Surfers Paradise ✈ Gold Coast (Coolangatta) Airport

Lamington National Park
☎ (07) 5544 0634 (Green Mountains ranger's office) or (1300) 881 164 (Beaudesert Country Tourism); www.epa.qld.gov.au 💲 Free (day visits)

2 The Great Barrier Reef

A submerged natural wonder of unparalleled beauty, the Great Barrier Reef is the world's biggest coral reef system, stretching for 2,300km (1,430 miles) from the Gulf of Papua along Queensland's golden eastern coast to just beyond the Tropic of Capricorn.

Snorkelling on the Great Barrier Reef

Encompassing nearly 3,000 individual reefs, more than 600 continental islands and 300 coral cays (low-lying sand islands), the Great Barrier Reef owes its existence to tiny coral animals called polyps, which provide the building-blocks for reef construction. As polyps die, their coral skeletons remain, which gradually form the hard reef.

Today's Great Barrier Reef – protected in a marine park larger than Great Britain – has been developing in this way for some 18,000 years, growing above the remains of much older reefs when sea levels rose at the end of the last Ice Age. Spectacular corals, however, are just part of the story: the reef is home to an incredible array of life forms including 400 kinds of soft and hard coral, riotously coloured fishes, giant turtles, dugongs (a distant marine relative of the elephant), humpback whales, manta rays, dolphins, sea birds and migratory wading birds. No place on land – not even the adjacent rainforests – has a greater variety of life.

Getting There

To see this underwater world at its best you need to head to the outer reef, which is most easily accessible from **Cairns** (► 124), just 50km (30 miles) distant: at its southern end, the outer reef is up to 300km (186 miles) from the mainland. There are dozens of Cairns- and Port Douglas-based day trip options, with major operators such as Sunlover Reef Cruises and Quicksilver offering the smoothest rides to outer-reef pontoons aboard luxuriously appointed, fast catamarans. You'll see the full range of coral and other marine life by scuba diving or snorkelling, but if you prefer not to get wet, you can still get a good view from a semi-submersible or glass-bottomed boat. You can also take a scenic flight in a helicopter that leaves from landing platforms moored at the outer reef. It's not cheap, but the perspective is pure magic.

Agincourt Reef is the closest of the pristine ribbon reefs, while a trip to **Arlington Reef** is also a very worthwhile experience. If you're comfortable with night diving or snorkelling and your visit coincides with late spring or early summer, do not miss the opportunity of seeing the coral spawning, when the reef's coral polyps reproduce in a technicolour explosion of billions of tiny eggs and sperm. One of the natural world's most dramatic events, it occurs for a few nights after a full moon in October or November, and has been likened to an underwater snowstorm.

Island Resorts

Idyllic palm-fringed islands, whose white-sand beaches are lapped by warm turquoise waters, are as much a part of the Great Barrier Reef experience as the coral itself. Though most of the reef's islands and coral cays are uninhabited, a number cater for visitors with accommodation that ranges from luxury resorts to basic camping. At the luxury end of the market are the resorts on **Lizard, Green, Bedarra, Hinchinbrook,**

The reef is surrounded by glorious blue sea

A diver and a potato cod, a species native to Australia

Orpheus and Hayman islands. Although the fulfilment of every romantic's dream, these "fantasy" resorts come at a hefty price and good-value alternatives include **Great Keppel, Long, Dunk, Hamilton and Brampton**.

Only four island resorts – Lizard, Green, Heron and Lady Elliot – offer the reef directly off their shoreline and of these, tiny (12ha/30-acre) Green Island, a beautiful coral cay with thick tropical vegetation just 27km (17 miles) from Cairns, is the most easily accessible for day trippers. (In fact, Heron Island is the exclusive domain of resort guests.) For that reason Green Island can be crowded, but if you don't mind sharing your beach, coral and rainforest with numerous fellow holidaymakers, it makes a great day trip. For those who're happy to leave resort facilities behind, the **Frankland Islands** – entirely national parkland – are a less well-known day trip destination from Cairns offering excellent snorkelling, diving, beaches and leisurely rainforest walks without the crowds.

With Time to Spare…

If you've got a week or so to spare, treat yourself to one of the most magical of Great Barrier Reef experiences – a

VIEWING THE REEF

- **Diving** Without doubt, **scuba diving** is the best way to appreciate the reef. Whether you're an experienced diver or a beginner, there is a **range of diving options**, from simply walking off the beach into a coral garden to wall, wreck, drift and eco dives – the latter accompanied by marine ecologists or reef guides who explain the reef's rich and complex life forms. If you've always wanted to learn to dive, this is the place to do it, with the best schools found in Cairns, Port Douglas, Townsville and Airlie Beach. To get your basic open-water certification you'll need to undertake a five-day course, consisting of two days' pool and classroom training and three days on the reef. For those with less time, resort dives – a single dive with an instructor, available on most day cruises and island resorts – are an excellent alternative.
- **Snorkelling** The next best thing to diving on the reef is snorkelling on the surface where coral reefs are shallow. Day cruises to the outer reef generally provide masks, snorkels and fins as part of the package as well as buoyant vests for less-confident swimmers. Unlike diving, it takes only a few minutes to learn the basics.
- **"Dry" options** If you really don't want to get wet, you can still get a good view of the reef from a **glass-bottomed boat or semi-submersible and underwater observatories**. Alternatively, you can take a **scenic flight** over the reef in a helicopter or fixed-wing craft.

leisureley sail around the **Whitsunday Islands** (www.whitsundaytourism.com), off Queensland's central coast. Scattered on both sides of the Whitsunday Passage, the 74 "emerald" islands that make up the group are the forested peaks of a drowned mountain range. Most are wholly or largely national parkland with several offering beach camping. There is a good range of **island resorts** too, from luxurious Hayman to family-style Club Crocodile on Long Island and low-key Hook. Collectively the Whitsundays offer a paradise of sandy beaches, clear turquoise waters, rainforests and colourful reefs that can be explored by staying on the islands or cruising around them. Most vessels leave from Shute Harbour or Airlie Beach, with day cruises generally stopping at a few islands and offering snorkelling and resort visits.

Other day cruise options have a more specialized focus such as **whale-watching** (July to November), fishing, diving or exploring secluded coves. Extended cruises cover similar territory. For experienced sailors, **bareboat (sail-yourself) chartering** is the way to go. If you choose this option, be sure to include the following highlights: Whitsunday Island's stunning **Whitehaven Beach**, by far the best in the group with 6km (4 miles) of fine white sand and good snorkelling at its southern end; fiord-like **Nara Inlet at Hook Island** for superb coral trout fishing; and the magnificent fringing coral at Butterfly Bay, Manta Ray Bay and Langford Reef.

Opposite: A school of grunt fish

✠ 211 E3

Tourism Queensland
☎ (07) 3535 3535; www.tq.com.au ▯ Proserpine, Townsville, Cairns
✖ Whitsunday Coast, Hamilton Island, Townsville, Cairns

THE GREAT BARRIER REEF: INSIDE INFO

Top tips The best time to visit the northern Great Barrier Reef is from **May to October** when the days are sunny, the humidity low and the seas calm. Rain and storms are common from November to April. However, tours to the reef run all year.

■ When snorkelling or diving, **take care not to stand on or touch any coral**: the delicate polyps are easily crushed. Such attentiveness to the reef's health will also help you avoid coming in contact with marine nasties such as the extremely poisonous stonefish, which lies on the bottom looking like a rock or lump of coral.

■ For Reef and World Heritage information visit www.gbrmpa.gov.au

3 Tropical North Queensland

Two of Australia's greatest natural treasures – the Wet Tropics rainforests and the Great Barrier Reef, both World Heritage listed – come together in Tropical North Queensland to create one of the country's most alluring holiday destinations.

Here are golden palm-fringed beaches, azure waters brimming with coral and marine life and luxuriant rainforests inhabited by rare wildlife and glistening with rushing streams. Amid this natural splendour resort towns provide the creature comforts with accommodation that ranges from the simple to the idyllic, sophisticated restaurants and casual cafes. The region offers a multitude of holiday experiences and the best place to begin your exploration is in its "capital", Cairns.

Cairns

Founded in 1876 as the port for inland goldfields, Cairns today is a modern city set between the twin backdrops of rainforest-clad hills and the waters of Trinity Bay. In some ways a victim of its own popularity, it has lost much of its laid-back atmosphere and its main attraction nowadays is as a base for exploring the surrounding region. That said, there are still places in town that are well worth visiting. Begin with a stroll along **The Esplanade**, which is flanked by parkland and a man-made lagoon on its bay side and a busy cafe and restaurant strip on the other. It's the hub of the city and the place where people come to eat and watch sea birds feeding on the tidal mudflats.

Just a short distance from The Esplanade, down Shields Street, is the excellent **Cairns Regional Gallery**, which features the work of local artists as well as touring exhibitions from major galleries. After visiting the gallery, spend some time wandering the city streets, browsing in the shops and relaxing with a cooling drink at one of the alfresco cafes.

Come sundown, head for one of the many restaurants on The Esplanade, Shields Street or Grafton Street (such as Perrotta's at the Gallery on the corner of Shields Street) then sample the best of **Cairns nightlife** at Johno's Blues Bar, (corner of Abbott and Aplin Streets) which has live music every night until late.

Rainforest

While based in Cairns, rent a car and explore the rainforest. Head north along the **Captain Cook Highway** for a beautiful 75km (47-mile) drive past isolated beaches, around headlands and through archways of tropical forest

to the sugar-milling town of Mossman, then continue for another 35km (22 miles) to Daintree Village. Be sure to stop at **Rex Lookout** along the way – a popular haunt for hang-gliders, it offers superb views over the Coral Sea and the coastline. Just before reaching the village, stop at the **Daintree River Cruise Centre** for an hour's drift along this pristine waterway, which forms the southern border of the Cape Tribulation section of Daintree National Park. Apart from giving you a fascinating insight into rainforest and mangrove ecology, the cruise provides the perfect vehicle for spotting a multitude of wildlife, including crocodiles, birds, fruit bats, tree snakes, butterflies and frogs.

Above: Cairns Botanical Gardens

Below: Palm Grove is Cairns' main beach

Continue on to Daintree Village for lunch then backtrack to Mossman, the gateway to the magnificent **Daintree National Park** (www.daintreevillage.asn.au). Part of the Wet Tropics rainforests, the Daintree is home to a remarkable array of plants and animals including the rare Bennett's tree kangaroo, the flightless cassowary, enormous birdwing butterflies and

thousands of orchid species. The
most easily accessible part of
the Daintree is **Mossman Gorge**
where you can take a short walk
through ancient rainforest to
the boulder-strewn river and its
crystal-clear swimming holes.

On the way back to Cairns,
make a detour off the highway to
Port Douglas, a one-time fishing
settlement turned resort village.
Despite its transformation into a
fashionable tourist enclave, the
village still retains its close-knit
community atmosphere and is
well worth a visit, even if only to enjoy the golden perfection
of its **Four Mile Beach** or to take in the sweeping views from
overlooking **Flagstaff Hill**. Port Douglas is also a departure
point for cruises to the outer reef.

Mirage
Marina,
Port Douglas

TAKING A BREAK

At **Daintree Discovery Centre** (tel: (07) 4098 9171), 10km
(6 miles) north of Daintree ferry, enjoy rainforest views with
a coffee and a snack.

✚ 211 D3

Tourism Tropical North Queensland Visitor Information Centre
✚ 211 D3 ✉ 51 The Esplanade, Cairns ☎ (07) 4051 3588;
www.tropicalaustralia.com.au ⏰ Daily 8:30–6:30, public holidays 10–6;
closed Good Fri, 25 Dec, 1 Jan 🚌 Reef Fleet Terminal (interstate buses);
Lake Street Terminus (local buses) 🚉 Cairns ✈ Cairns

Cairns Regional Gallery
✚ 211 D3 ✉ Corner of Abbott and Shields streets, Cairns ☎ (07) 4046
4800; www.cairnsregionalgallery.com.au ⏰ Mon–Sat 10–5, Sun and public
holidays 1–5; closed 1 Jan, Good Fri, 25 and 26 Dec 💲 Inexpensive

---

TROPICAL NORTH QUEENSLAND: INSIDE INFO

Top tips From late October to June is the **marine stinger (jellyfish) season**, when
the safest place to swim is a hotel pool. At beaches, swim only in netted
enclosures when lifeguards are present. Marine stingers are rarely found on
the reef itself or on island beaches.
■ **Avoid getting sunburn**, especially on reef trips: wear a hat and use factor 30+
sunscreen.
■ It is cheaper to buy **disposable underwater cameras** on the mainland.

In more depth At the **Rainforest Habitat Wildlife Sanctuary** (tel: (07) 4099 3235;
www.rainforesthabitat.com.au), on Port Douglas Road, Port Douglas, you can
observe more than 140 bird, butterfly, marsupial and reptile species from
elevated boardwalks winding through recreated rainforest, wetlands, woodland
and grassland habitats.

At Your Leisure

4 Gold Coast Theme Parks

For sheer fun and thrills, albeit at a price, there is no better place than the Gold Coast's theme parks. **Sea World** includes the antics of polar bears, trained dolphins and the water-ski team's stunts, while its star ride is the Corkscrew Rollercoaster. For a slice of Hollywood, visit **Warner Bros Movie World** where you can tour the movie sets and watch live shows. Here, too, are two of the coast's best rides – the Lethal Weapon suspended roller-coaster and Batman Adventure. **Wet'n'Wild Water World's** giant slides offer the ultimate in aquatic fun, while adrenaline junkies get thrills on **Dreamworld's** fast rides.

Sea World
🔢 215 F5 ✉ Sea World Drive, Main Beach
☎ 13 33 86; www.seaworld.myfun.com.au
🕐 Daily 10–5:30; closed 25 Dec, Anzac Day
💲 Expensive 🚌 Surfside 715

Warner Bros Movie World
🔢 215 F5 ✉ Pacific Motorway, Oxenford
☎ 13 33 86; www.movieworld.myfun.com.au
🕐 Daily 10–5:30; closed 25 Dec, Anzac Day
💲 Expensive 🚌 Surfside TX1 TX2

Wet'n'Wild Water World
🔢 215 F5 ✉ Pacific Motorway, Oxenford
☎ 13 33 86; www.wetnwild.myfun.com.au
🕐 Daily 10–5 in summer; 10–4 in winter;
Dec–Jan 10–9; closed 25 Dec, Anzac Day
💲 Expensive 🚌 Surfside TX1, TX2

Dreamworld
🔢 215 F5 ✉ Dreamworld Parkway, Coomera
☎ (07) 5588 1111; www.dreamworld.com.au
🕐 Daily 10–5; Anzac Day 1–5; closed 25 Dec
💲 Expensive 🚌 Surfside TX1, TX2
ℹ For all theme parks, Gold Coast
Tourist Shuttle bus can collect you from your accommodation

5 Fraser Island

UNESCO World Heritage listed for its catalogue of natural wonders that include fantastically sculpted cliffs of coloured sands, freshwater lakes, mighty sand blows, surf beaches and rainforests, Fraser Island – off southern Queensland's coast – is the perfect holiday destination for nature lovers and those in search of peace and quiet. At 123km (76 miles) in length, it is the world's largest sand island, making four-wheel-drive vehicles an essential means of exploration. Fraser Island is also famous for its large dingo population, but remember these are wild animals that can be aggressive and unpredictable. Do not miss driving along the east coast's 75-Mile Beach, swimming in the fresh waters of Lake McKenzie, gazing at the 70m (230-foot) high satinays (a type of turpentine tree, related to eucalypts) in Pile Valley, admiring the coloured sand-cliffs at The Cathedrals and strolling along Wanggoolba Creek's fern-fringed boardwalk. You can see the highlights in a rushed day trip, but stay for a few days to appreciate the island's beauty.
🔢 211 F1

Hervey Bay Visitor
Information Centre
✉ 262 Urraween Road, Hervey Bay ☎ (07)
4125 9855; www.frasercoastholidays.info
🕐 Daily 9–5; closed Good Fri, 25 Dec
🚢 From Hervey Bay, River Heads or Inskip Point

Lake Mackenzie, Fraser Island

❻ Undara Lava Tubes

The largest lava tube system in the world, Undara Lava Tubes are a four-hour drive southwest of Cairns. They were formed some 190,000 years ago when a now-extinct volcano erupted. The outer layers of lava quickly cooled and hardened while inside, fiery streams gradually drained away, leaving behind long, hollow tubes. Ancient roof collapses have since created fertile pockets in which prehistoric rainforest plants thrive – an incongruous sight amid the surrounding dry scrub. Join a tour to explore these awesome tubes, the largest of which is 23m (75 feet) wide and 17m (55 feet) high.

➕ 211 D3 ✉ Undara Volcanic National Park, near Mount Surprise ☎ Undara Experience: (07) 4097 1900 and (1800) 990 992 in Australia; www.undara.com.au 🕐 Daily tours: 2-hour, half-day or full-day tours and scenic flights 💲 Expensive ❗ There are return daily bus and flight services between Cairns and Undara or you can self-drive in a conventional vehicle. Accommodation is available for overnight stays

❼ Atherton Tableland

Providing a cool retreat from the hot, humid coast, the Atherton Tableland behind Cairns is a serene upland region of rolling farmlands, rainforests, volcanic lakes, waterfalls and pretty villages. Its most popular attraction is the rainforest village of Kuranda, which though slightly spoiled by tourism is still worth visiting. Highlights include the colourful markets, butterfly sanctuary, bird aviaries and Rainforestation Nature Park. Though you can reach Kuranda by car, the most spectacular way to arrive is by train on the famous Kuranda Scenic Railway, or in a gondola on the Skyrail Rainforest Cableway, gliding for 7.5km (5 miles) above the rainforest canopy.

➕ 211 D3

Atherton Tableland Information Centre
✉ Corner of Main Street and Silo Road, Atherton ☎ (07) 4091 4222; www.athertoninformationcentre.com.au 🕐 Daily 9–5; closed 1 Jan, Good Fri, Easter Sun, 25 and 26 Dec 🚍 Kuranda 🚉 Kuranda

❽ Tjapukai Aboriginal Cultural Park

The park provides an excellent introduction to Aboriginal culture. With three theatres, a museum, an art gallery and a gift shop, the park is both fun and educational. Highlights include the **Creation Theatre** where giant holograms bring Dreamtime stories to life, performances of Tjapukai corroborees and songs and the Camp Cultural Village where you can throw spears and boomerangs, play the didgeridoo and sample bush foods and medicines.

➕ 211 D3 ✉ Kamerunga Road, Smithfield, 17km (11 miles) north of Cairns ☎ (07) 4042 9900; www.tjapukai.com.au 🕐 Daily 9–5 and from 7 for evening shows; closed 25 Dec 💲 Expensive 🚍 Sunbus 1, 1A or the Park shuttle service (call for details)

Millaa Millaa Falls in the rainforest of the Atherton Tableland

Where to... Stay

Prices
Prices are for the least expensive double room in high season:
$ under A$150 **$$** A$150–A$280 **$$$** over A$280

GOLD COAST AND HINTERLAND

The Bearded Dragon $–$$
Set on farmland on the forested Tamborine Plateau, this good-value country lodge has 18 rooms, as well as an on-site restaurant and bar.
215 F5 Lot 2 Tamborine Mountain Road, Tamborine (07) 5543 6888; www.beardeddragon.com.au

BreakFree Diamond Beach Resort $$
This popular resort, set in tropical gardens and a short walk from the beach, is very good value. There is a choice of fully self-contained one-, two- or three-bedroom apartments, and facilities include an outdoor pool, spa and barbecue area.
215 F5 10–16 Alexandra Avenue, Broadbeach (07) 5570 0000; www.diamondbeachresort.com.au

Hotel Watermark Gold Coast $$–$$$
Watermark has 385 well-appointed rooms, spectacular views, and facilities such as two pools, a day spa, gymnasium, two bars/restaurants and conference rooms.
215 F5 3032 Surfers Paradise Boulevard, Surfers Paradise (07) 5588 8333; www.hotelwatermarkgoldcoast.com.au

Sheraton Mirage Resort and Spa Gold Coast $$$
This luxurious hotel has beautifully furnished rooms with antiques and tapestries. A network of pools winds around the complex.
215 F5 Sea World Drive, Main Beach (07) 5591 1488; www.starwoodhotels.com/sheraton

AIRLIE BEACH

Coral Sea Resort $$–$$$
In a spectacular location near the marina, this place overlooks boats on their way to the Whitsundays. The secluded pool, bar and open dining deck all face the sea.
211 E3 25 Oceanview Avenue, Airlie Beach (07) 4964 1300; www.coralsearesort.com.au

Whitsunday Terraces Resort $–$$
Verandahs with ocean views make the most of cooling breezes in these quiet units just off the main street. The apartments feature queen-size beds and air-conditioning.
211 E3 Golden Orchid Drive, Airlie Beach (07) 4946 6788; www.qresorts.com.au

CAIRNS/PORT DOUGLAS

Cairns Reef 'n' Rainforest B&B $$
Wake to the songs of native birds and the sounds of the nearby waterfall at this new B&B set in a tropical rainforest. All mod cons are on offer and it is only minutes from Cairns City. Helpful owners will assist with your sightseeing plans.
211 D3 112 Mansfield Street, Earlville (0448) 209 022; www.cairnsreefbnb.com.au

Rydges Sabaya Resort Port Douglas $$
This comparatively inexpensive resort has 192 rooms and one- or two-bedroom apartments. Just minutes from Port Douglas, and close to Four Mile Beach, the resort offers a lagoon-style swimming pool, day spa and kids' club.

Where to...
Eat and Drink

Prices
Prices per person for a meal, excluding drinks, tax and tip:
$ under A$20 $$ A$20–A$30 $$$ over A$30

BRISBANE, GOLD COAST AND HINTERLAND

e'cco $$$

This glamorous venue is one of Queensland's most prestigious restaurants and has won many culinary awards. The well-presented food is simple and stylish, such as roast venison, duck breast and seared scallops. The desserts are brilliant and there is a perfectly formed wine list.

➕ 215 F5 ⊠ 100 Boundary Street, Brisbane ☎ (07) 3831 8344; www.eccobistro.com ⏰ Tue–Fri 12–2:30, Tue–Sat 6pm–late

Mermaids Dining Room/Bar $

With a beachside location at the surfing mecca of Burleigh Point, Mermaids offers idyllic and casual alfresco dining at its best. Start the day with a hearty beachfront breakfast, or choose from a variety of light luncheon salads, seafood dishes, and fresh fruit desserts. Seasonal dinner menus include vegetarian dishes, as well as beef, poultry, and seafood specialities.

➕ 215 F5 ⊠ 43 Goodwin Terrace, Burleigh Heads ☎ (07) 5520 1177; www.mermaidsonburleigh.com ⏰ Daily from 7:30 breakfast, lunch, Wed–Sun dinner

Moo Moo The Wine Bar + Grill $$–$$$

Serving innovative modern Australian cuisine and specializing in steak dishes, this relaxed restaurant and wine bar is a favourite with locals and visitors. Other choices include seafood, kangaroo, duck, and vegetarian dishes. Desserts are tempting, but if you don't have a sweet tooth, you can try excellent cheeses.

➕ 215 F5 ⊠ 2685 Gold Coast Highway, Broadbeach ☎ (07) 5539 9952; www.moomoorestaurant.com ⏰ Daily lunch from noon, dinner from 6

Ristorante Fellini $$$

Gaze across the marina at this top restaurant. The food is modern Italian drawing on abundant seafood and the rich produce of the hinterland. Desserts are sumptuous and there is an extensive wine list.

➕ 215 F5 ⊠ level 1, Marina Mirage, Seaworld Drive, Main Beach ☎ (07) 5531 0300; www.fellini.com.au ⏰ Daily 12–3, 6–10:30

➕ 211 D3 ⊠ 87–109 Port Douglas Road, Port Douglas ☎ (07) 4099 8900; www.rydges.com

Shangri-La Hotel, The Marina, Cairns $$$

As you enter, you'll be impressed by the waterfalls in the lobby and a tropical aquarium. Overlooking Trinity Bay, it's close to Pier Marketplace, and also to Marlin Marina and Trinity Wharf, both departure points for cruises to the Great Barrier Reef.

➕ 211 D3 ⊠ Pierpoint Road, Cairns ☎ (07) 4031 1411; www.shangri-la.com

DAINTREE

Daintree Eco Lodge & Spa $$$

This stylish lodge has 15 raised villas that make the most of the tropical setting. Designed to harmonize with the environment, it promises an enchanting stay.

➕ 211 D3 ⊠ 20 Daintree Road, Daintree ☎ (07) 4098 6100; www.daintree-ecolodge.com.au

Where to... Shop

GOLD COAST

The **Centro Surfers Paradise** on Cavill Mall opposite the beach is the place to do any general shopping; in addition to the supermarket there are more than 100 speciality shops, duty-free stores and cafes. You can also enjoy ten-pin bowling, rides and the games arcade. The area's Sunday craft market is held by local beaches, rotating between Broadbeach, Coolangatta and Burleigh Heads; check with the visitor centre (tel: (07) 5538 4419).

BRISBANE

Brisbane's main shopping precinct is the **Queen Street Mall**, with six shopping centres, arcades and

CAIRNS/PORT DOUGLAS

2 Fish Seafood Restaurant $$–$$$

As its name implies, this happening Port Douglas establishment specializes in seafood, with Asian and Mediterranean influences. The menu includes oysters, king prawns, mussels, and tropical fish such as barramundi and coral trout, but also vegetarian, chicken and meat dishes.

➕ 211 D3 ✉ 7/20 Wharf Street, Port Douglas ☎ (07) 4099 6350; www.2fishrestaurant.com.au ⏰ Daily 12–2, 6–10

Barnacle Bill's Seafood Inn $$–$$$

People flock to this waterfront restaurant, which has both indoor and outdoor dining areas. Seafood, including prawns, oysters, scallops, crayfish, mud crabs and barramundi, and fish dishes, such as bouillabaisse, are the main attraction here, but the menu

also offers pasta, steak, chicken, vegetarian, kangaroo and crocodile dishes. Book ahead.

➕ 211 D3 ✉ 103 The Esplanade, Cairns ☎ (07) 4051 2241; www.barnaclebills.com.au ⏰ Daily 5–late

L'Unico Trattoria Italiano $$

Just a 15-minute drive north of Cairns, this Italian restaurant with water views is the heart of Trinity Beach's social scene. Known for its friendly service, L'Unico offers pastas, pizzas, seafood, antipasto and much more. In addition to lunch and dinner, snacks are served all day, and drinks are available on the verandah. BYO is permitted.

➕ 211 D3 ✉ 75 Vasey Esplanade, Trinity Beach ☎ (07) 4057 8855; www.lunico.net.au ⏰ Lunch and dinner daily from 12

Ochre Restaurant $$–$$$

A wide variety of native bush ingredients are used in the menu of this exciting restaurant. Dine on the Heritage-listed verandah or inside, where the wide windows provide

a relaxing view. Dishes range from crisp-fried calamari to kangaroo stir fry, as well as crocodile and emu.

➕ 211 D3 ✉ Corner of Shields and Sheridan streets, Cairns ☎ (07) 4051 0100; www.ochrerestaurant.com.au ⏰ Mon–Fri 12–3, daily 6–10

DAINTREE

Julaymba Restaurant & Gallery $$$

Part of the award-winning Daintree Eco Lodge (▶ 130), Julaymba specializes in tropical gourmet cuisine. Using local produce, and incorporating indigenous nuts, berries, leaves and seeds, the menu is truly unusual. Their signature dish is wild barramundi served with native herbs and a salad. The restaurant is adorned with Aboriginal artworks and has a terrace overlooking a lagoon.

➕ 211 D3 ✉ Daintree Eco Lodge & Spa, 20 Daintree Road, Daintree ☎ (07) 4098 6100; www.daintree-ecolodge.com.au ⏰ Breakfast, lunch and dinner daily

speciality shops. At the top end is the six-level **Myer Centre**, which has 200 shops, and an eight-screen cinema complex. Over the bridge is **South Bank Parklands**, for souvenir shopping, craft markets and food outlets. At **Eagle Street Pier** are the Sunday Riverside and Eagle Street Pier markets, specializing in arts and crafts. See also www.ourbrisbane.com

CAIRNS

Cairns is geared towards the tourist market, with souvenir shops proliferating. However, **Cairns Regional Gallery** at the corner of Abbott and Shields streets is housed in a heritage building and includes a fine arts and crafts shop and gourmet foods outlet in the cafe. For more general shopping, head to **Cairns Central** on the corner of McLeod and Spence streets; it incorporates a supermarket, two department stores, 180 speciality shops and a cinema complex.

Where to...
Be Entertained

Brisbane's main performance venue is the **Queensland Performing Arts Centre** (tel: (07) 3840 7444, or 13 62 46 within Australia). Part of the South Bank's vast Queensland Cultural Centre, which includes the city's museum, art gallery and the State Library, the centre has five performance spaces including the 1800-seat Concert Hall.

Free outdoor performances are staged in **South Bank Parklands** on Brisbane River Foreshore, where you can also wander through the weekend market, relax in cafes or take a scenic cruise. At Surfers Paradise, the **Gold Coast Arts Centre** at 135 Bundall Road (tel: (07) 5581 6500) features

MUSIC AND THEATRE

theatre, cinema, drama, comedy, dance and concerts.

NIGHTLIFE

Conrad Jupiters Casino (tel: (07) 5592 8100) at Broadbeach on the Gold Coast is open 24 hours a day and offers seven live shows each week in addition to its gaming tables. The same company owns Brisbane's leading **Conrad Treasury Casino** (tel: (07) 3306 8888) on Queen Street. When in Cairns, head to the **Hotel Sofitel Reef Casino Cairns** (tel: (07) 4030 8888).

SPORTING EVENTS AND SHOWS

Queensland has endless major one-off international sports events,

whether it be rugby union, tennis, cricket, swimming or golf.

Brisbane's **Winter Racing Carnival** runs from May to July at venues around the city. In September, the **Brisbane River Festival** has regattas, dragon boats and other aquatic activities.

The **Royal Queensland Show**, "The Ekka", primarily an agricultural event and fun fair, is held at Brisbane Showground during August. The **Wintersun carnival** at Coolangatta on the Gold Coast, in early June, specializes in outdoor concerts, particularly rock'n'roll revival acts.

The Brisbane Courier-Mail offers music and film details on Thursday, outdoor activity information on Friday and what's on in the arts scene on Saturday. Check the *Gold Coast Sun* or *Cairns Post* for entertainment news in those regions.

Northern Territory

Getting Your Bearings

With its wide open spaces, sparse population, isolation and uncompromising climate, the Northern Territory is still a frontier land. Its boundaries encompass areas of exceptional natural beauty, ancient Aboriginal culture and extraordinary landforms including that most recognizable of Australian icons, Uluṟu, and Kakadu National Park.

Just over 50 per cent of the Territory's 1,346,200sq km (525,018 square miles) is Aboriginal-owned land and a greater number of traditional communities have survived here than anywhere else in Australia, making it the place to learn more about their culture. Most Territorians live in the two major population centres: Darwin in the tropical Top End and Alice Springs in the arid Red Centre. Historically a site of great devastation, Darwin was bombed by the Japanese in World War II and almost destroyed by Cyclone Tracy in 1974. Today's Darwin, closer to Asia and far more laid back than the cities of Australia's southern half, is a colourful, multicultural place that is home to more than a few Outback "characters". Equally modern Alice Springs has undergone a rapid, albeit less drastic, evolution from dusty frontier settlement to modern township. Both centres are not only great destinations in their own right, but perfect bases for exploring the Territory's many natural attractions.

★ **Don't Miss**

At Your Leisure

Croker Island

Garig Gunak Barlu National Park

Melville Island

Cobourg Peninsula

Bathurst Island

Van Diemen Gulf

0   50 km
0   30 miles

Crocodylus Park

DARWIN 🛫 **5**
Aquascene ☐ Howard Springs

Jabiru ☐

36

Arnhem Land

Litchfield National Park 6
☐ Adelaide River

son Bay

STUART HIGHWAY

21

Kakadu National Park **1**

Page 133:
Standley
Chasm, Alice
Springs

Opposite: The
road to Uluṟu
(Ayers Rock)

7
Gemtree

5

1531
▲ Mount Zeil

West MacDonnell National Park
8

🛫 **2 Alice Springs**

M a c D o n n e l l

2

R a n g e s

Watarrka National Park 9

Finke Gorge National Park

6

STUART HIGHWAY

0   50 km
0   30 miles

87

1069
▲ Mount
Olga

🛫 ☐ Yulara

Uluṟu-Kata Tjuṯa
National Park 3

863
▲ Uluṟu (Ayers Rock)

4

In Five Days

If you're not quite sure where to begin your travels, this itinerary recommends a practical and enjoyable five days exploring the Northern Territory, taking in some of the best places to see using the Getting Your Bearings map on the previous page. For more information see the main entries.

Day 1

Set out early from Darwin, the Top End's cosmopolitan capital, for the 250km (155-mile) drive along the Arnhem Highway to the spectacular **Kakadu National Park** (➤ 138–141). Visit ancient Aboriginal rock-art galleries, walk along bush tracks to superb lookouts and appreciate the magnificent scenery (and perhaps spot a crocodile) during a Guluyambi Cultural Cruise. Spend the night at the Gagudju Crocodile Holiday Inn in Jabiru.

Day 2

Start the day with a peaceful Yellow Water boat cruise (above) then continue your exploration of the park, not only on the ground, but from the air with a scenic flight from Cooinda airstrip. Late in the afternoon, return to Darwin the same way you came in, stopping en route at the Bark Hut Inn on the Arnhem Highway for dinner.

Day 3

Get up with the birds for an early two-hour morning flight to **2 Alice Springs** (➤ 142–143), founded in the 1870s as a repeater station on the Overland Telegraph Line and now a thriving modern town in the continent's bone-dry heart. Spend the day soaking up the Outback atmosphere while enjoying a tour of the town's highlights, including the Royal Flying Doctor Service Base (right). Spend the night in or near Alice Springs (➤ 149 for accommodation).

Day 4

A 40-minute flight from Alice Springs brings you to Ayers Rock Resort (Yulara), from where you can make an afternoon pilgrimage to Uluṟu (Ayers Rock), below, one of Australia's greatest icons. Standing sentinel over the sandplains of **3 Uluṟu–Kata Tjuṯa National Park** (➤ 144–146), this ancient rock has a compelling presence that, once experienced, will never be forgotten. The best place to stay the night is at Yulara's Sails in the Desert Hotel but other choices are available, including Ayers Rock Resort (➤ 149).

Day 5

Put on your walking shoes for a morning exploration of Kata Tjuṯa (The Olgas), left, the lesser-known but equally impressive cluster of monoliths west of Ayers Rock Resort. After returning to Yulara for a refreshing swim and lunch, join Aboriginal Aṉangu guides to learn about Uluṟu's sacred significance, Tjukurpa (Aboriginal law, creation stories) and local bush foods and medicines.

Kakadu National Park

UNESCO World Heritage listed for its outstanding cultural and natural values, Aboriginal-owned Kakadu National Park, 250km (155 miles) east of Darwin, is the jewel of the Top End. Protected within its 20,000sq km (7,800 square miles) is an entire tropical river system, an incredible diversity of plants and animals, breathtaking scenery and one of the most extensive collections of rock art in the world.

The national park's main physical feature is the 600km (370-mile) sandstone escarpment of the **Arnhem Land Plateau**, providing a dramatic backdrop for the forested lowlands, rocky outcrops, floodplains and tidal flats below. From here, during the wet season, water cascades some 200m (650ft) at the spectacular **Jim Jim Falls**. Much of the film *Crocodile Dundee* was set in this landscape. It is also the setting for two controversial uranium mines: Ranger and Jabiluka. Aboriginal people have lived continously in the region for at least 50,000 years and their history can be traced through the rock art of an estimated 5,000 or more sites, some of which are out of bounds to visitors.

The two finest accessible sites are **Ubirr and Nourlangie Rock**; but for a deeper understanding of Aboriginal culture, visit the **Warradjan Cultural Centre**.

Most people visit Kakadu in the dry season months of June, July and August when the climate is most comfortable and creeks and floodplains have dried up, concentrating wildlife on the permanent wetlands. This is a particularly good time to see crocodiles and birds, but the land is drier than most would expect.

To arrive in the wet season, however, is to see Kakadu at its most dynamic. Road access is restricted to some areas and you'll have to bear with uncomfortable humidity and frequent rain, but the park is at its verdant best.

Making the Most of the Wet and Dry

The Dry (May–October)
Day 1 After arriving at the park entrance station, drive on to the **Bowali Visitor Centre**. Here you can check road conditions, pick up a map, have morning tea, and get an excellent overview of the region's habitats through displays, slides and videos. Continue to the Border Store, 39km (24 miles) to the northeast, for a picnic lunch at nearby Cahills Crossing then explore the 1.5km (1-mile) circular **Manngarre rainforest walk** that starts at the car park.

Waterlillies in a billabong, Yellow Waters

Return in time for a 3pm **Guluyambi Cultural Cruise** of the East Alligator River (a free shuttle bus to the boat ramp leaves from the Border Store). On reaching dry land again, drive the short distance to **Ubirr** for some of the park's best rock art and a superb sunset view over the Nardab floodplain.

Day 2 It's some 56km (35 miles), about 45 minutes' drive, from Jabiru to Cooinda, so leave in plenty of time to get to Gagudju Lodge Cooinda, where you can buy a ticket for an early morning **Yellow Water boat cruise** – the bird life is

most active at this time. After the cruise, spend a half hour or so at the nearby **Warradjan Aboriginal Cultural Centre**, then drive to Cooinda airstrip for an hour-long scenic flight.

Yellow River at sunset

Have lunch at the lodge, then continue on to the Nourlangie car park where a 1.5km (1-mile) circular walk takes you past the ancient **Anbangbang rock shelter** and several outstanding art sites. A moderately steep climb to **Gunwarddehwardde Lookout** provides impressive views of Kakadu's escarpment and Nourlangie Rock. After leaving the car park, take the first road to the left to reach Anbangbang Billabong – one of Kakadu's most attractive waterholes – where you can enjoy a 2.5km (1.5-mile) circular walk.

WITH TIME TO SPARE...

If you've got an extra day up your sleeve, head south to Jim Jim and Twin Falls. This is dry season only territory, reached by a four-wheel-drive track off the Kakadu Highway. A bumpy 60km (37-mile) drive and a rocky 1km (0.5-mile) walk will bring you to Jim Jim Falls. Twin Falls is a further 10km (6 miles) from Jim Jim and involves crossing the Jim Jim Creek. If you're not comfortable with four-wheel driving, join a commercial tour of the area.

During the wet season, head for Gubara, in the Nourlangie area, for a 6km (4-mile) return walk to shady monsoon forest pools. Alternatively, drive south to sample the Yurmikmik walks. The area, offering interconnecting walks ranging from 2 to 11km (1 to 7 miles), is reached by turning east off the Kakadu Highway on to the unsurfaced Gunlom road and travelling 13km (8 miles).

The Wet (November–April)

Day 1 Follow the dry season itinerary until you leave Bowali Visitor Centre, then drive to the Gagudju Crocodile Holiday Inn for check-in and a midday pick-up by Kakadu Parklink for a 2.5 hour **Guluyambi Cultural Cruise**.

The cruise takes you through the stunning Magela Creek system and includes a short bus trip to Ubirr – it's the only guaranteed means by which wet season visitors can view this excellent art site. Return to Gagudju Crocodile Holiday Inn for the night.

Day 2 Follow the dry season itinerary with the exception that your hour-long scenic flight includes the Jim Jim and Twin Falls in full flood and that the Anbangbang Billabong walk is likely to be closed. An alternative is to take the second road to the left after the Nourlangie car park and visit Nawurlandja Lookout. The 600m (650-yard) climb offers good views of the escarpment and Anbangbang Billabong.

TAKING A BREAK

Stay at the **Gagudju Crocodile Holiday Inn**, in Jabiru, and feast on the restaurant's excellent Aussie tucker.

✚ 209 F4

Bowali Visitor Centre
✉ Kakadu Highway ☎ (08) 8938 1121; www.environment.gov.au/parks/kakadu
⏰ Daily 8–5 🍴 Visitor Centre cafe ($) 🚌 From Darwin ✈ To Jabiru
🎫 Park entry and Visitor Centre: free

Warradjan Cultural Centre
✉ Kakadu Highway ☎ (08) 8979 0145; www.kakadu-attractions.com/warradjan ⏰ Daily 9–5

Guluyambi Cultural Cruises
☎ (08) 8979 2411 or (1800) 089 113 within Australia; www.guluyambi.com.au

---

KAKADU NATIONAL PARK: INSIDE INFO

Top tips Wear a hat, use sunscreen and **always carry ample water** – a litre per person per hour is recommended when walking.

■ Use **insect repellent** at all times – mosquitoes can carry viruses such as the Ross River virus.

■ **Beware of crocodiles**; obey the "No Swimming" warnings. Swimming anywhere in the park is actively discouraged by the rangers. Crocodiles can be present even in small pools and have been known to attack unsuspecting tourists. Always keep away from the water's edge.

■ Animals tend to be less active during the heat of the day. **Mornings and evenings** are the best times to see birds and animals such as wallabies.

■ To avoid missing out, **book boat cruises and scenic flights 24 hours before your visit**.

Hidden gem After leaving the Nourlangie car park, the first road to the right leads to an easy 3.4km (2-mile) return walk to Nanguluwur, a little-visited, but fascinating **Aboriginal rock art site**.

2 Alice Springs

Built upon parched red desert dust, and subjected to
scorching summer heat, freezing winter nights and bone-
jarring electrical storms, Alice Springs is the original symbol
of the Australian pioneering spirit. Founded as an Overland
Telegraph station in the 1870s and immortalized in Nevil
Shute's novel *A Town Like Alice*, the rough-and-ready town of
old has evolved into a popular tourist destination.

Now a thriving metropolis of some 28,000 people, Alice
Springs boasts quality shops and services, including a casino.
But "the Alice" has lost none of its charm. Eccentric events
like the Henley-On-Todd Regatta (September), where teams
use leg power to race their bottomless "boats" along the dry
Todd River, and the Camel Cup, a series of camel races in July,
are highlights of an offbeat social calendar.

Exploring the Town

The hub of the town's central business district is Todd Mall,
and if you're after cafes, souvenirs or authentic indigenous
artworks, you'll find them in abundance here. For a great
view of the town and its rugged backdrop, the MacDonnell
Ranges, head for Anzac Hill, a steep walk or a short drive
at the northern end of Todd Street. More adventurous
souls can enjoy a bird's-eye view of the Red Centre from a
hot-air balloon as they drift above the southern flanks of
the MacDonnell Ranges in the cool, calm morning air. To
really come to grips with the character of this remote region,
use some of your time in Alice Springs to visit two famous
Outback institutions: the **Royal Flying Doctor Service
base** and the **School of the Air**, which broadcasts lessons to
children on remote stations and in isolated communities.

Another must-see is the **Telegraph Station Historical
Reserve**, where meticulously restored buildings and displays

**Opposite:
Kings Canyon,
south of Alice
Springs**

**Below: Camel
riders outside
the town**

evoke the settlement's early years. Here, too, are shady picnic grounds and the original Alice Springs – actually a waterhole on the Todd River.

TAKING A BREAK

For Mediterranean and "good old Aussie" food, visit **Bar Doppio Cafe Mediterranean** in Todd Mall (tel: (08) 8952 6525).

✚ 210 A2

Central Australian Tourism Industry Association
✉ 60 Gregory Terrace ☎ (08) 8952 5800 or (1800) 645 199; www.centralaustraliantourism.com ⏰ Mon–Fri 8:30–5:30, Sat–Sun 9:30–4; closed 25 Dec, 1 Jan

Alice Springs Telegraph Station Historical Reserve
✉ 4km (2.5 miles) north of Alice Springs ☎ (08) 8952 3993; www.nt.gov.au/nreta/parks ⏰ Reserve: daily 8am–9pm; buildings: daily 8:30–5; closed 25 Dec 💲 Inexpensive

Alice Springs School of the Air
✉ 80 Head Street ☎ (08) 8951 6834; www.assoa.nt.edu.au ⏰ Mon–Sat 8:30–4:30, Sun 1:30–4:30; closed 25 Dec–2 Jan 💲 Inexpensive

Royal Flying Doctor Service Visitor Centre
✉ 8–10 Stuart Terrace ☎ (08) 8952 1129; www.flyingdoctor.org/about-us/visitor-centres/ ⏰ Mon–Sat 9–5, Sun and holidays 1–5; closed 25 Dec, 1 Jan 💲 Inexpensive

ALICE SPRINGS: INSIDE INFO

Top tips Take a tour to see the main attractions quickly. **Tailormade Tours** (tel: (08) 8952 1731 or (1800) 806 641; www.tailormadetours.com.au) offers a guided half-day tour in a minibus, lasting 3–4 hours, while the **Alice Explorer** (tel: (08) 8952 2111 or (1800) 722 111; www.alicewanderer.com.au) is a "hop-on, hop-off" shuttle bus tour (daily 9–4) that takes in all the major sights.
■ Come prepared for **extreme temperatures**, ranging from a low of -7°C (19°F) on winter nights, to summer highs that regularly exceed 40°C (104°F).

In more depth Alice Springs Desert Park, on Larapinta Drive (tel: (08) 8951 8788; www.alicespringsdesertpark.com.au), is a spectacular showcase of the landscapes, animals and plants of Australia's deserts.
■ Also on Larapinta Drive is the **Alice Springs Cultural Precinct** (tel: (08) 8951 1120; www.nt.gov.au/nreta/arts/ascp). The many attractions here include the Museum of Central Australia, the Strehlow Research Centre, art galleries and a craft centre.
■ If it isn't too hot, **rent a bicycle** in Alice Springs and cycle 18km (11 miles) to Simpsons Gap through the West MacDonnell National Park.

③ Uluṟu–Kata Tjuṯa National Park

Two of the world's most dramatically beautiful landmarks – Uluṟu (Ayers Rock) and Kata Tjuṯa (The Olgas) – are encompassed in the spectacular World Heritage listed Uluṟu–Kata Tjuṯa National Park. The most famous of these, Uluṟu, is justifiably one of Australia's greatest attractions and the reason hundreds of thousands of international visitors make the journey each year to Australia's hot and desolate interior.

The rock's vast bulk is an extraordinary and overwhelming sight. With a base circumference of 9.4km (6 miles), this **sandstone monolith** rises a towering 348m (1,142 feet) from the surrounding spinifex and desert oak-studded sandplain. At around 600 million years old, its ancient presence is heightened by the amazing sunset and sunrise colour changes – through shades of red, mauve, pink and blue.

In 1985 a land rights battle ended in victory for the local Aṉangu people, giving them title deeds to the land. Today, they lease the land to the government and jointly manage the park with the Federal Government's Parks Australia.

There are many ways to see Uluṟu. You can take a scenic flight over the rock and the surrounding area in a helicopter or small plane, travel around it in a chauffeur-driven limousine or on the back of a Harley Davidson motorbike, ride a camel to view it at sunrise or sunset, or join one of a multitude of bus- or walking-tours. If you intend to climb Uluṟu, be aware that it is a **sacred site** and doing so shows disrespect for the Anangu culture. The hazardous 1.6km (1-mile) route, which takes about two hours there and back, is extremely strenuous and not for the faint-hearted. The first section is very steep and the summit frequently windy. Far more relaxing, and culturally respectful, is the self-guided base-walk, which takes 3–4 hours, and allows you a fascinating view of the caves, paintings and weather-sculpted surface.

The stunning view of the red rock of Uluṟu

Cultural Centre

The best way to start your Uluṟu experience, however, is to visit the **Uluṟu-Kata Tjuṯa Cultural Centre**, just 1km (0.6 miles) from the rock, offering dynamic displays of Anangu culture and housing a cafe, shop, gallery and national park information centre. The free daily ranger-guided **Mala Walk** (2km/1.25 miles) is also recommended as an introduction to Aboriginal perceptions of Uluṟu, but it is even better to join one of the excellent **Anangu cultural tours** (www.ananguwaai.com.au). The **sunset view** of the rock is obligatory, though you will share the experience with hundreds of others, most carrying cameras, and all crammed into the official viewing areas. **Sunrise viewings** also tend to be mass-spectator events.

Kata Tjuṯa

Like Uluṟu, Kata Tjuṯa, 50km (31 miles) to the west, is the visible tip of a huge slab of rock that extends possibly as far as 5 or 6km (3 or 4 miles) beneath the ground. Its composition, however, is quite different.

The Aboriginal name for these remarkable **boulder conglomerates** means "many heads", an apt description of its 36 rounded domes divided by valleys and gorges. The largest of these, Mount Olga, is actually about 200m (650 feet) higher than Uluṟu. The domes of Kata Tjuṯa – a site sacred to the Anangu – are strictly off limits to visitors. Show your respect for the local culture by not entering sacred sites. Also be aware that many Aboriginal people do not want their photograph taken. Do not photograph people without asking permission.

ULURU–KATA TJUTA NATIONAL PARK: INSIDE INFO

Top tips Climbing Uluru is strongly discouraged, but some people still insist on ascending. Be aware that many visitors over-estimate their capabilities and numerous deaths have resulted from heart failure. **Do not attempt the climb** if you suffer from a heart condition, breathing difficulties or fear of heights.

■ Large tour buses tend to visit Uluru in the morning and Kata Tjuta in the afternoon. For more **peaceful exploration**, visit Kata Tjuta first then Uluru.

■ **Arrive early to watch sunset on Uluru**. You'll be amazed at the range of colours reflected on the rock.

Hidden gem If you've got more time, visit **Mount Conner** (859m/2,818 feet), the region's third monolith, about 100km (62 miles) east of Uluru, on the **Curtin Springs cattle station** (www.curtinsprings.com). This ancient mesa is impressive, rising some 250m (820 feet) above the plain, and a visit here will also give you a chance to see how an Outback cattle station is run.

Your base for exploring the 1,325sq km (512-square mile) national park is **Ayers Rock Resort**, an ultra-modern complex offering everything from grassy camping areas, self-catering and luxury hotels to restaurants, cafes, bars and shops. The **Tour and Information Centre** in the Resort Shopping Centre is the place to book all kinds of tours, while the **Visitors Centre**, adjacent to Desert Gardens Hotel, has excellent displays on the area's history, geology, plants and animals.

Aboriginal rock art

Of the many activities on offer here, from stargazing to guided walks, one counts as near-essential: the nightly **Sounds of Silence dinner** in the desert. Perched on the dunes, diners take in a 360-degree sunset view that includes Kata Tjuta and Uluru while sipping champagne, then enjoy a sumptuous gourmet feast. Book well in advance for this popular event.

TAKING A BREAK

For a quick bite or leisurely lunch and Yulara's best coffee, try **Geckos Cafe**, in the Resort Shopping Centre.

🕂 209 F1 ✉ Ayers Rock Resort ☎ Visitors Centre (08) 8957 7377; www.ayersrockresort.com.au 🕐 Daily 9–5 ☎ Tour and Information Centre (08) 8957 7324 🕐 Daily 9:30–4:30 🍴 Cafes and restaurants ($–$$$) 💰 Park entry fee: moderate ✈ Connellan Airport, about 7km (4 miles) from the Resort

Uluru–Kata Tjuta Cultural Centre

✉ Yulara Drive ☎ (08) 8956 1128; www.environment.gov.au/parks/uluru 🕐 Daily 7–6 💰 Free 🍴 Initi Souvenirs and Cafe ($)

At Your Leisure

❹ Crocodylus Park

Close encounters with Australia's saltwater crocodile, the world's largest reptile, are not advisable. It is far better to observe these amazing, yet dangerous, creatures in a safe environment, and Crocodylus Park is just the place. The best time to visit is during the daily feeding sessions when the 70-odd salties in the park's lagoon are coaxed into action with chunks of meat. The Crocodile Museum is worth a good look, and the park also contains big cats, monkeys, and Australian birds and other wildlife.

🗺 209 F4 ✉ 815 McMillans Road, Berrimah ☎ (08) 8922 4500; www.crocodyluspark.com ⏱ Daily 9–5; closed 25 Dec 🚶 Moderate 🚌 No 5 (Sat and holidays: No 4 or 10 to Casuarina, then No 9) ℹ Feeding and tour times: 10, 12, 2 and 3:30

❺ Aquascene

Every day hundreds of fish ride in on the high tide to Doctors Gully, a short walk from Darwin's centre, for a feeding frenzy that has become one of the city's most popular attractions. It all began in the 1950s when a local threw scraps of food to a few mullet. Today, an astonishing number of fish species including metre-long (3ft) milkfish, mullet, catfish, bream, rays and batfish arrive for their fix of stale bread, fed to them by the tourist's hand.

🗺 209 F4 ✉ 28 Doctors Gully Road, Darwin ☎ (08) 8981 7837 for feeding times; www.aquascene.com.au ⏱ Daily (opening times change daily with the tide); closed 25 Dec 🚶 Inexpensive

❻ Litchfield National Park

Cascading waterfalls plunging over sandstone escarpments and surrounded by patches of rainforest are the main attraction of Litchfield National Park, less than two hours' drive from Darwin. Swimming in the crystal-clear waterholes is popular, but be warned: crocodiles are sometimes found in waterholes, so heed all "No Swimming" signs. Wangi Falls, the park's most popular waterfall, flows all year round, though wet season visitors are unable to swim in its pool due to dangerous undertows. Buley Rockhole and Florence Falls offer two good alternatives. Other highlights include bushwalking tracks, giant magnetic termite mounds and the intriguing sandstone formations of the Lost City.

🗺 209 F4 ✉ Litchfield National Park ☎ Parks and Wildlife Service of the NT Batchelor Office: (08) 8999 4555; www.nt.gov.au/nreta/parks ⏱ Daily 🚶 Free ℹ The only way to see the park is in your own transport or by organized tour. Sections of the park are accessible May–Nov only

❼ Gemtree

Novice and experienced fossickers (gem searchers) will enjoy rich pickings in the gem fields near Gemtree Caravan Park, 140km (87 miles) northeast of Alice Springs. The park runs regular "tag-along" driving guided tours, with all equipment included, to the nearby Mud Tank zircon field and to a garnet deposit.

Visitors relax in freshwater rapids at Buley Rockhold, Litchfield National Park

Beehive dome landforms in NT

If you're not joining a tour, you'll need a fossicking licence, available from Gemtree, and your own equipment. Gemtree offers cabin and caravan accommodation, a gem room and gallery, bushwalks and birding. Bookings are essential for tours.

⊞ 210 A2 ⊠ Plenty Highway (70km/44 miles off the Stuart Highway) ☎ (08) 8956 9855; www.gemtree.com.au ⊙ Daily; closed 25 Dec. Zircon and garnet fossicking tours depart Gemtree at 9 (6 in summer) 🖩 Gemtree: inexpensive. Fossicking tours: expensive; fossicking licence: free 🅸 Tour bookings are essential; the zircon field and several garnet fields can be reached by conventional vehicle (if it hasn't been raining). Tours are "tag-along", ie you use your own vehicle and follow the guide

❽ West MacDonnell National Park

The West MacDonnell Ranges offer an ancient landscape of brilliant colours, shady gorges and refreshing waterholes. You can visit all the major attractions in a day, starting with Simpsons Gap, just 18km (11 miles) west of Alice Springs. Here, a short walk leads you past white river sands and huge ghost gums (a species of eucalyptus with white bark) to a shady, red-cliffed cleft and waterhole, beside which you can sit and watch black-footed rock wallabies come to drink in the afternoon. Those looking for a cool break can enjoy a swim in Ellery Creek Big Hole, a large waterhole lined with river red gums. Just outside the park boundary, Standley Chasm, a spectacular narrow break in the MacDonnell Ranges, lights up at

midday when the sun briefly paints both walls a brilliant orange.

⊞ 209 F2

Parks and Wildlife Service of the Northern Territory, Alice Springs Region
⊠ Tom Hare Building, South Stuart Highway, Alice Springs ☎ (08) 8955 0310; www.nt.gov. au/nreta/parks ⊙ Mon–Fri 8–4:20 🖩 Free 🅸 Without transport, organized tours are the only way to see the park ⊠ Standley Chasm ☎ (08) 8956 7440; www.standleychasm.com.au ⊙ Daily 8–5; closed 25 Dec 🖩 Inexpensive

❾ Watarrka National Park

The remote, rugged Watarrka National Park, three hours' drive north of Uluṟu, is best known for Kings Canyon – a spectacular sandstone gorge with walls that rise 100–150m (330–490ft) to a plateau of rocky domes. It's worth taking the 6km (4-mile) loop-walk to the canyon rim for the views. Along the way explore an eerie collection of weathered rock formations known as the Lost City, and the Garden of Eden – an oasis of waterholes and lush vegetation. If you don't feel up to the canyon climb, there are two 2.6km (1.5-mile) return walks: the Kings Creek Walk, along the valley floor to a lookout or the Kathleen Springs Walk, to a spring-fed waterhole.

⊞ 209 F2

Parks and Wildlife Service of the Northern Territory, Alice Springs Region
⊠ Tom Hare Building, South Stuart Highway, Alice Springs ☎ (08) 8951 8250; www.nt.gov.au.nreta/parks ⊙ Mon–Fri 8–4:20 🖩 Free 🅸 Without transport, organized tours are the only way to see the park

Where to...
Stay

Where to...
Eat and Drink

Prices

Prices are for the least expensive double room in high season:

$ under A$150 $$ A$150–A$280 $$$ over A$280

Prices

Prices are per person for a meal, excluding drinks, tax and tip:

$ under A$20 $$ A$20–A$30 $$$ over A$30

DARWIN AND KAKADU

Aurora Kakadu $–$$

A comfortable hotel set amid 10ha (25 acres) of bushland at the heart of the Kakadu National Park. There are nature walks, a pool, spa pool and tennis courts.

🚩 209 F4 ⊠ Arnhem Highway ☎ (08) 8979 0166; www.auroraresorts.com.au

Holiday Inn Esplanade Darwin $–$$$

This hotel on the harbour foreshore has good facilities and rooms.

🚩 209 F4 ⊠ The Esplanade, Darwin ☎ (08) 8980 0800; www.ichotelsgroup.com

---

ALICE SPRINGS AND ULURU

Ayers Rock Resort $–$$$

The only option near the rock, but it does offer different accommodation, a hotel, hostel and campsite.

🚩 209 F1 ⊠ Yulara ☎ (1300) 134 044 or (02) 8296 8010; www.ayersrockresort.com.au

Chifley Alice Springs Resort $–$$$

This attractive low-rise resort offers a range of rooms. Facilities include a pool, restaurant, bar, bicycle rental and guest laundry

🚩 210 A2 ⊠ 34 Stott Terrace ☎ (1300) 134 044; www.chifleyhotels.com.au

---

DARWIN

Crustaceans on the Wharf $$–$$$

On Darwin's wharf precinct, with magnificent ocean views and outside seating, Crusty's is one of Darwin's leading seafood restaurants. The menu includes oyster, prawn, barramundi and lobster offerings, vegetarian options and a children's menu. Signature dishes include Cajun barramundi with prawns and chilli mango sauce, chilli crab, and fresh oysters. There is a licensed bar, and wine is available by the glass.

🚩 209 F4 ⊠ Stokes Hill Wharf ☎ (08) 8981 8658 🕐 Mon–Sat dinner 6–10

Hanuman $$–$$$

Enjoy Thai, Malay, Chinese and Indian dishes at this elegant venue, which features exotic furnishings and artwork from around the world. Inside seating and outside dining on the deck, plus a stylish cocktail bar. The service is excellent and there are many delicious seafood, meat and vegetarian dishes.

🚩 209 F4 ⊠ Holiday Inn Esplanade Darwin, 93 Mitchell Street ☎ (08) 8941 3500; www.hanuman.com.au 🕐 Mon–Fri 12–3, daily from 6pm

Where to... Shop

DARWIN

Darwin's city centre is to be found in the Smith Street Mall and Knuckey Street. Take a special look at Mitchell Street's Aboriginal Fine Arts Gallery (tel: (08) 8981 1315) for good Aboriginal arts and crafts.

From April through to October you can visit **Mindil Beach Sunset Markets** on Thursday and Sunday evenings.

ALICE SPRINGS/RED CENTRE

In the Red Centre, Aboriginal arts and crafts are the best finds. Alice Springs' shopping centre is quite small and can easily be covered on foot. The **Ayers Rock Resort** has good souvenirs.

Pee Wee's at the Point $$

This unique restaurant offers swaying palms, sweeping views across the bay, plenty of wildlife and a peaceful ambience on outdoor deck, lawn, and patio areas. Renowned for its first-class food and service, Pee Wee's Modern Territorian cuisine specializes in fresh local seafood and produce.

🚩 **209 F4** ✉ **Alec Fong Lim Drive, East Point Reserve, Fannie Bay** ☎ **(08) 8981 6868; www.peewees.com.au** 🕐 **Daily 5–10**

ALICE SPRINGS

Oscars Café and Restaurant $–$$

Mediterranean dishes, including slow-cooked treats from Portugal and Spain, feature alongside pizzas and salads at this popular eatery. Fresh seafood is flown in. Drop by for a morning or a late-night coffee.

🚩 **210 A2** ✉ **Shop 1, Cinema Complex, 86 Todd Mall, Alice Springs** ☎ **(08) 8953 0930** 🕐 **Daily 9–late**

Where to... Be Entertained

DARWIN

Darwin's outdoor **Deckchair Cinema** (tel: (08) 8981 0700; www.deckchaircinema.com) is open from Apr–Nov. Indoor cinemas are focused on Mitchell Street, which is also the place for nightlife. **Darwin Community Arts** on Smith Street (tel: (08) 8981 5522; www.darwincommunityarts.org.au) offers outdoor theatre from May–Oct.

The **Beer Can Regatta** at Mindil Beach in July or August features races between boats made from drink cans and bottles. The **Darwin Festival** of performance and visual arts is held during August.

The **SkyCity Darwin Casino** (tel: (08) 8943 8888; www.skycitydarwin.com.au) on the edge of Mindil Beach offers restaurants, bars, concerts and stage shows, as well as gambling.

ALICE SPRINGS

Alice Springs' **Lasseters Hotel Casino** (tel: (08) 8950 7777; www.lassetershotelscasino.com.au) is the focus of that area's most glamorous evening entertainment.

Visitor information:
Alice Springs, tel: (08) 8952 5800;
www.centralaustraliantourism.com
Darwin, tel: (08) 8936 2499;
www.tourismtopend.com.au.
Also *Northern Territory News*.

South Australia

Getting Your Bearings

South Australia is a place of contrasts offering enormous variety in its scenery and range of experiences. It is the driest State in Australia with two-thirds of its nearly 1 million sq km (380,000 square miles) encompassed in the semi-arid Outback, a region of soaring temperatures, vast expanses, dry salt lakes and ancient mountain ranges.

The vast majority of South Australia's population lives in the capital, Adelaide, in the fertile southeast, enjoying a pleasant Mediterranean-style climate and easy access to sandy beaches, forested hills dotted with historic villages and some of Australia's best wine-producing regions. Founded in 1836, Adelaide is the only Australian State capital to be established without the aid of convict labour and one of the few to benefit from early planning, courtesy of its visionary designer Colonel William Light. Nowadays, this "City of Churches", formerly so-called because of its principles of religious freedom and great variety of congregations, is home to the internationally renowned biennial Adelaide Festival, a thriving restaurant and cafe scene, Australia's first legal nudist beach (Maslin Beach) and relaxed drug laws. You don't have to travel far from the city to see the State's premier attractions. On its doorstep lie the Adelaide Hills and the Barossa, a region famous for its Germanic traditions and superb wines, while a little farther afield are the natural wonderlands of Kangaroo Island and the rugged Flinders Ranges.

★ Don't Miss
❶ The Barossa ➤ 156
❷ Adelaide ➤ 158

At Your Leisure
❸ Glenelg ➤ 159
❹ Adelaide Hills ➤ 159
❺ Flinders Ranges ➤ 160
❻ Kangaroo Island ➤ 160

Previous page: Vineyards, Barossa Valley
Above: South Australia's fertile landscape

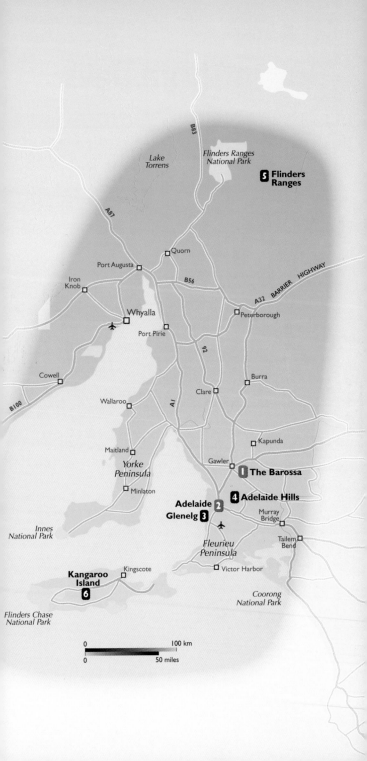

In Three Days

If you're not quite sure where to begin your travels, this itinerary recommends a practical and enjoyable three days exploring South Australia, taking in some of the best places to see using the Getting Your Bearings map on the previous page. For more information see the main entries.

Day 1

2 Adelaide (➤ 158), set on the River Torrens, is a very liveable city that, unlike Sydney and Brisbane, is not burdened with traffic chaos during peak times of the day. Use this day to discover the many fine old buildings housing galleries and museums, including the Art Gallery of South Australia, with its fine Australian collection, and the Aboriginal artefacts in the South Australian Museum (above). Join residents enjoying their laid-back urban lifestyle, as you stroll the leafy streets, and experience the city's thriving and artistic cultural life. The inner city suburbs are particularly vibrant with great speciality shopping. Just 10 minutes from the Adelaide CBD is the Brickworks Markets, where the 100 permanent stalls are centred around an old brick kiln dating from 1912. Be sure to enjoy a fine dining experience in the evening.

Day 2

Rise early to collect your rental car for a two-day driving tour of **1 The Barossa** (top right, ➤ 156–157), starting via Main North Road through Elizabeth and Gawler. By the time you reach Tanunda to check out the Barossa Visitor Information Centre, you'll be ready for a refreshment stop. Perhaps get the makings for a picnic lunch, before heading for some

vineyards cellar door tasting rooms, where you can chat with winemakers, sample various wines, and enjoy your picnic. Chateau Tanunda has lovely old stone winery buildings and a popular cellar door sampling room. You could also take a tour of the historic Seppelt family winery, with its stunning gardens, palm-lined driveways and heritage buildings. Towards the end of the day, drive to Mengler Hill Lookout for superb views of the valley, before checking into one of the many guest houses, motels, or B&Bs (➤ 162).

Day 3

After a leisurely breakfast, continue your exploration of the valley, returning to Adelaide via the Eden Valley, Gumeracha and the Torrens Gorge. Start at Angaston, where the Angus Park fruit shop sells an extensive range of premium dried fruit products, and the Saturday morning farmers market has enough tasty food to set you up for the day. The nearby Kaiserstuhl Conservation Park preserves a part of the Mount Lofty Ranges, and has varied birdlife and kangaroos that feed near the parking area. Next, head for the picturesque small township of Eden Valley, with its magnificent old red gums, many small vineyards, and beautiful stone buildings, including the St Petri Lutheran Church. This is a good stopping place for lunch. The drive back to Adelaide (right) is arguably the most scenic approach to any capital city in Australia.

❶ The Barossa

With its rolling hills adorned with grape vines, charming old towns filled with storybook churches, festivals and fine food, the Barossa – Australia's best-known wine-producing region – is a place to indulge the senses.

The best way to savour the Barossa, which comprises the Barossa and Eden valleys, is to get off the main road and explore the countryside. But before you hit the trail, get your bearings and an overview of the region's history at the **Barossa Visitor Information Centre** in Tanunda. Here you'll learn how the region owes its distinctive character to a blend of two cultures: English and German. Although English colonists were the first to settle in the valley in the 1830s, successive waves of German-speaking Silesians and Prussians fleeing religious intolerance followed. The Lutheran farmers and artisans took their cue from the Mediterranean climate and planted vineyards.

Wine and Specialist Foods

Nowadays, the Barossa is home to more than 600 grape growers, some now sixth generation, who supply about 65,000 tonnes of grapes to the valley's 60 or more wineries each vintage. Between **wine tastings**, savour other Barossa specialities (see www.foodbarossa.com): fresh bread and pastries, dried fruits, cheeses and smoked meats. Schulz Butchers in Angaston is renowned for its delicious "mettwursts", while the Apex Bakery in Tanunda, built in 1924, still uses its original wood-fired oven.

Well worthwhile is a visit to **Seppeltsfield** – Australia's most historic operational winery. If you take an 11:30am guided tour, you'll avoid the large bus groups that tend to arrive in the afternoon. Afterwards, enjoy a picnic lunch in its picturesque grounds with goods bought in the bakeries and delicatessens at Tanunda.

A view across the Barossa Valley

The rest of the day is yours to satisfy your own taste at the many wine stores. Try to reach Mengler Hill Lookout in the late afternoon for a sunset view of the valley. An evening meal at **Vintners Bar & Grill** (➤ 163) in Angaston is recommended, then retire to one of the Barossa's many B&Bs. The following day, continue your exploration before taking the Angaston Road to Eden Valley for the drive back to Adelaide via Birdwood, Gumeracha and the scenic Torrens Gorge.

TAKING A BREAK

Enjoy fine local produce and a menu that reflects the Barossa's traditions at **Kabminye Wines' Krondorf Road Cafe**, located at Krondorf Road, Krondorf.

➕ 214 B3

Wine tasting at the Old Block Cellars in the valley

Barossa Visitor Information Centre
✉ 66–68 Murray Street, Tanunda ☎ (08) 8563 0600 or (1300) 852 982; www.barossa.com ⏱ Mon–Fri 9–5, Sat–Sun 10–4; closed Good Fri, 25 Dec
🚌 From Adelaide

THE BAROSSA: INSIDE INFO

Top tips First stop in the Barossa must be the **Visitor Centre in Tanunda**. Pick up a map, get advice on accommodation and tap the local knowledge of the staff for the best wineries to visit according to your preference and taste.

■ Highly recommended is **Grant Burge Wines**, Tanunda, a small, good quality winery famous for its reds, which can be sampled in a beautifully restored tasting room.

■ **Drinking and driving do not mix**. Police conduct random breath-tests in Australia, and you should limit your alcohol consumption when wine-tasting.

■ The famous **Whispering Wall** – the Barossa Reservoir's retaining wall – is shaped in such a way that messages whispered at one end carry audibly to the other end 140m (153 yards) away.

2 Adelaide

Adelaide has a charm that few Australian cities can match. Laid out on either side of the River Torrens in a neat grid system of streets and squares, the city is ringed by parkland and set against the rolling hills of the Mount Lofty Ranges, giving it a relaxed, almost country-like atmosphere. Added to that are a Mediterranean-style climate, great food and wine, fine colonial buildings and a thriving cultural life.

The best way to get around the compact centre is on foot. Begin your exploration in Rundle Mall, a feast of shops and colourful street life. Where the mall ends, Rundle Street begins – an arty cafe strip for the hip and happening.

Just around the corner is North Terrace, Adelaide's grandest avenue and home to two of the city's most impressive institutions: the **Art Gallery of South Australia** and the **South Australian Museum**. Gallery highlights include the nation's best collection of 19th-century colonial art and Western Desert Aboriginal dot paintings, but it is also noted for its fine collection of British art from the 16th century to the present and a considerable collection of Southeast Asian ceramics.

At the **natural and cultural history museum**, next door the highlight of the museum is its world-renowned collection of Australian Aboriginal artefacts.

For a different perspective of the city, board a **Popeye Motor Launch** and take a cruise on the placid River Torrens then head to Lights Vision, a lookout on Montefiore Hill, for a captivating afternoon view.

TAKING A BREAK

Slip into the cafe at the State Library, next to the South Australian Museum.

Adelaide Arcade

➕ 214 B3

Art Gallery of South Australia and South Australian Museum
✉ North Terrace ☎ Gallery (08) 8207 7000; www.artgallery.sa.gov.au; museum (08) 8207 7500; www.samuseum.sa.gov.au 🕐 Both daily 10–5; closed 25 Dec (Museum closed Good Fri also) 💲 Free 🍴 Art Gallery Restaurant ($$) 🚌 City Loop or Bee Line

Popeye Motor Launches
✉ River Torrens, departs from Elder Park wharf ☎ (08) 8295 4747 or 8223 5863 🕐 Departure times vary seasonally but generally from 10:30/11am to 4/5pm 💲 Inexpensive 🚌 City Loop or Bee Line

At Your Leisure

The marina at Glenelg

3 Glenelg

This is Adelaide's most popular beach suburb, with attractions such as dining and shopping, the Bay Discovery Centre, The Beachouse for the children, and dolphin-watching cruises. The best way to get here is via a 30-minute tram ride from Adelaide. Sleek modern vehicles run on most days, but you can travel on a vintage tram on weekends and public holidays.

🚷 214 B3

Glenelg Visitor Information Centre
✉ Moseley Square, Glenelg ☎ (08) 8294 5833; www.glenelg.com.au 🚊 Glenelg – free, tram – inexpensive 🚊 Adelaide Metro (1300) 311 108; www.adelaidemetro.com.au

4 Adelaide Hills

Tumbling green countryside and historic towns make the Adelaide Hills popular. Overt tourism overshadows some of the region's charm, but you'll find much that is worthwhile. Notable attractions include Mount Lofty Summit for panoramic views, Cleland Wildlife Park, the National Motor Museum, wineries and restaurants, the scenic drive through Torrens Gorge, and Hahndorf, Australia's oldest German settlement.

🚷 214 B3

Adelaide Hills Visitor Information Centre
✉ 41 Main Road, Hahndorf ☎ (08) 8388 1185 and (1800) 353 323; www.visitadelaidehills.com.au 🕐 Mon–Fri 9–5, Sat–Sun and public holidays 10–4; closed Good Fri, 25 Dec 🚌 From Adelaide

Barrett Vineyard in the Adelaide Hills

5 Flinders Ranges

One of Australia's finest natural features, the Flinders Ranges are starkly beautiful. The area is a place of intense blue skies, purple-hued hills and rugged ranges, valleys carpeted in wildflowers, and a rich Aboriginal and European heritage. Beginning only 200km (125 miles) north of Adelaide, the Flinders are on the edge of the Outback. Stretching 480km (300 miles) from Crystal Brook in the south to Mount Hopeless in the north, the ranges are the remains of a mountain chain thrust up from the sea some 500 million years ago, then gradually eroded to spectacularly sculpted quartzite ridges and peaks. To get a feel for the region's geological history while enjoying an attractive drive, explore the 20km (12-mile) Brachina Gorge Geological Trail, where interpretative signage leads you through a 130-million-year corridor.

The heart of this region – and its major draw – is Wilpena Pound. A vast natural amphitheatre rimmed by sandstone and quartzite peaks, it offers some of Australia's most stimulating walks and wildlife encounters. First stop should be the Visitor Centre at Wilpena for details on accommodation (camping is permitted), walks and guided tours. If you do only one walk into the Pound, make it the 2.5-hour return stroll to Hills Homestead – a potent reminder of the early settlers' ill-fated efforts to grow wheat.

The Flinders are astonishingly rich in wildlife. Galahs, corellas, rosellas and wedge-tailed eagles are common, and dawn and dusk are the best times to see wallabies and kangaroos. Aboriginal rock art can be viewed at Sacred Canyon or Arkaroo Rock.
🔲 214 B4

Wilpena Pound Visitor Information Centre
✉ Flinders Ranges National Park ☎ (08) 8648 0048; www.wilpenapound.com.au and www.parks.sa.gov.au/parks ⏰ Daily 8–4 💲 Inexpensive ℹ Renting a four-wheel drive is recommended. Information from the Wadlata Outback Centre ✉ 41 Flinders Terrace, Port Augusta ☎ (1800) 633 060 or (08) 8642 4511; www.wadlata.sa.gov.au

6 Kangaroo Island

There is much to love about Kangaroo Island. Nowhere else in Australia will you see such an abundance and variety of native animals in their natural habitat, while also able to enjoy spectacular scenery,

The view from St Mary Peak over the ABC Range in the Flinders Ranges

The Remarkable Rocks, Kangaroo Island

friendly small towns and excellent fishing and swimming. Separated from the mainland during the last Ice Age, it is free of predators such as dingoes and foxes and, today, about one-third of the island is protected in national and conservation parks.

The island's peaceful demeanour belies its renegade past. Sealers, escaped convicts and runaway sailors sought refuge on its shores several years before explorer Matthew Flinders officially discovered and named it in 1802. It was formally colonized in 1836 when Kingscote, today the island's main town, became the first free settlement in Australia. Four years later, however, Kingscote was all but abandoned in favour of Adelaide and the island was left in peace for more than a century. There were no Aboriginal people on the island at the time of European settlement, but dating of campfire-remains indicate they occupied the island at least as early as 10,000 years ago. Why they disappeared from an island so rich in game remains a mystery.

You can see the highlights in a day if you fly from Adelaide, but you'll need several days to explore this large island which has no public transport. A rental car or personalized four-wheel-drive tour (such as offered by Kangaroo Island Wilderness Tours) are the recommended options.

"Must sees" include Little Sahara's sand dunes; Seal Bay, to see Australian sea lions; and Flinders Chase National Park, where the major attractions are the aptly named Remarkable Rocks and Admirals Arch. A few docile kangaroos usually hang around the Rocky River park headquarters. While you will be lucky to spot the shy platypus, koalas are widespread and found wherever the big gums of the river systems are located. For swimming or fishing, stop at stunning Vivonne Bay or head for the north coast beaches.

➕ 214 B3

Kangaroo Island Gateway Visitor Information Centre – Penneshaw
✉ Howard Drive, Penneshaw ☎ (08) 8553 1185; www.tourkangarooisland.com.au
🕐 Mon–Fri 9–5, Sat, Sun and holidays 10–4; closed 25 Dec 🚢 From Cape Jervis ✈ From Adelaide

Kangaroo Island Wilderness Tours
✉ Parndana, Kangaroo Island ☎ (08) 8559 5033; www.wildernesstours.com.au
💲 Expensive

Yellow-footed rock wallabies in an encounter

Where to...
Stay

Prices
Prices are for the least expensive double room in high season:
$ under A$150 $$ A$150–A$280 $$$ over A$280

THE BAROSSA

Langmeil Cottages $$

These four quaint German-style stone cottages are within walking distance of several wineries and offer good-value accommodation. Each cottage sleeps three and has a private bathroom and kitchen. Other facilities include a pool, sauna, spa and laundry room. Take a ride along the pleasant cycle track to visit the local places of interest.

✚ 214 B3 ⊠ 89 Langmeil Road, Tanunda ☎ (08) 8563 2987; www.langmeilcottages.com

Stonewell Cottages $$

Three romantic, stone cottages furnished with Barossa antiques, the "Haven" has two private apartments, while the "Hideaway" is a two-bedroom cottage and "Cupid's Cottage" is a one-bedroom retreat. All three have kitchens, wood fires, air conditioning and private double spas. The owners supply hearty, country breakfast provisions including fresh farm eggs, home-made jam and bread. There are also barbecue facilities, and guests can row across the lake to a private island.

✚ 214 B3 ⊠ Stonewell Road, Tanunda ☎ (08) 8562 8628; www.stonewellcottages.com.au

ADELAIDE AND SURROUNDS

Breakfast on Hindley $$

In Adelaide's busy West End, this 4-star hotel offers studios and two-bedroom apartments. All have facilities and large private balconies, and there is security parking and 24-hour reception.

✚ 214 B3 ⊠ 255 Hindley Street, Adelaide ☎ (08) 8217 2500; www.breakfree.com.au

North Adelaide Heritage Group $$–$$$

The 21 self-contained historic properties are within walking distance of Adelaide's Central Business District. Accommodation ranges from a cosy 19th-century cottage to a former fire station, complete with 1942 fire engine. All properties are beautifully furnished, and breakfast provisions are included in the price.

✚ 214 B3 ⊠ Various north Adelaide locations ☎ (08) 8272 1355; www.adelaideheritage.com

Rockford Adelaide $-$$

This boutique-style West End hotel is close to the city's arts precinct, the casino, Rundle Mall and many other attractions. The 68 guest rooms, some with spa baths, are stylishly decorated and there is also a restaurant and bar.

✚ 214 B3 ⊠ 164 Hindley Street, Adelaide ☎ (08) 8211 8255; www.rockfordhotels.com.au

KANGAROO ISLAND

Ozone Seafront Hotel $-$$

Located right on the waterfront, the good-value Ozone is Kangaroo Island's most famous hotel. There is a choice of room styles, with good facilities, a popular bistro, swimming pool, sauna and barbecue area.

✚ 214 B3 ⊠ The Foreshore, Kingscote ☎ (08) 8553 2011; www.ozonehotel.com

Where to...
Eat and Drink

Prices

Cost per person for a meal, excluding drinks, tax and tip:

$ under A$20 $$ A$20–A$30 $$$ over A$30

THE BAROSSA

Vintners Bar & Grill $$–$$$

Australia's finest timber, jarrah, has been used in the flooring here. Open fireplaces, roof beams and plenty of glass complete the effect. The modern menu showcases the heritage of the Barossa, with produce, such a veal loins and grain-fed chickens and fresh fish supplied by local farms, merchants and vineyards.

🔢 214 B3 ✉ Nuriootpa Road, Angaston ☎ (08) 8564 2488; www.vintners.com.au ⊙ Daily from 12, Mon–Sat from 6

ADELAIDE AND SURROUNDS

Art Gallery Restaurant $$

Take a courtyard seat to enjoy Adelaide's balmy weather at this charming cafe. To suit the easy-going sophistication of the place, dishes such as pasta with fresh tuna are simple but modern and made from good-quality ingredients.

🔢 214 B3 ✉ Art Gallery of South Australia, North Terrace, Adelaide ☎ (08) 8232 4366 ⊙ Lunch and snacks daily, 10–4:30

Auge Ristorante $$$

This city centre bar and restaurant is very popular with locals: drop in for morning coffee, or enjoy an excellent Italian lunch or dinner. The menu includes classics such as antipasto, risottos and pastas plus some dream desserts.

🔢 214 B3 ✉ 22 Grote Street, Adelaide ☎ (08) 8410 9332; www.auge.com.au ⊙ Tue–Fri 12–3, dinner Tue–Sat 6–late

Hotel Richmond $$

Located in Adelaide's main shopping street, this lively pub offers an imaginative Australian menu in its First Restaurant & Bar, serving everything from hearty breakfasts to fine dinners. The menu has an Italian bent, and includes steak, rabbit, pasta and vegetarian dishes.

🔢 214 B3 ✉ 128 Rundle Mall, Adelaide ☎ (08) 8215 4441; www.hotelrichmond.com.au ⊙ Breakfast 7am; Mon–Sat 12–3; Mon–Thu, Sat 6–9

The Summit $–$$$

Located in the Adelaide Hill. The Summit cafe and restaurant offer great food and wines from the local area, plus wonderful views out over Adelaide. The food is fresh, with familiar ingredients in mouth-watering combinations, including west coast oysters on the half shell, sautéed prawns in garlic cream sauce, and grilled kangaroo fillet on sweet potato purée.

🔢 214 B3 ✉ Summit Road, Mount Lofty ☎ (08) 8339 2600; www.mtloftysummit.com ⊙ Restaurant: daily 12–3. Wed–Sun dinner from 6pm. Cafe: Mon–Tue 9–5, Wed–Sun 9am–late

KANGAROO ISLAND

Sorrento's Restaurant $$

Focusing on fresh local produce such as lobster, oysters and steak, this is one of the island's best restaurants. It is part of the Kangaroo Island Seafront Resort, a good option for accommodation.

🔢 214 B3 ✉ 49 North Terrace, Penneshaw ☎ (08) 8553 1028; www.seafront.com.au ⊙ Breakfast and dinner daily; lunch served on a seasonal basis

Where to...
Shop

ADELAIDE CENTRE

Rundle Mall is the city's main shopping centre, and includes the Italianate **Adelaide Arcade**, built in the 1880s. Also in this area is an Adelaide institution – **Haigh's Chocolates**, open since 1915 – and the **R M Williams** bush clothing store at 6 Gawler Place. **JamFactory Contemporary Craft and Design Centre** (19 Morphett Street) is the place for jewellery and crafts. The **Olympic Opal Company** (tel: (08) 8211 8757) in the Rundle Mall handles everything from mining and cutting the opals, to making and selling jewellery. Another good retailer is the **Opal Field Gems Mine & Museum** (33 King William Street; tel: (08) 8212 5300).

VICTORIA SQUARE AREA

Adelaide's **Central Market** in Gouger Street is open Tuesday to Saturday. It offers some insight into the multicultural communities with its diverse range of fresh produce.

THE BAROSSA

The Barossa is known for its fine foods, arts, crafts and antiques. Some great places for local produce are **Maggie Beer's Farm Shop** in Nuriootpa (tel: (08) 8562 4477), the **Barossa Valley Cheese Company** in Angaston (tel: (08) 8564 3636), and Angaston's Saturday morning **Barossa Farmers Market**. Quality art and crafts can be found at the **McCrae Gallery** in Tanunda (tel: (08) 8563 0709).

Where to...
Be Entertained

ADELAIDE

Culture vultures are never short of entertainment in Adelaide, which is considered to be one of Australia's leading cities of the arts.

The **Adelaide Festival**, held biennially (in even-numbered years) during February and March, ranks with Edinburgh as one of the greatest arts festivals in the world and features around 500 performances of traditional and contemporary opera, dance, theatre and music, plus a writers' week. The Adelaide Cabaret Festival, a major annual event in the Adelaide Festival Centre in King William Road (tel: (08) 8216 8600), highlights the world's best cabaret artists, with classic and contemporary performances.

THE BAROSSA

The Barossa hosts several annual festivals, among them the **Barossa Vintage Festival** – a week-long celebration with more than 100 events and activities around Easter (odd-numbered years) – and the February **Barossa Under the Stars** open-air concerts.

This wine region has become almost as well known for its produce and gourmet food, celebrated during the August **Barossa Gourmet** weekend.

The Advertiser is the state's leading newspaper and features entertainment on Thursdays and Saturdays. Check also with local visitor information centres for details of what's on.

Western Australia

Getting Your Bearings

Covering roughly a third of the continent, yet with less than a tenth of the nation's population, Western Australia is an expansive region of immense contrasts and natural beauty. Great deserts dominate the interior, tall forests and springtime wildflowers flourish in the southwest; white, sandy beaches and rugged cliffs rim the coast, and extraordinary rock formations rise from the untamed wilderness of the Kimberley in the far north.

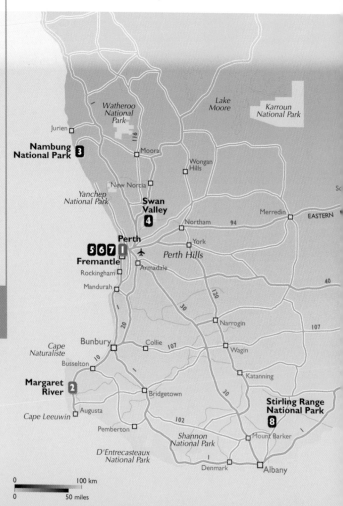

Above: Street lights on Hay Street, Perth

Page 165: Waterfall, Hamersley Gorge in Western Australia

The earliest European visitors, who landed on the west coast in the 17th century, never explored farther than the coastal dunes and were unenthusiastic about the region's potential. It wasn't until 1829 that the first British settlers arrived in the Swan River Colony, later Perth. Today, the State capital is a city of space and light – built and rebuilt with the proceeds of vast mineral wealth – that celebrates its glorious climate with a relaxed, outdoor lifestyle. Its nearby port, Fremantle, is a much more historic city with 19th-century buildings, great street cafes and irresistible charm. But it is the Margaret River region in the southwest that is the jewel of WA's holiday destinations, offering an unbeatable combination of natural beauty, legendary surf beaches, world-class wineries and tasteful tourist facilities.

★ Don't Miss

At Your Leisure

In Four Days

If you're not quite sure where to begin your travels, this itinerary recommends a practical and enjoyable four days exploring Western Australia, taking in some of the best places to see using the Getting Your Bearings map on the previous page. For more information see the main entries.

Day 1

Spend a relaxed day in ❶ Perth (above, ➤ 170–171), a modern city with an exuberant climate and an outdoor orientation. Visit two of its most interesting institutions – the Western Australian Museum and Perth Mint – then head to beautiful Kings Park for lunch in Fraser's Restaurant (➤ 177) and a stroll through its gardens and bushland.

Day 2

Board a boat at Perth's Barrack Street Jetty for the short trip down the Swan River to ❶ Fremantle (top right, ➤ 170–171), one of the world's best preserved 19th-century ports. Along the way, sights include the impressive Swan Bell tower, the restored Swan Brewery, Kings Park, and many magnificent homes on the riverbank. Spend the day exploring Fremantle's quaint streets, the outstanding maritime and shipwreck museum, the old prison, and other historical buildings. Don't miss the old Victorian building that houses the Fremantle Markets, where you can buy the ingredients for a picnic on the waterfront. The cafes of South Terrace are perfect for an alfresco snack.

Day 3

Set off early for the 290km (180-mile) drive south along the Southwestern Highway, Bussell Highway and scenic Caves Road to the **2 Margaret River Region** (below; ➤ 172–173). Spend the first day touring vineyards, such as the Voyager Estate Winery, and the gourmet food outlets, including those selling cheeses, olive oil, venison and

fruits. There's plenty of boutique accommodation for staying in the region. Before heading off the next day for Augusta, stroll the main street, with its galleries and gift shops.

Day 4

Drive through the beautiful forests and pretty country roads, to the town of Augusta, with its superb coastal scenery and famed lighthouse on Cape Leeuwin. This is the most southwesterly tip of Australia, where the Indian and Southern Oceans meet, and where you can watch migrating humpback whales from June to September. After lunch, travel to Caves Road, where the local tourism body operates daily tours (9:30–3:30) of three accessible limestone caves, each with their own unique formations, Lake, Mammoth, and Jewel. Drive back to Perth later in the afternoon.

❶Perth and Fremantle

Delightfully located on the broad Swan River, Perth is a youthful, modern city with a warm, sunny climate and an outdoor lifestyle. It is also one of the world's most isolated cities, closer to Southeast Asia than its own national capital.

Perth

Glass-and-concrete skyscrapers dominate Perth's skyline and it is, indeed, a busy "happening" city, albeit with a population of just 1.5 million people. The vibrant Northbridge district, around the art gallery and museum and filled with cafes, restaurants, bars and clubs, is lively day and night.

Perth's chief attractions are easily visited in a day and the first of these – the **Perth Mint** – is east of the centre, in Hay Street. Opened as a branch of London's Royal Mint in 1899 to turn gold from Western Australia's goldfields into sovereigns, this historic building now produces proof coins and specialist precious-metal coins, which you can watch being minted. Arrive in time for the hourly gold pour.

Next stop is the **Western Australian Museum Perth**, where the highlights are the Katta Dijnoong Aboriginal gallery and Land & People, which tells the story of WA from dinosaurs onwards. When you've finished exploring the museum, head down to St Georges Terrace and catch a bus to **Kings Park**, a 400ha (990-acre) expanse of native bushland, a botanic garden and manicured parklands threaded with walking tracks and scenic drives.

If you're visiting in spring, you'll be treated to a colourful display of wild flowers, but at any time of the year you can enjoy superb views of the city from the park's eastern end.

Looking to the city skyline and Swan River from Kings Park

Fremantle

Take a cruise down the Swan River to the port town of Fremantle. Jazzed up for an influx of tourists anticipated for the 1987 America's Cup yacht race series, "Freo" is still a town of old-world charm, its quaint streets filled with renovated

PERTH AND FREMANTLE: INSIDE INFO

Top tips A fun way to explore Perth is to take a ride on the **wooden replica trams** that trundle between Burswood Entertainment complex and Kings Park, stopping off at some of the main city sights en route. Similar trams operate in Fremantle, departing from the Town Hall frequently from 9:45am.

■ Explore **Kings Park** in Perth by bicycle, which you can rent from a couple of outlets in the city. It's also a good way to work off lunch!

historic buildings, alfresco cafes, restaurants, galleries and bustling markets. While strolling around and soaking up the maritime atmosphere is the best approach here, there are a few sights worth closer inspection, starting with the **Fremantle Prison**. Built by convicts between 1850 and 1860, it operated as a maximum security prison until 1991 and now you can take day or night tours of the forbidding, but fascinating, complex. If it's market day (Friday, Saturday or Sunday), make your next stop the famed **Fremantle Markets**, housed in a grand old Victorian building in South Terrace and selling everything from fresh produce to quality Australiana. Near by are the inviting alfresco cafes of Freo's "cappuccino strip" (South Terrace), the perfect place for lunch.

Devote some time to the **Western Australian Maritime Museum** and its **Shipwreck Galleries**. The museum, housed in a striking modern building at Victoria Quay, highlights the State's maritime heritage, from pearling luggers to racing yachts. The relics in the nearby Shipwreck Galleries include timbers from the Dutch ship Batavia, wrecked off present-day Geraldton in 1629.

TAKING A BREAK

Enjoy imaginative Modern Australian cuisine at **Fraser's Restaurant** (➤ 177).

Perth ✛ 212 B2
Fremantle ✛ 212 B2

Perth Mint
✉ 310 Hay Street, East Perth
☎ (08) 9421 7223; www.perthmint.com.au ⏰ Mon–Fri 9–5, Sat–Sun 9–1; closed 1 Jan, Good Fri, 25 Apr, 25 Dec. Gold-pouring hourly Mon–Fri 10–4, Sat–Sun 10–noon
🚋 Moderate 🚌 The Red CAT

Western Australian Museum Perth
✉ James Street, Perth ☎ (08) 9212 3700; www.museum.wa.gov.au ⏰ Daily 9:30–5; Anzac Day and 26 Dec 1–5, closed Good Fri and 25 Dec 🚋 Donation 🚌 The Blue CAT
🚉 Perth City Railway Station

Fremantle Prison
✉ 1 The Terrace ☎ (08) 9336 9200; www.fremantleprison.com.au ⏰ Daily 9–5; closed Good Fri, 25 Dec 🚋 Expensive 🚌 Fremantle
🚉 Fremantle

Western Australian Maritime Museum
✉ Victoria Quay, Fremantle ☎ (08) 9431 8444; www.museum.wa.gov.au/maritime ⏰ Daily 9:30–5; Anzac Day and 26 Dec 1–5; closed Good Fri, 25 Dec 🚋 Inexpensive 🚌 Fremantle
🚉 Fremantle

Western Australian Maritime Museum Shipwreck Galleries
✉ Cliff Street, Fremantle ☎ (08) 9431 8444 ⏰ As above 🚋 Donation

2 Margaret River Region

With a ruggedly beautiful coastline, majestic native forests, rolling pastureland and vineyards, the Margaret River region is one of Western Australia's most picturesque landscapes.

Running the length of its coast is the **Leeuwin-Naturaliste National Park**, which encompasses soaring coastal cliffs with panoramic views, world-class surfing beaches, secluded bays perfect for fishing and swimming, caves filled with spectacular formations, lofty karri forests and springtime wild flowers. Complementing this natural grandeur are more than 160 wineries, restaurants, galleries, craft shops and quaint towns whose residents have perfected the art of relaxed living.

Caves Road

The best way to approach the region is via Caves Road, which branches off the Bussell Highway at the town of Busselton and brings you directly to the Willyabrup Valley where most of the wineries are found. **Vasse Felix** – Margaret River's oldest winery and vineyard – has an excellent restaurant and is a great place to stop for lunch. After sampling the local foods and wines, continue along Caves Road to the signposted turn-off to the Margaret River Mouth, where you can watch surfers riding the legendary waves. Then, if it's a hot day, continue on to nearby **Gnarabup Beach** for sheltered swimming in an idyllic bay. From here, return to Caves Road for the short drive to Margaret River township – the perfect base for exploring the region – and spend time browsing through the numerous galleries and shops.

The shoreline at Prevelly Park, Margaret River

Explore the Southwest

Head back to Caves Road and drive south to find the **Boranup Gallery**, which sells quality furniture handmade from local timbers. Backtrack the short distance to the Boranup Forest turn-off and enjoy a sublime drive (along a well-graded dirt road) through 50m (165-foot) high karri trees, then rejoin the main road and continue to **Jewel Cave**. Take a guided tour of the region's best cave, which features a stunning array of limestone formations including a fragile 6m (19-foot) long straw stalactite that is estimated to be about 3,370 years old. Don't miss a visit to the nearby **CaveWorks** eco-centre (free admission with your cave ticket), featuring impressive displays and a cafe. Be sure to visit Cape Leeuwin, the most southwesterly point of Australia: it's a great place for spotting migrating humpback and southern right whales in July, October and November. The lighthouse is worth a climb.

For the return drive to Margaret River, take the Bussell Highway and stop first at **Fox Studio Glass**, in Karridale, where you can observe glass-blowers. Then continue to the Redgate Road turn-off, which leads to **Leeuwin Estate**, one of the region's premier wineries with an excellent restaurant (► 177). Finish your day at the **Voyager Estate**, worth a visit as much for the rose gardens as for the wine.

TAKING A BREAK

For cheap, fresh food, head for **The Arc of Iris** (tel: (08) 9757 3112) in the main street. If you're ready to spend a little more, try **Vat 107** restaurant on the Bussell Highway.

✚ 212 A2

Margaret River Visitor Centre
✉ 100 Bussell Highway ☎ (08) 9780 5911; www.margaretriver.com 🕐 Daily 9–5; closed 25 Dec 🚌 Trans WA or South-West Coachlines from Perth

Jewel Cave
✉ Off Caves Road ☎ CaveWorks: (08) 9757 7411; www.margaretriver.com 🕐 Daily 9:30–3:30; closed 25 Dec 💲 Moderate

MARGARET RIVER REGION: INSIDE INFO

Top tips As a rule, **the restaurant scene here is very busy on Saturday nights**: avoid disappointment by making early reservations at the restaurant of your choice.

■ Western Australia's best dairy products are made at **The Margaret River Dairy Company** and **Fonti Farm**, both on Bussell Highway, where you can taste speciality cheeses and yoghurts, and watch cheese being made through a viewing window.

■ **Eagles Heritage Raptor Wildlife Centre**, on Boodjidup Road, has a huge collection of birds of prey and free-flight displays.

Hidden gem For a chance to pick your own berries, sample fruit wines and ports and buy delicious jams, preserves, pickles and vinegars, visit **The Berry Farm**, at 222 Bessell Road, Margaret River.

At Your Leisure

Rock formations, Nambung NP

🄱 Nambung National Park

Nambung National Park, 245km (152 miles) north of Perth, has a wealth of natural attractions, from beautiful beaches and coastal dune systems to stunning wildflower blooms in spring – but it is the extraordinary Pinnacles Desert that is its main attraction. Here, thousands of weather-beaten limestone pillars – some jagged sharp-edged columns, others resembling tombstones – rise up to 4m (13 feet) from the stark landscape of yellow sand. A one-way track winds around them, but for the best views of these eerie giants, park the car and wander around them on foot. In the early morning or late in the afternoon, the sun casts long shadows, enhancing their surreal effect.

➕ 212 A2 ✉ Nambung National Park, via Cervantes ☎ Ranger's office at Cervantes: (08) 9652 7043; www.australiascoralcoast.com 🕐 Daily 💲 Inexpensive

🄲 Swan Valley

This is Western Australia's oldest wine region and famous for its fortified varieties. The Swan Valley may not match most of Margaret River's (► 172–173) vintages, but it does offer a pleasant day's wine tasting within easy reach of Perth. Centred on the Swan River, at the foot of the Darling Range, the valley boasts not just wineries, but gourmet produce and excellent restaurants, tea rooms and galleries displaying local handicrafts. The historic town of Guildford, at its entrance, is worth a stop for a look at the many well-preserved 19th-century buildings and the various arts, crafts and antiques shops.

The best way to explore the Swan Valley is to follow the signposted Swan Valley Food and Wine Trail, which loops up one side of the river and down the other, past the best of the region's wineries.

➕ 212 B2

Swan Valley and Eastern Region Visitor Centre
✉ Corner of Meadow and Swan streets, Guildford ☎ (08) 9379 9400; www.swanvalley.com.au 🕐 Daily 9–4; closed 25 Dec 💲 Tours: expensive 🚌 Feature Tours or Australian Pinnacle Tours available from Perth 🚉 Midland, Guildford ⛴ Boat tours from Barrack Street Jetty, Perth

🄴 Swan River and Ocean Sailing

If sailing is your passion – or just an unrealized urge – then Perth and Fremantle are the places to indulge yourself. Blessed with dependable winds and a warm sunny climate, the waters here offer some of Australia's best sailing. Operators cater for all levels of experience, with options ranging from an invigorating sail on the Swan River in a hired 4.5m (15-foot) catamaran and windsurfing at Pelicans Point to joining a skippered day-sail to Rottnest Island. Offshore yachts can be chartered in Fremantle for both day and overnight trips, and similar arrangements can be made for Swan River jaunts.

Western Australian Visitor Centre
✉ Forrest Place (Corner Wellington Street) ☎ (08) 9483 1111 or (1800) 812 808; www.westernaustralia.com, www.wavisitorcentre.com and www.experienceperth.com

🕓 May–Aug Mon–Thu 8:30–5:30, Fri 8:30–6, Sat 9:30–4:30, Sun 11–4:30; Sep–Apr Mon–Thu 8:30–6, Fri 8:30–7, Sat 9:30–4:30, Sun 11–4:30; closed all public holidays

Fremantle Visitor Centre
✉ Town Hall, Kings Square ☎ (08) 9431 7878; www.fremantlewa.com.au 🕓 Mon–Fri 9–5, Sat 10–3, Sun 11:30–2:30; closed public holidays

⑥ Cottesloe Beach

With its lively cafes, picturesque fringe of Norfolk pines, deep clear water and wide stretch of white sand, Cottesloe is the most popular of Perth's city beaches and the perfect place for an early-morning or late-afternoon swim. Just 11km (7 miles) southwest of the city centre, it is one of a string of glorious ocean beaches that stretch north along the Sunset Coast for some 30km (18 miles). For wave action, head north of Cottesloe to the less-crowded surf beaches, but if it's an all-over tan you're seeking, try Swanbourne's nude-bathing area. At the end of the day, however, it doesn't matter which beach you sit on to watch the vivid spectacle of an Indian Ocean sunset – anywhere on the Sunset Coast is a ringside seat.

🏛 212 B2 ✉ Marine Avenue, Cottesloe
🕓 24 hours daily 🎟 Free 🚌 102, 103, 107
🚆 Cottesloe

⑦ Rottnest Island

Idyllic Rottnest, 18km (11 miles) west of Fremantle, offers something for everyone. Pristine beaches, turquoise waters, and some of Western Australia's best coral reefs provide opportunities for fishing, swimming, snorkelling and diving, while the dearth of traffic (private vehicles are not permitted) makes renting a bicycle and cycling from one white, sandy beach to another particularly pleasant. Also on offer are a museum, historical walking tours, bus tours, golf, restaurants and accommodation and a chance to see quokkas – the unique marsupials that 17th-century Dutch explorer Willem de Vlamingh mistook for rats; hence his name for the island: "rats" nest.

🏛 212 A2 ✉ Rottnest Island Visitor Centre, Thomson Bay ☎ (08) 9372 9732; www.rottnestisland.com 🕓 Daily 8–5
🚢 Rottnest Island (from Perth and Fremantle)
✈ Rottnest Island (15 mins from Perth)

⑧ Stirling Range National Park

With its powerful mountain scenery and brilliant springtime wildflower displays, the national park, 450km (280 miles) southeast of Perth, is one of Australia's outstanding reserves. Its rugged peaks rise abruptly to more than 1,000m (3,280ft) from the surrounding plain, providing a cool, humid environment in which around 1,500 flowering plant species thrive. The Stirling Range is Western Australia's best alpine-walking area, and for enthusiasts, Bluff Knoll, at 1,095m (3,593ft) the highest peak in the range, offers a 3- to 4-hour (6km/ 4-mile) return walk to the summit. More relaxing, and no less rewarding, is the unsurfaced Stirling Range scenic drive, which winds for 40km (25 miles) from Chester Pass Road to Red Gum Pass Road.

🏛 212 B2 ✉ Ranger Station, Moingup Springs Campsite, Chester Pass Road ☎ (08) 9827 9230; www.naturebase.net
🕓 Daily 🎟 Inexpensive

Cottesloe Beach, Perth

Where to... Stay

Prices

Prices are for the least expensive double room in high season:

$ under A$150	**$$** A$150–A$280
$$$ over A$280	

PERTH AND FREMANTLE

City Waters $

For the price-conscious traveller, this collection of self-catering studios, only ten minutes' walk from the city, is ideal. There is a friendly atmosphere and one-bedroom or family studios are available. WiFi is on offer.

✚ 212 B2 ⊠ 118 Terrace Road, Perth
☎ (08) 9325 1566; www.citywaters.com.au

Duxton Hotel Perth $$–$$$

The award-winning Duxton, located on Perth's main thoroughfare, is one of the city's best hotels. Its five-star facilities include 306 spacious rooms, many with river views; a gym and pool; a bar and fine-dining restaurant; and excellent service.

✚ 212 A2 ⊠ 1 St Georges Terrace, Perth
☎ (08) 9261 8000; www.duxtonhotels.com

Esplanade Hotel $$

This 4.5 star hotel, just a two-minute walk from the centre of Fremantle, has 300 well-appointed rooms and suites, most with private balconies and parkland views. It has a heated swimming pool, three outdoor spas, a fitness centre, a business centre, and WiFi. On Sunday, make a reservation for the High Tea.

✚ 212 A/B2 ⊠ Corner Marine Terrace and Essex Street, Fremantle ☎ (08) 9432 4000; www.esplanadehotelfremantle.com.au

Mantra on Hay $$

One- and two-bedroom apartments with large balconies, fully equipped kitchens, bathroom and laundry facilities, lounge and dining areas. Close to the WACA cricket ground, Gloucester Park, Burswood Casino, and Queens Gardens, as well as premier shopping and multicultural dining choices.

✚ 212 A2 ⊠ 201 Hay St, Perth
☎ (07) 5665 4450; www.mantra.com.au

MARGARET RIVER REGION

Heritage Trail Lodge $$

A romantic hideaway with private verandahs offering superb forest views. Breakfast, served in the conservatory, features locally produced foods.

✚ 212 A2 ⊠ 31 Bussell Highway, Margaret River ☎ (08) 9757 9595; www.heritage-trail-lodge.com.au

Hidden Valley Forest Retreat $$–$$$

Set among forest and wetlands, Hidden Valley offers a choice of accommodation and personalized services, such as massage, spa treatments, and even a private chef. Tours can be arranged.

✚ 212 A2 ⊠ Haag Road, Margaret River
☎ (08) 9755 1066; www.yourhiddenvalley.com

Margaret River Hotel $$

A perfect base from which to explore the region, this hotel offers traditional country-style accommodation, with a range of rooms including a deluxe spa room. There is a bistro, rooms have WiFi, and it's just a short stroll to the weekend farmer's market.

✚ 212 A2 ⊠ 125 Bussell Hwy, Margaret River ☎ (08) 9757 2655; www.margaretriverhotel.com.au

Where to...
Eat and Drink

Prices
Prices per person for a meal, excluding drinks, tax and tip:
$ under A$20 $$ A$20–A$30 $$$ over A$30

PERTH AND FREMANTLE

44 King Street $–$$
An imaginative menu and nearly 50 wines by the glass has brought acclaim to this contemporary bistro. Greek and Italian dishes predominate.

➕ 212 B2 🖂 44 King Street, Perth ☎ (08) 9321 4476 🕑 Breakfast, lunch and dinner daily from 7am

Fraser's Restaurant $$–$$$
Fine city and river views, award-winning food and an extensive wine list unite to make a visit to Fraser's a priority for any Perth visitor. The modern menu is extensive and changes daily according to what local produce is available. Breakfast served on weekends.

➕ 212 B2 🖂 Fraser Avenue, Kings Park, West Perth ☎ (08) 9481 7100; www.frasersrestaurant.com.au 🕑 Sun 8am–10pm, Mon–Sat 12–10

Indiana $$
Perth's trendy beachside suburb of Cottesloe is the perfect place to watch the sun set over the Indian Ocean. Once a grand old teahouse, Indiana has an innovative bistro menu based on fresh WA produce, pours its own-brew tap beers, and has a comprehensive wine list.

➕ 212 A2 🖂 99 Marine Parade, Cottesloe ☎ (08) 9758 8877; www.indiana.com.au 🕑 Daily 8–late

Kailis Fish Market Cafe $
Experience the sights and bustle of this long-established working fish market on the Fremantle waterfront. Enjoy fresh fish and chips, lobster and salad, or garlic prawns, or the cakes and bread.

➕ 212 B2 🖂 Fishing Boat Harbour, 46 Mews, Fremantle ☎ (08) 9335 7755; www.kailis.com 🕑 Daily 8am–late

Rialtos $$–$$$
This popular restaurant serves excellent Italian fare in a contemporary setting, complete with funky furniture and a cocktail bar. Italian and Australian wines are available.

➕ 212 B2 🖂 424 Hay Street, Subiaco ☎ (08) 9382 3292; www.rialtos.com.au 🕑 Mon–Sat 12–3, Tue–Sat 6–10

MARGARET RIVER REGION

Leeuwin Estate Winery Restaurant $$$
A favourite of visitors and residents, the brasserie has both verandah and alfresco seating. Wines come from the estate, which is one of the country's largest table-wine producers, but the menu looks fasrther afield to Europe.

➕ 212 A2 🖂 Stevens Road, Margaret River ☎ (08) 9759 0000; www.leeuwinestate.com.au 🕑 Daily 12–3, Sat 6–10

Must $$
This classy offshoot of the Perth restaurant of the same name features classic French cuisine based on fresh local produce. Dishes featuring tender, select beef adorned with a choice of bearnaise sauce or green pepper jus are popular. The wine selection is phenomenal. Booking advised.

➕ 212 A2 🖂 107 Bussell Hwy, Margaret River ☎ (08) 9758 8877; www.must.com.au 🕑 Daily 12–late

Where to...
Shop

PERTH AND FREMANTLE

The heart of Perth is an attractive shopping centre. The two main department stores are **Myer** and **David Jones**. London Court is a Tudor-style collection of more than 1,200 speciality shops, off St Georges Terrace, which is also home to **Costello's** (tel: (08) 9325 8588), an excellent retailer of opals, Argyle diamonds and pearls. For good Aboriginal art and crafts, try the **Aboriginal Art and Craft Gallery** in Kings Park (tel: (08) 9481 7082).

Kailis Australian Pearls (tel: (08) 9239 9330) in Fremantle is the top place for Broome pearl jewellery. Visit the **Fremantle Markets** on the corner of Henderson Street and South Terrace (Friday to Sunday), where more than 150 stallholders offer fresh produce, antiques and crafts.

Fremantle also has art and craft galleries, and some good bookshops, including **Elizabeth's Secondhand Bookshop** (High Street Mall tel: (08) 9430 6700).

MARGARET RIVER

In the main street of Margaret River, **Jahroc Mill Gallery** (83 Bussell Highway), specializes in wooden products. At **The Fudge Company** (152 Bussell Highway) you can watch fudges and chocolates being made in small batches. A range of hemp clothing for men and women and other natural hemp products can be found at the **Margaret River HempCo** (133 Bussell Highway).

Where to...
Be Entertained

PERTH AND FREMANTLE

The hub of Perth nightlife is in Northbridge's William and James streets. Closer to the water is **His Majesty's Theatre** at 825 Hay Street (tel: (08) 9265 0900), built in 1904 and host to drama, opera, ballet and stage musicals. Nearby, the **Perth Concert Hall** (tel: (08) 9231 9900) is the state's top fine music venue and home of the West Australian Symphony Orchestra.

A 10-minute drive from Perth is Burswood, and the architecturally stunning **Burswood Entertainment Complex and Casino** in Great Eastern Highway (tel: (08) 9362 7777; www.burswood.com.au). Concerts include pop and classical music, musical comedy and tribute shows. There is a cabaret lounge.

In Fremantle, the **Fremantle Arts Centre** at 1 Finnerty Street (tel: (08) 9432 9555; www.fac.org.au) has free open-air concerts on Sunday afternoons in addition to its regular exhibitions. The building, once an asylum and including a ground-floor social history museum, is worth a visit in itself.

For current entertainment news, check the *West Australian* newspaper, Monday to Saturday, or *The Sunday Times*.

MARGARET RIVER FESTIVALS

The area is famous for its wine and food festivals. The **Wine Festival**, held in November, is very popular. The **Leeuwin Estate Winery** holds a concert in February/March that attracts international musicians.

Tasmania

Getting Your Bearings

Australia's only island State is also its smallest, but within Tasmania's compact 67,800sq km (26,180 square miles) is a wealth of monumentally beautiful wilderness, gentle pastoral landscapes reminiscent of the English countryside, heritage towns and chilling convict history. It is the perfect holiday isle: distances are small, the locals friendly, hospitality old-fashioned and welcoming, the local foods outstanding and the pace of life decidedly relaxed.

Home to the world's first Green political party, the Tasmanian Greens, Tasmania cherishes its landscapes – a major attraction for nature lovers. Those spending time in the vast World Heritage area – a place of wild rivers, temperate rain forest, buttongrass plains and glacially carved mountains and tarns – will find the air fragrant and the water sweet in what is still one of the cleanest places on earth. For many years after its founding in 1804, Van Diemen's Land, as Tasmania was first known, was used as a place of secondary punishment for errant convicts from New South Wales. Today, the State's violent convict past presents its most brutal face at Port Arthur, while its capital, Hobart, combines a stunning harbour setting with the most picturesque elements of its history.

**Page 179:
Walkers at
the start of
the Overland
Track**

Furneaux
Group

Cape Barren
Island

Clarke Island

Banks Strait

Cape Portland

Mount William
National Park

Eddystone
Point

B82

Bridport

Bay of Fires

George
Town

Port
Sorell

Beauty Point

Derby

Beaconsfield

A8

Scottsdale

St Helens

trobe

A7

A3

South Esk

eld

Deloraine

4 Launceston

Cataract ✈
Gorge
Reserve

Ben Lomond
National Park

Evandale

St Marys

Creek

Fingal

B51

Macquarie

A4

Douglas Apsley
National Park

of Jerusalem
al Park

Great
Lake

Arthurs
Lake

Campbell Town

B34

Bicheno

Ross

A3

Lake
Echo

Swansea

Coles Bay

Great
Oyster
Bay

Freycinet
National Park

raleah

A10

A5

Bothwell

Oatlands

Freycinet
Peninsula

Hamilton

Kempton

B31

Triabunna

Orford

Darlington
Maria Island

Derwent

Cadbury's
Factory Cruise

9 Richmond

A3

Maria Island
National Park

ydena

Mt Wellington

8

Sorell

A9

Cascade
Brewery

6 7 2

Lauderdale

Forestier
Peninsula

Huon

Hobart

Port Arthur
Historic Site 3

Tasman
Peninsula

Huonville

Geeveston

Storm
Bay

Cape
Raoul

Cape
Pillar

Dover

A6

Bruny Island

Southport

South Bruny
National Park

South East
Cape

| 0 | | 50 km |
| 0 | | 30 miles |

**Opposite:
Looking over
the harbour in
Hobart from
Mount Nelson**

In Five Days

If you're not quite sure where to begin your travels, this itinerary recommends a practical and enjoyable five days exploring Tasmania, taking in some of the best places to see using the Getting Your Bearings map on the previous page. For more information see the main entries.

Day 1

If you arrived in Tasmania at Launceston airport, in the state's north, make the 2.5-hour drive via Deloraine and Sheffield to **1 Cradle Mountain** (above, ▶ 184) – part of the Tasmanian Wilderness World Heritage Area. If you arrive on the ferry, then you can drive to Cradle Mountain in 90 minutes from Devonport.

Day 2

Arrive in **5 Strahan** (left, ▶ 188), a peaceful fishing village on the rugged West Coast, via Rosebery and Zeehan, and take a scenic flight over the Franklin-Gordon Wild Rivers National Par. Spend the rest of the day exploring Strahan's picturesque main street and Visitor Centre. A good place to stop, stretch your legs and have lunch is the Lake St Clair National Park, where you can take a short, scenic walk from the visitor centre.

Day 3

Leave early for the 300km (186-mile) drive, via Queenstown, along the scenic Lyell Highway, which winds between the magnificent Cradle Mountain-Lake St Clair and Franklin-Gordon Wild Rivers national parks on its way to **2 Hobart** (above, ➤ 186).

Day 4

Wander around historic Hobart and explore famous Victoria Dock with its associated marine craft, and the restored Henry Jones IXL buildings. The city's heritage streetscapes are infused with old-world charm, and colonial buildings house museums, public offices, and a variety of shops, galleries, cafes and restaurants. On Saturday, Salamanca Place has a thriving art, crafts, food and produce market of over 300 stalls.

Day 5

Step back in time to Australia's harsh and fascinating convict past at the **3 Port Arthur Historic Site** (right, ➤ 187), a 90-minute drive from Hobart. If time permits, take in historic Richmond, with its old convict-built bridge, then stop at Eaglehawk Neck for refreshments, stunning coastal views, and the interesting Tessellated Pavement. Explore the ruins of Port Arthur, cruise to the Isle of the Dead, and finish with a "ghost tour".

❿ Cradle Mountain

Whether shrouded in cloud, resplendent under a clear sky, or reflected in the mirror surface of tranquil Dove Lake, Cradle Mountain is the epitome of a wild alpine landscape. When mountaineer and botanist Gustav Weindorfer first surveyed the countryside from its 1,545m (5,069-foot) summit in 1910, he declared: "This must be a national park for the people for all time."

Today, Cradle Mountain's moorland, heath, deep gorges, forested valleys, lakes and tarns are protected in the northern section of the World Heritage-listed Cradle Mountain–Lake St Clair National Park.
Spectacular scenery and sublime bushwalks are the mountain's major attractions. If you're fit, the six- to eight-hour return walk to the summit is well worth the effort and takes you a short way along the **Overland Track**, one of Australia's most popular long-distance bushwalks. Weather conditions can alter dramatically and quickly – come prepared with layered clothing and a snug, waterproof jacket.

Lake Oenone and Lake Helen and nearby peaks seen from the summit of Mount Olympus

However, you don't have to stand atop the mountain to appreciate the region's beauty. Simply sitting on a bench in the **Dove Lake car park** – a great place for a picnic lunch on a sunny day – will afford you one of the most stunning views of the area. Of the many short walks on offer, the **Dove Lake Loop Track** is the most outstanding. This two-hour return walk weaves through ancient rainforest and past quartzite beaches, offering a variety of mountain views – especially if you walk in a clockwise direction.

TAKING A BREAK

The Tavern Bar at Cradle Mountain Lodge, just outside the park boundary, offers informal bistro meals in a country-pub atmosphere. For more sophisticated fare try the lodge's **Highland Restaurant**.

✚ 215 D1

Cradle Mountain Visitor Centre
✉ Cradle Mountain Road ☎ (03) 6492 1110; www.parks.tas.gov.au
🕐 Daily 8:30–4:30 💵 Inexpensive 🍴 Cradle Mountain Lodge Tavern Bar and Bistro ($) 🚌 From Launceston, Devonport and Hobart

2 Hobart

Hobart's great strengths are the splendour of its natural setting, between Mount Wellington and the River Derwent, and the preservation of its colonial past. Many of its beautiful Georgian buildings were constructed by the convicts who formed the bulk of its founding population, and past and present merge, rather than clash, in many of its heritage streetscapes.

With one of the world's finest deep-water harbours, it is also a city with strong maritime ties and shows its prettiest face to those approaching from the sea. But the best way to soak up the **historic atmosphere** of this small, uncluttered city is on foot. Just a stone's throw from the city's heart is **Sullivans Cove**, hub of the waterfront, and a good place to begin your exploration.

In the late 19th century barques, square-riggers or whaling boats would have been chafing at their moorings here, but today's **Victoria Dock** is the peaceful home to much of Hobart's fishing fleet while neighbouring **Constitution Dock** really comes to life around the end of each year as the finishing point for the famous Sydney to Hobart Yacht Race. Here you can buy cheap fish and chips from punts permanently moored alongside Mures Fish Centre, a two-level complex containing a restaurant, a sushi bar, a bistro and several food outlets.

Looking from the rocks at Mount Welllington to Ralph Bay

Behind Victoria Dock, Hunter Street's **pretty row of old warehouses** is fodder for photographers, while those with an artistic bent should visit the former IXL Jam Factory, now home to galleries, a design store, the Tasmanian School of Art and the Henry Jones Art Hotel.

On the other side of the cove you will find **Salamanca Place**, a delightful line-up of restored colonial warehouses filled with shops, art galleries, cafes, and pubs full of character. This is the place to be on a Saturday when the open-air Salamanca Market attracts bargain-hunting crowds to its medley of quality Tasmanian arts and crafts, books, clothing, flowers, organic food and bric-a-brac.

About two-thirds of the way along the front of the warehouses is an alleyway leading to Kellys Steps, which link the waterfront area with residential **Battery Point**. This former mariners' village has changed little in the past 100 years and its narrow, cottage-lined streets are an inviting lesson in social history.

For sheer quaintness, you need go no further than **Arthurs Circus** with its 15 single-storey Georgian cottages set around a village green, but if it's window-shopping or antique browsing you're after, take a walk along Hampden Road on the far side of the green.

In this most maritime of cities, you should end your day where you began – down on the waterfront – where all that remains is to explore Tasmania's culinary delights in one of the many restaurants you passed by earlier.

Racing yachts in Constitution Dock, the venue for the finish of the Sydney to Hobart annual yacht race

TAKING A BREAK

Great for breakfast, lunch and dinner, the **Retro Café** (➤ 191) in Salamanca Place has a relaxed air and a clientele ranging from students to politicians.

➕ 215 E1

Tasmanian Travel and Information Centre
✉ Corner of Davey and Elizabeth streets ☎ (03) 6283 4222 or 1800 990 440; www.discovertasmania.com, www.hobarttravelcentre.com.au
🕐 Mon–Fri 8:30–5:30, Sat, Sun and public holidays 9–5; closed 25 Dec

HOBART: INSIDE INFO

Top tips The **Tasmanian Museum and Art Gallery**, in Macquarie Street (tel: (03) 6211 4177; www.tmag.tas.gov.au), has an excellent collection of Tasmanian colonial art while its museum displays include convict and Aboriginal history.
■ For a break from city sightseeing, visit the beautiful **Royal Tasmanian Botanical Gardens** (tel: (03) 6236 3075; www.rtbg.tas.gov.au), set high above the river and just a short walk from the centre. The highlights include a large collection of temperate plants, Japanese Gardens and the Botanical Discovery Centre.

3 Port Arthur Historic Site

One of Australia's most infamous convict settlements, Port Arthur, was established on the Tasman Peninsula in 1830. It quickly gained a reputation as a "hell-on-earth" and by the time it closed its doors in 1877, about 12,000 sentences had been served here.

The church in Port Arthur Historic Site

Tragically, the closure did not mark the end of its violent history: in April 1996 a lone gunman massacred 35 tourists and locals. Today, Port Arthur has regained its peaceful character and is a place of picturesque stone ruins and restored buildings set amid old English-style gardens and lawns that roll to the water's edge.

Begin your exploration in the Visitor Centre's interactive **Interpretation Gallery**, where you'll discover what life in the convict era was really like, then join one of the regular site-introduction walks. You'll end up at the former "lunatic" Asylum, built in 1867 and now housing a museum displaying grim relics like the notorious cat-o'-nine-tails. Next door's **Model Prison** is one of the site's highlights. Opened in 1852, it replaced floggings with a system of isolation and total silence, and if you stand inside the claustrophobic punishment cell, you'll know why a stint in here pushed several prisoners to the brink of insanity.

The hour-long guided tour of Port Arthur's burial ground – the Isle of the Dead – offers fascinating stories about the colourful characters buried there. At exploration's end, the 20-minute harbour cruise is a great way to sit back and take in the grandeur of the historic site. The **Historic Ghost Tours** that run after dusk are great fun, highlighting the site's rich repertoire of other-worldly tales and strange occurrences.

TAKING A BREAK

The **Museum Coffee Shop** is a snug setting for coffee, cakes or light meals, while **Felons Restaurant** in the Visitor Centre offers a more extensive menu.

➕ 215 E1 ☎ (03) 6251 2378 or (1800) 659 101; www.portarthur.org.au
🕐 Site: daily 8:30–dusk; visitor centre: daily 8:30 until end of Ghost Tour
💷 Moderate–Expensive 🍴 Museum Coffee Shop ($) 🚌 Buses from Hobart

At Your Leisure

❹ Cataract Gorge Reserve

Carved by the South Esk River, the spectacular Cataract Gorge – just 15 minutes' walk from central Launceston – is the star feature of one of Australia's most alluring urban reserves. To see the best of the gorge, start at Kings Bridge, which offers a stunning view of the almost vertical cliffs rising from the river. From here you can take the 30-minute (one-way) Cataract Walk along the northern side of the gorge to the Victorian garden at Cliff Grounds, which is linked to the south side by a suspension bridge, a 457m (1,500ft) long chairlift and a footpath.

➕ 215 E1 ✉ Cataract Gorge Reserve ☎ (03) 6323 3610; chairlift: (03) 6331 5915; www.launcestoncataractgorge.com. au ⏰ Chairlift: daily from 9am (hours vary; call for details) 🎟 Reserve: free; chairlift: inexpensive 🚌 No 51B to First Basin; Nos 40, 41, 42, 43, 44 to Cataract Gorge 🚢 Tamar River Cruises operates cruises into the gorge from Home Point cruise terminal, tel: (03) 6334 9900; www.tamarrivercruises.com.au

❺ Strahan

The once-bustling mining and timber port of Strahan is today a pretty fishing village best known as a stepping-off point for cruises of Macquarie Harbour – including a stop at Sarah Island to visit the ruins of a penal settlement for "incorrigibles" – and the pristine Gordon River, part of the World Heritage Franklin-Gordon Wild Rivers National Park. Scenic flights offer an alternative, equally spectacular view of the area: one of the most exciting includes a seaplane landing at Sir John Falls on the Gordon River.

The Franklin River, a tributary of the Gordon River, was the centre of intense political debate in the 1970s and early 1980s between the Tasmanian government, who put forward a proposal to build a dam on the Gordon River, and the (Liberal) Federal government who opposed it. The election of a Federal Labor government in 1983 resulted in cancellation of the project. Another attraction is the scenic 1896 West Coast Wilderness Railway, running from Strahan to Queenstown.

➕ 215 D1

Strahan Visitor Centre

✉ The Esplanade ☎ (03) 6472 6800; www.westcoast.tas.gov.au ⏰ Daily 10–6 🎟 West Coast Reflections exhibition at the Visitor Centre: inexpensive 🚌 TassieLink to Strahan

❻ Cascade Brewery

Beer lovers should not miss watching some of Australia's finest brews being produced in the country's oldest brewery (1824) – the Cascade plant on the slopes of Mount Wellington. The 90-minute site tours reveal the entire brewing process, from malting to packaging, finishing with a tasting session and a visit to the Cascade Visitor Centre. Even if you're not a beer connoisseur, the brewery's stone façade and beautiful Woodstock Gardens make a visit worthwhile.

➕ 215 E1 ✉ 140 Cascade Road, South Hobart ☎ (03) 6224 1117; www.cascadebrewery. com.au ⏰ Tours: several times daily 🎟 Moderate 🚌 43, 44, 49 ℹ Bookings are essential. The Cascade Brewery is a fully operational worksite – visitors must wear flat, preferably enclosed, footwear

❼ Mount Wellington

Hobart's impressive backdrop – 1,270m (4,167-foot) Mount Wellington – is well known for its panoramic views. On clear days you'll see most of the city and southern Tasmania from the summit, and if the weather is really good, many of the mountains of central and southwestern Tasmania too. The Mount Wellington Visitor Centre has panels identifying major features of

A passenger ferry making its way along Cataract Gorge

he view and nearby boardwalks lead to open-air lookouts. The easiest way to reach the top of Mount Wellington is by car, but those with a bent for strenuous bushwalking may prefer to tackle the slopes via a track on the eastern slopes.

➕ 215 E1 ✉ Visitor Centre: daily 8–8 in summer; 8–4:30 in winter; www.wellingtonpark. as.gov.au 💲 Free; tours: expensive 🚌 Nos 48, 49 to Fern Tree provide access to the main walking tracks. Experience Tasmania (☎ (03) 6234 3336; www.experiencetas.com.au) runs ours including Mount Wellington on Tue, Thu, Fri and Sat

🟦 Cadbury's Factory Cruise
The most scenic and direct route to chocoholic heaven is the Cadbury's Cruise from Hobart's Brooke Street Pier. Billed as the "sweetest cruise in Australia", it is the appetite-sharpening prelude to a guided tour of the country's best-smelling factory – Cadbury's – established in 1922 and now producing 90–100 tonnes of chocolate a day. You'll be led for 2km (1 mile) through a labyrinth of corridors and stairs to rooms filled with the machinery – and a delicious smell of chocolate-making. Along the way, you're encouraged to sample to your heart's content, until you arrive replete, or feeling slightly ill, at the factory shop where you can snap up a variety of sweet bargains.

➕ 215 E1 ✉ The Cruise Company, Brooke Street Cruise Centre ☎ (03) 6234 9294 🕐 Mon–Fri 9 (back at pier by 12); closed public holidays 💲 Expensive ℹ Book early to avoid disappointment; tour numbers are limited. Also, as the factory is an industrial worksite, you must wear fully enclosed footwear and appropriate clothing

🟦 Richmond
Once a key military post and convict station on the route between Hobart Town and Port Arthur, Richmond today is Australia's finest historic village. Just 24km (15 miles) from Hobart, it owes its 19th-century character to the building of the Sorell Causeway in 1872, bypassing the village. Development slowed to a snail's pace until tourism boomed and most of its 50 or so historic buildings now house galleries, craft shops, cafes and guest-houses. A stroll around the village will reveal Australia's best-preserved convict prison – the 1825 Richmond Gaol – and its oldest Catholic church (St John's, 1836) and oldest bridge, Richmond Bridge, built by convicts between 1823 and 1825.
➕ 215 E1

Richmond Gaol
✉ 37 Bathurst Street ☎ (03) 6260 2127; www.richmondvillage.com.au 🕐 Daily 9–5; closed 25 Dec 💲 Inexpensive 🚌 Tassielink coaches from Hobart

Where to...
Stay

Prices

Prices are for the least expensive double room in high season:

$ under A$150 $$ A$150–A$280 $$$ over A$280

CRADLE MOUNTAIN

Cradle Mountain Lodge $$–$$$

This luxurious sanctuary has views across Tasmania's World Heritage wilderness area. Guests stay in comfortable wood cabins.

✚ 215 D1 ◈ Cradle Mountain Road
☎ (03) 6492 2103 or (1300) 806 1924;
www.cradlemountainlodge.com.au

GEORGE TOWN

Belles Bed and Breakfast $

Situated opposite the foreshore of the Tamar River, in the charming old port village of George Town, Belles offers a queen size bedroom, with ensuite and private lounge room. Enjoy a delicious home cooked breakfast, fresh flowers in your room and plenty of home-made treats.

✚ 215 E2 ◈ 1 Macquarie Street,
George Town ☎ (03) 6382 2574;
www.bellesbedandbreakfast.com.au

HOBART

Avon Court Apartments $$

Conveniently situated on Battery Point and an easy walk from Salamanca Place, these good-value apartments attract regular customers.

✚ 215 E1 ◈ 4 Colville Street, Battery Point
☎ (0466) 594 571; www.avoncourt.com.au

Henry Jones Art Hotel $$$

This multi award-winning hotel is housed within a row of historic warehouses on Hobart's waterfront, and showcases the work of some of Tasmania's top artists. The hotel's rooms, restaurants and bars are furnished with more than 250 original artworks and the hotel itself, an exciting and innovative combination of the ultramodern and the antique, has all amenities including WiFi.

✚ 215 E1 ◈ 25 Hunter Street, Hobart
☎ (03) 6210 7700; www.thehenryjones.com

Riverside Glaziers Bay $$

Situated in the tranquil Huon Valley, just 45 minutes' drive south of Hobart, this comfortable, spacious cottage accommodates up to six guests. Panoramic views of the Huon River and mountains can be enjoyed from every room and a generous breakfast is provided.

✚ 215 E1 ◈ 35 Graces Road,
Glaziers Bay ☎ (03) 6295 1952;
www.huonriverside.com.au

Somerset on Salamanca $$

The Somerset offers spacious serviced apartments, all with a private balcony or courtyard. The decor is modern and stylish and the kitchens are fully-equipped.

✚ 215 E1 ◈ 8 Salamanca Place, Hobart
☎ (03) 6220 6600 or (1800) 766 377;
www.somersetonsalamanca.com

PORT ARTHUR

Stewarts Bay Lodge $$

Set in natural bushland, this is the ideal place to try bushwalking, fishing or photography. The Lodge is a leisurely stroll along a shoreline trail to Port Arthur Historic Site.

✚ 215 E1 ◈ 6955 Arthur Highway,
Port Arthur ☎ (03) 6250 2888;
www.stewartsbaylodge.com

Where to...
Eat and Drink

Prices

Prices per person for a meal, excluding drinks, tax and tip:
$ under A$20 $$ A$20–A$30 $$$ over A$30

STRAHAN

Franklin Manor $$

Franklin Manor offers boutique accommodation and the finest restaurant on Tasmania's west coast. Local produce is the staple, fish particularly. Visit the cellar to pick your own wine.

➕ 215 D1 ✉ The Esplanade, Strahan ☎ (03) 6471 7311; www.franklinmanor.com.au ⏱ Dinner daily

Risby Cove $$–$$$

One of Strahan's finest licensed restaurants, Risby Cove's scenic location, alongside the marina and harbour, is perfect for viewing the spectacular west coast sunsets. The menu lists local seafood teamed with Tasmanian wines. Don't miss the Barilla Bay oysters and seared Tasmanian scallops.

➕ 215 D1 ✉ The Esplanade, Strahan ☎ (03) 6471 7572; www.risby.com.au ⏱ Daily 7am–10am, 6pm–late

HOBART

Marque IV $$–$$$

The award-winning Marque IV offers one of Hobart's best dining experiences, along with a great waterfront location and outdoor dining. The Modern Australian menu includes fine meat, game and seafood dishes.

➕ 215 E1 ✉ Elizabeth Street Pier, Hobart ☎ (03) 6224 4428; www.marqueiv.com.au ⏱ Lunch Wed–Fri, dinner daily

Retro Café $–$$

The best breakfasts in Hobart and super-fine coffee are among the treats in this popular cafe. Lunchtime sees a blackboard menu with daily changing specials. You can bring your own alcohol. This cafe only accepts cash payments.

➕ 215 E1 ✉ Corner of Salamanca Place and Montpelier Retreat, Hobart ☎ (03) 6223 3073 ⏱ Daily 8–6

LAUNCESTON

Mud Bar and Restaurant $$–$$$

Exclusively furnished and elegantly designed, this popular eatery at the Old Launceston Seaport has superb waterfront views. The menu features fresh local produce in dishes with authentic Italian flavours, along with specialities like Atlantic salmon, pork and veal meatballs, braised lamb fettucine, grilled fish, confit duck leg and steamed mussels.

➕ 215 E2 ✉ 28 Seaport Boulevard, Launceston ☎ (03) 6334 5066; www.mudbar.com.au ⏱ Daily from 11am

RICHMOND

Prospect House $$

Sample a variety of foods from Tasmania's rich harvest in this mansion, built using convict labour in 1830. Polished timber, crisp white tablecloths and a log fire create the setting for dining on succulent venison or duck served with garden-fresh vegetables, followed by delicious desserts. Tasmania's unique pinot noirs and rieslings are on the wine list.

➕ 215 E1 ✉ 1384 Richmond Road, Richmond ☎ (03) 6260 2207; www.prospect-house.com.au ⏱ Dinner daily

Where to...
Shop

TASMANIA

There is some unique shopping here, particularly at the many galleries, where traditional handicrafts are made with wool, glass, clay, leather and wood. **The Design Centre** (cnr Tamar and Brisbane streets, Launceston, tel: (03) 6331 5506) sells the finest wood designs. In Evandale, **Lake Leather** (3 Russell St, tel: (03) 6391 8888) has the state's best leather products. Popular weekend markets are held at **Evandale** (Sun 8–1), Launceston (Sun 9–2), Sorrell (Sun 7–1), and Wynyard (third Sun 9–3).

HOBART

The city has pleasant shopping arcades with fashion and gift stores.

For exclusive shopping, head to the Murray and Liverpool streets precinct. The Cat and Fiddle Arcade, between Liverpool and Collins streets malls, has speciality shops, including jeweller **Michael Hill** (tel: (03) 6236 9545). **Art Mob** (29 Hunter St, tel: (03) 6236 9200) has Aboriginal art, and Masterpiece @IXL has fine art and antiques.

Take a trip to Salamanca Place (www.salamanca.com.au) to find the best arts and crafts (try the **Salamanca Arts Centre** at No 77, tel: (03) 6234 8414), as well as a range of Tasmania's gourmet foods. **Masons Studio Jewellers** (No 33) design, facet and set Tasmanian topaz. This is also the venue for Hobart's lively Saturday **Salamanca Market** (8:30–3), arguably Australia's best outdoor market.

Where to...
Be Entertained

HOBART

The **Theatre Royal** (29 Campbell Street, tel: (03) 6233 2299), built in 1837, is the country's oldest theatre, and its traditional charm is a satisfying counterpoint to the contemporary style of theatre at the Salamanca Arts Centre.

Hobart's main festivals and events are held between December and February. Top of the list is the party marking the conclusion of the **Sydney to Hobart yacht race**, at the end of December. Other highlights are the **Taste of Tasmania** (late December/early January), **Hobart Summer Festival** (late December to mid-January) and **Royal Hobart Regatta** (February).

The **Royal Hobart Show** in October is a good draw for families. On display are the best livestock the state has to offer, and the produce of large and small industries, including craft and food products. There is also a fun fair.

Entertainment is also to be found at the **Wrest Point Hobart** in Sandy Bay (tel: (03) 6225 7001; www. wrestpoint.com.au). The resort is sited on a promontory overlooking the Derwent River and, along with games and bars, offers several restaurants and cafes, nightclubs, a theatre and a revolving restaurant.

For information on entertainment during your visit, check the pages of the local *Mercury* newspaper, which has an entertainment section called "Pulse" on Thursdays.

Walks and Tours

1 THE SHORES OF MOSMAN BAY

Walk

Threading through the leafy shoreline of Mosman Bay, this tranquil walk – one of Sydney Harbour's prettiest – combines a ferry ride with easy footwork. Best walked in the morning or early afternoon, it offers magnificent views of the city and harbour and a close-up look at harbourside living, with mansions, houses and colourful gardens on one side and bushland, yacht anchorages and secluded fishing and picnicking spots on the other.

1–2

Start at Circular Quay, just a few minutes' walk southwest of the Opera House, and take a ferry to **Cremorne Point Wharf**. After leaving the ferry, cross the road and climb the steps. Follow the path into the park, past the playground until you reach a bench on the right from where you can enjoy a superb view of the Opera

DISTANCE Approximately 2km (1.25 miles) **TIME** 30–40 minutes **START POINT** Cremorne Point Wharf **END POINT** Mosman Bay Wharf **FERRY DEPARTURES** Ferries to Cremorne Point Wharf and Mosman Bay Wharf depart from Circular Quay (⊞ 217 B4) approx every 30 minutes Mon–Sat and every 40 minutes on Sun. They take about 10 minutes to Cremorne Point, 20 minutes to Mosman

Harbour Bridge (▶ 48–51). Continue along the path to **Robertsons Point**, for a sweeping harbour vista.

2–3

Retrace your track to the steps leading up from the wharf and take the right fork in the path, which will lead you past a row of fine old apartment buildings.

3–4

Soon you'll reach the enchanting **Lex and Ruby Graham Gardens**, which spill down the slope on your right in a lush tangle of vegetation with palms and tree ferns as well as splashes of colour from cliveas, hydrangeas and other flowering plants. A highlight of the walk, these National Trust of Australia-listed gardens were originally created by Lex and Ruby Graham, a local couple, in 1957. From here there are delightful views into Mosman Bay, with its boats and the attractive harbourside houses in the exclusive suburb of Mosman.

4–5

Reid Park

Harnett Avenue

Avenue Road

7 Mosman Rowing Club

8 The Barn

9 Mosman Bay Wharf

10 Sculpture of HMS Sirius

MOSMAN

Mosman Bay

Bromley Ave

6

CREMORNE

5

0   200 metres
0   200 yards

gazebo, head towards Old Cremorne Wharf as indicated by the sign. The path on your right leads to **Sydney Amateur Sailing clubhouse.**

5–6

Once past the wharf you soon reach the top of a slight rise and a lovely view of the end of the bay. A little farther on, you'll come to the Bromley Avenue sign, which points you down the path to a dense grove of trees. Here the path splits three ways. Take the lower one down the steps and over a small timber bridge.

6–7

At the end of this path, descend the steps to reach the roadway outside the **Mosman Rowing Club.** Here, neatly dressed visitors may enjoy a drink and bistro-style snacks on the verandah overlooking the yachts in the marina.

7–8

Leaving the rowing club, stroll down Centenary Drive past the parking areas then around the end of the bay to meet up with Avenue Road. Cross over to look at Mosman's oldest building, **The Barn.** Built in 1831 for use as a

whaling storehouse, it is now home to the 1st Mosman Scouts.

8–9

Cross back over the road to view the sculpture of **HMS Sirius**, the principal naval escort of the First Fleet, which arrived in Port Jackson (Sydney Harbour) on 26 January 1788. A bronze plaque gives some historical notes.

9–10

Continue to **Mosman Bay Wharf**, where there are lavatories, a shop and a cafe, and enjoy the views as you wait for the ferry back to Circular Quay.

TAKING A BREAK

Relax at Mosman Rowing Club: in addition to bar snacks, there is also the Rowers Restaurant, which serves lunch (Wed–Sun). Mosman Bay, tel: (02) 9953 7966. Note that to enter here, you need to be smartly dressed.

Mosman Bay

2 THE DANDENONG RANGES

Tour

Following winding roads through soaring forests and tree-fern gullies, stopping at magnificent public gardens and quaint villages, this scenic tour of the Dandenong Ranges makes a relaxed day's outing from Melbourne.

DISTANCE 105km (65 miles)* **TIME** Three hours without stopping, but a whole day to really appreciate the region's many attractions **START POINT** Upper Ferntree Gully ✚ 215 D2 **END POINT** Montrose ✚ 215 D2
(*Includes travel from and to Melbourne's city centre)

1–2

Drive from Melbourne along the Burwood Highway (Route 26) then start your tour proper at **Upper Ferntree Gully**, gateway to the beautiful Dandenong Ranges. Continue along the highway to Belgrave, home to *Puffing Billy*, a vintage steam train that runs for 25km (16 miles) through forests, ferns and farmlands to Gembrook.

2–3

On reaching the roundabout, continue along Monbulk Road for a drive through the of Sherbrooke Forest, part of the Dandenong Ranges National Park (www.dandenongrangestourism.com.au). **Grants Picnic Ground**, signposted on the right near the end of this road, has abundant bird life.

3–4

Soon after leaving the picnic ground, you'll come to another roundabout. Turn left on to Sherbrooke Road and drive for a few kilometres to the **George Tindale Memorial Gardens** at Sherbrooke, which feature flowering plants, lawns and rock gardens under a canopy of mountain ash.

4–5

A couple more bends in the road to the west is the **Alfred Nicholas Gardens**, also at Sherbrooke. Noted for its exotic and indigenous plants, this 13ha (32-acre) garden includes a picturesque lake,

Five Ways Lookout

Kalorama

Mt Dandenong Observatory

William Ricketts Sanctuary

DANDENONG TOURIST ROAD

Dandenong Ranges National Park

National Rhododendron Gardens

Mt Dandenong

Dandenong Ranges National Park

Montrose ROAD

CANTERBURY

Melbourne

5-6

At the intersection of Sherbrooke and Mount Dandenong Tourist roads, take a right turn and follow the route to Olinda. The first town you'll reach is **Sassafras**. This popular resort is packed with enticing arts-and-crafts galleries, antiques shops, cafes, and tea rooms, including the quintessentially English Miss Marple's. Back on the tourist road, continue to **Olinda**, which offers yet more antiques shops, galleries, tea rooms and restaurants. If you're ready for refreshment, stop at either of these villages.

6-7

Before leaving Olinda, take a short detour down the Olinda-Monbulk Road, then turn left into The Georgian Road to the world-renowned **National Rhododendron Gardens**. Spring (September–November) sees them at their most spectacular, but at any time of the year they offer one of the best views in the

Aboriginal figures amid rocks, tree-ferns, huge eucalypts and trickling waterfalls.

8-9

From here, it's a short drive along the tourist road to Kalorama and the **Five Ways Lookout**, which offers extensive views across Silvan Reservoir and the Upper Yarra Valley.

9-10

After leaving the lookout car park, make an immediate left turn from the tourist road on to Ridge Road. After a few kilometres you'll reach the signposted one-way loop road to **Mount Dandenong Observatory**. At 633m (2,077ft), this is the highest point in the Dandenongs, with views across Melbourne and Port Phillip.

10-11

Backtrack along Ridge Road and make a left turn to rejoin the tourist road.

11-12

The route descends through bushland and past nurseries to Montrose, the northern gateway to the Dandenongs. Turn left into Canterbury Road (Route 32) and return to the city.

7-8

Rejoin the Mount Dandenong tourist road and continue for several kilometres to the **William Ricketts Sanctuary** at Mount Dandenong. A Dandenongs highlight, this tranquil garden on the side of a steep hill features sculptures of

Dandenongs – the Australian Alps forming a dramatic backdrop to Silvan Reservoir Park.

MOUNT TOUR

Melbourne
Upper Ferntree Gully
1

Alfred Nicholas Gardens **5**

SHERBROOKE
Sherbrooke **George Tindale Memorial Gardens** **4**

Dandenong Ranges National Park

Sherbrooke RD

Grants Picnic Ground **3**

Forest

Sherbrooke

MONBULK ROAD

Puffing Billy **2**
Belgrave

1 Mile

3 THE SOUTHERN HIGHLANDS

Tour

With its blend of sandstone escarpments, wild bushland, farmland and historic villages, the **Southern Highlands has been a popular weekend retreat for Sydneysiders since the 1920s.** This scenic drive passes through prime rural landscapes to lookouts with views of waterfalls, valleys and mountains. Along the way you can stop and explore villages with art and antiques shops and, if you're visiting in spring or autumn, see gardens resplendent in their seasonal hues.

DISTANCE 320km (200 miles)* **TIME** One day
START POINT Mittagong ➕ 215 E3
END POINT Berrima ➕ 215 E3 (*Includes return travel from Sydney's city centre)

1–2

From Sydney, drive for 112km (70 miles) along the South Western Freeway and Hume Highway (Routes M5 and 31) until you reach the Mittagong (Tourist Drive 14) exit. **Mittagong**, Gateway to the Highlands, is the site of the main visitor centre (Tourism Southern Highlands, tel: (02) 4871 2888 or (1300) 657 559; www.southern-highlands.com.au).

Highway) and turn left at the clock onto Bowral Road then turn left again into Bessemer Street. Pass under the railway line, cross Railway Parade, then veer left into Waverley Parade and right into Oxley Drive, which winds through Mount Gibraltar Reserve to the 864m (2,835ft) summit of Mount Gibraltar. Turn right at the "Bowral via Lookouts" sign to reach the four **lookouts** on the mountain's rim, which offer excellent views right over the region.

Drive downhill to reach the intersection with Mittagong Road, then turn left and drive into Bowral. Founded in the 1860s, **Bowral**

soon became a summer retreat for wealthy Sydney residents, who left a legacy of stately mansions with cool-climate gardens. Tulip Time, in September to October, is the region's leading floral festival when many private gardens, ranging from formal English to country Australian, are open for inspection. Antiques, crafts and speciality shops line Bong Bong Street, the main road, but Bowral's chief claim to fame is as the boyhood home of cricketing legend Sir Donald Bradman. The Bradman Museum of Cricket and Oval in St Jude Street

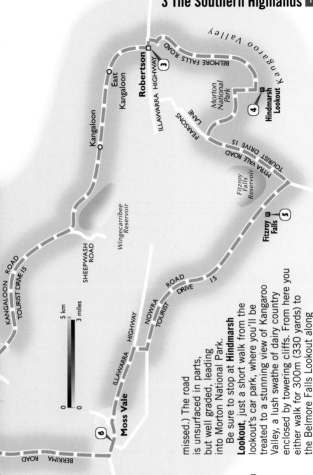

2–3

At the end of Bong Bong Street is a roundabout. Take the Kangaloon Road exit (Tourist Drive 15) and drive for several kilometres east to the Kangaloon Road/Sheepwash Road intersection. Turn left here, following the Tourist Drive 15 sign, and continue past the Wingecarribee Reservoir and picnic area. The route winds up the hillside through pastureland dotted with grazing cattle. Proceeding through the villages of Kangaloon and East Kangaloon, you'll soon reach a grove of huge gum trees that marks the entrance to **Robertson**, a quaint town best known as the setting for the film *Babe*. A highlight here is The Old Robertson Cheese Factory where you can try the local cheeses and also have lunch at the Pig and Whistle cafe.

3–4

On reaching the Illawarra Highway intersection soon after entering the town, turn left and follow the signs to Belmore Falls. (After turning right into South Street, take the first left into Belmore Falls Road – the sign here is partly obscured and the turn-off easily missed.) The road is unsurfaced in parts, but well graded, leading into Morton National Park. Be sure to stop at **Hindmarsh Lookout**, just a short walk from the lookout's car park, where you'll be treated to a stunning view of Kangaroo Valley, a lush swathe of dairy country enclosed by towering cliffs. From here you either walk for 300m (330 yards) to the Belmore Falls Lookout along the escarpment track or return to the car and drive to the next car park.

The lookout offers a clear view of the upper and lower falls, which cascade over the escarpment in a dramatic drop.

4–5

Continue to the intersection with Pearsons Lane, where the dirt road ends, and turn left into Myra Vale Road. Drive past the Fitzroy Falls Reservoir to the intersection with Nowra Road. Turn right here and continue for a few kilometres to **Fitzroy Falls**, also in Morton

Belmore Falls, Morton National Park

National Park. A short boardwalk from the National Parks and Wildlife Service Visitor Centre leads to several lookouts offering spectacular views of the 81m (266-foot) falls and deep sandstone gorges.

5–6

From Fitzroy Falls, continue along Nowra Road until you reach the signposted route to **Moss Vale** (Tourist Drive 15). Turn right here, then left at the Illawarra Highway intersection. Soon you'll reach a roundabout. Turn left again and head down Argyle Street, the town's winding main road.

A prime rural centre for sheep, cattle, goats and champion horses, Moss Vale has a real "villagey" atmosphere with pretty tree-lined streets and plenty of cafes, restaurants, galleries and speciality shops.

6–7

From Moss Vale, make a right turn from Argyle Street into Waite Street then left into Berrima Road and drive through countryside until you reach the intersection with the Old Hume Highway. Turn right and cross the Wingecarribee River into Berrima.

The most charming and historic of the Southern Highlands' villages, **Berrima** is considered to be one of the best remaining examples of a small Australian town built in the 1830s, its numerous restored buildings now trading as stylish craft shops, galleries and restaurants. The Surveyor-General Inn, established in 1834 and claiming to be the oldest continuously licensed (legally permitted to sell alcohol) pub in Australia, has roaring log fires in winter and is a cosy place to stop for late-afternoon refreshment.

7–8

From Berrima, continue north along the Old Hume Highway, joining the Hume Highway, then the South Western Freeway for the return drive to Sydney (125km/78 miles).

TAKING A BREAK
The **Pig and Whistle** at the Old Robertson Cheese Factory serves snacks and light meals as well as "Devonshire" teas and cakes.

Practicalities

BEFORE YOU GO

WHAT YOU NEED

		UK	Germany	USA	Canada	France	Ireland	Netherlands	
● Required ○ Suggested ▲ Not required	Some countries require a passport to remain valid for a minimum period (usually at least six months) beyond the date of entry – check before you travel.								
Passport/National Identity Card		●	●	●	●	●	●	●	●
Visa or Australian Electronic Travel Authority (ETA)		●	●	●	●	●	●	●	●
Onward or Return Ticket		▲	▲	▲	▲	▲	▲	▲	▲
Health Inoculations (tetanus and polio)		▲	▲	▲	▲	▲	▲	▲	▲
Health Documentation (➤ 206, Health)		●	▲	▲	▲	●	▲	●	▲
Travel Insurance		○	○	○	○	○	○	○	○
Driving Licence (national) and International Driving Permit		●	●	●	●	●	●	●	●

WHEN TO GO

Sydney

High season   Low season

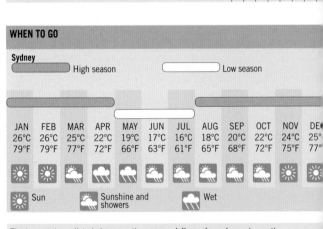

JAN	FEB	MAR	APR	MAY	JUN	JUL	AUG	SEP	OCT	NOV	DE●
26°C	26°C	25°C	22°C	19°C	17°C	16°C	18°C	20°C	22°C	24°C	25°
79°F	79°F	77°F	72°F	66°F	63°F	61°F	65°F	68°F	72°F	75°F	77°

☀ Sun   ⛅ Sunshine and showers   🌧 Wet

The temperatures listed above are the **average daily maximum** for each month.
Australia has a **range of climates** because of its size, geographical location and lack of high mountain ranges.
During the summer months (December to February) the southern states are the best places to visit, while Western Australia, the Northern Territory and Queensland can be very **hot and humid**.
Between November and April it is the **wet season** in parts of Western Australia and the Northern Territory, and in northern Queensland. Tropical cyclones occur at this time.
Most of the rainfall on the Great Barrier Reef occurs in January and February.
Winter (June to August) is the best time to visit the north, west and Red Centre.
The **ski season** is from June to October.

GETTING ADVANCE INFORMATION

Websites
■ Tourism Australia:
www.australia.com
■ Australian Tourism Net:
www.atn.com.au

■ Australian Regional Tourist Associations:
http://members.ozemail.com.au/~fnq/rta/
■ Northern Territory:
www.travelnt.com

In Australia
Tourism Australia
GPO Box 2721
Sydney 1006
☎ (02) 9360 1111

GETTING THERE

From the UK Flying time to the Australian East Coast from the UK is normally in excess of 22 hours with flights to the Australian West Coast about 3–4 hours shorter. From Europe carriers usually fly via the Middle East or an Asian city. Major airlines operating from London include: **British Airways** (tel: 0870 850 9850), **Qantas** (tel: 0845 77 477 67), **Air New Zealand** (tel: 0800 028 4149) and **Singapore Airlines** (tel: 0870 60 888 86).

From North America Flying time to the Australian East Coast from the US West Coast is normally 15 hours. From North America, carriers fly via the US West Coast or Vancouver. Major carriers that fly daily include: **Qantas** (tel: 1-800 227 4500), **Air New Zealand** (tel: 1-800 262 1234) and **United** (tel: 1-800 538 2929).

Ticket prices Within Europe and North America, a number of airlines offer competitive fares. Summer (December to February) is the **most popular time to visit**, so fares are more expensive and flights tend to be booked well in advance. Independent packages offer combination air fare, accommodation and car rental. Fares are generally cheaper from May to August (autumn and winter). Consult a specialist travel operator, the internet or the travel sections of newspapers and magazines for the best current deals. Non-direct routes and round-the-world tickets can offer savings.

TIME

Australia has three major time zones. **Eastern Standard Time**, 10 hours ahead of GMT (GMT+10), operates in Queensland, the Australian Capital Territory, New South Wales, Victoria and Tasmania. **Central Standard Time** (GMT+9.5) operates in South Australia and the Northern Territory. **Western Standard Time** (GMT+8) operates in Western Australia. **Daylight Saving**, when clocks are put forward by 1 hour at the beginning of summer, operates in New South Wales, Victoria, Tasmania, the Australian Capital Territory, Western Australia and South Australia.

CURRENCY AND FOREIGN EXCHANGE

Currency The monetary unit of Australia is the Australian dollar ($A) and the cent 100 cents = 1 $A).
Coins come in 5 cent, 10 cent, 20 cent, 50 cent and $1 and $2 denominations, and there are $5, $10, $20, $50 and $100 notes.

Exchange Most airports, banks and large hotels have facilities for changing foreign currency and travellers' cheques (commissions and fees may be charged). A passport is usually adequate for identification. **Cash withdrawals** can be made at automatic teller machines (check with your bank for details of where your cards will be accepted). **Debit cards** may be accepted at retail outlets that are validated for international access, using a personal identification number (PIN). Major **credit cards** are accepted in all large cities. The most commonly accepted credit cards are American Express, Bankcard, Diners Club, MasterCard and VISA, and their affiliates. The use of ATM and credit cards may be restricted in smaller towns and rural areas, such as the Outback, where there are fewer banking establishments.

In the UK
Tourism Australia
Australia Centre
Australia House, 6th Floor,
Melbourne Place/Strand
London WC2B 4LG
☎ (020) 7438 4601

In the USA
Tourism Australia
6100 Center Drive
Suite 1150
Los Angeles CA90045
☎ 310/695 3200

In Canada
Tourism Australia
111 Peter Street,
Suite 630,
Toronto M5V 2H1
☎ 416/408 0549

WHEN YOU ARE THERE

NATIONAL HOLIDAYS

1 Jan	New Year's Day
26 Jan	Australia Day
Variable	Labour Day
Mar/Apr	Good Friday
Mar/Apr	Easter Monday
25 Apr	Anzac Day
Second Mon in Jun	Queen's Birthday
(WA: last Mon in Sep)	
25 Dec	Christmas Day
26 Dec	Boxing Day

Individual states have public holidays throughout the year for agricultural shows, regattas and race days.

ELECTRICITY

The power supply is 220/240 volts AC (50 cycles). Sockets accept three-flat-pin plugs so an adaptor is needed. 110v appliances will need a voltage converter. Universal outlets for 240v or 110v shavers are usually found in leading hotels.

OPENING HOURS

○ Shops   ● Post Offices
● Offices   ● Museums/Monuments
● Banks   ● Pharmacies

8am 9am 10am noon 1pm 2pm 4pm 5pm 7pm

□ Day   □ Midday   □ Evening

Shops Hours vary from state to state. Many supermarkets and department stores have late-night opening on Thu and Fri until 9 and are open Sat 9–5. Some shops in tourist centres and cities often open Sun.
Banks Mon–Fri 9:30–5. Some open Sat morning.
Post Offices Mon–Fri 9–5.
Museums Hours may vary.
Pharmacies Some offer a 24-hour service in cities.

TIPS/GRATUITIES

Tipping is optional; 10% for good service is standard.
Yes ✓   No ✗

Restaurants (service not included)	✓ 10%
Bar service	✗
Tour guides	optional
Hairdressers	✗
Taxis	✗
Chambermaids	✗
Porters	✓ $A1–2 per bag

GENERAL INFORMATION

- There is a smoking ban in all restaurants and other enclosed spaces.
- Police are strict about speeding and drink-driving. If you are arrested, you should give your name and address and then contact a lawyer or your consulate.

TIME DIFFERENCES

GMT	Australia (Sydney)	UK	USA (NY)	USA (West Coast)	Germany
12 noon	10pm	12 noon	7am	4am	1pm

STAYING IN TOUCH

ost offices, located in
ty centres, suburbs and
ombined with a general
ore in smaller places where
pening times vary, offer
ostal and *poste restante*
ervices. Most post boxes,
ainted red with a white
tripe, resemble litter bins.

ublic telephones

ong-distance calls within Australia (STD) and
ternational Direct Dialling (IDD) can be made
n public payphones (check with operator: dial
234 for charges). Public payphones accept cash
nd phonecards, available from retail outlets in
enominations of $5, $10 and $20. The *Telsta
elecard* is a cashless calling card that allows you to
ake calls to over 65 countries. *Telstra PhoneAway*
repaid card enables you
use virtually any phone
Australia with all calls
harged against the card.

ternational Dialling Codes
ial 0011 followed by

eland:	353
SA/Canada:	1
ermany:	49
etherlands:	3
pain:	34

Mobile providers and services

overage depends on your service provider, but the
ational carrier, Telstra, offers the best dual band
2G and 3G) coverage. Other providers include Optus,
odafone, and Virgin. In most popular destinations you
ill get good reception. When you head inland from the
bast or off the beaten track in national parks, don't
xpect to make calls with regular mobile phones.

WiFi and Internet

ou will find internet cafes wherever you go; usage fees
re around $5 per half-hour or $8 per hour. Generally,
ternet connections have reasonable download times,
ut to upload images or download music files, look for
facility with cable broadband. Nearly all hotels have
he option of internet connection in your room.

PERSONAL SAFETY

In crowded places, take the
usual safety precautions.
Walking in the bush and
swimming have their hazards.

- Hitch-hiking is strongly
  discouraged throughout
  Australia.
- Women should avoid
  walking alone at night.
- If bushwalking or camping,
  leave an itinerary with
  reliable friends. Wear
  boots, socks and trousers.
- In the bush take care with
  cigarettes – fires start
  easily in summer.
- As you would in busy areas,
  make sure your personal
  belongings are secure.
- Take care at ATMs when
  withdrawing cash.
- Take care and heed
  warning signs when
  swimming, whether in
  the sea or fresh water
  (crocodiles!).
- Swim where red and yellow
  flags are displayed – they
  show that a lifeguard is on
  duty at the beach.
- Do not swim in areas
  without a lifeguard.

Police assistance:
☎ 000 from any phone

EMERGENCY	
POLICE	000
FIRE	000
AMBULANCE	000

HEALTH

 Insurance British and certain other nationals are eligible for free basic care at public hospitals but it is strongly recommended that all travellers take out a comprehensive medical insurance policy. (See www.medicareaustralia.gov.au)

 Dental Services Dentists are plentiful and the standard of treatment is high – as are the fees. In an emergency go to the casualty wing of a local hospital, or locate a dentist from the local phone book. Medical insurance is essential.

 Weather The sun in Australia is extremely strong, especially in summer. Wear a hat to protect your face and sunglasses to protect your eyes. Avoid sunbathing in the middle of the day. Use high-factor sunscreen and cover up when sightseeing.

 Drugs Prescription and non-prescription drugs are available from pharmacies. Visitors may import up to three months' supply of prescribed medication: bring a doctor's certificate.

 Safe Water It is safe to drink tap water anywhere in Australia. Bottled mineral water is available throughout the country.

CONCESSIONS

Students/Youths Young visitors should join the International Youth Hostels Federation before leaving their own country. Australia has a widespread network of youth and backpacker hostels. International Student or Youth Identity Cards may entitle the holder to discounts on attractions.

Senior Citizens Many attractions offer a discount for senior citizens; the age limit varies from 60 to 65, and your passport should be sufficient evidence of your age. However, few discounts on travel are available to overseas senior citizens, as an Australian pension card is usually required to qualify.

TRAVELLING WITH A DISABILITY

Hotels, airlines, attractions and transportation carriers generally provide access for people with disabilities. Check with service providers. Contact National Disability Services (tel: (02) 6283 3200; www.nds.org.au) for details. Tourism Australia publishes a comprehensive fact sheet for people with disabilities.

CHILDREN

Most restaurants and cafes are child friendly, especially cheap eateries. Some offer a children's menu, and there are many fast-food outlets. As an alternative to hotels, houses and serviced apartments can be rented.

TOILETS

Free public toilets are found in most public places, such as museums, department stores, bus stations and railway stations. Toilets are generally clean and well serviced, and baby-changing facilities are found in many places, especially department stores.

LOST PROPERTY

For lost or misplaced items of personal property, contact the nearest police station.

EMBASSIES AND HIGH COMMISSIONS

 UK (02) 6270 6666

 USA (02) 6214 5600

 Ireland (02) 6273 3022

 Canada (02) 6270 4000

 New Zealand (02) 6270 421

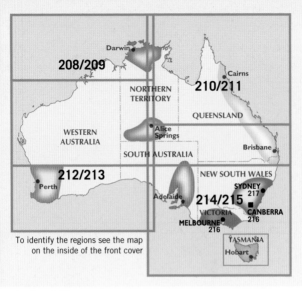

To identify the regions see the map
on the inside of the front cover

Regional Maps

═══	Major route	▢	Capital city
═══	Freeway	▫	City/town
───	Main/other road	▣	Featured place of interest
───	Untarred road	✈	Airport
───	Railway	▲	Height in metres
───	State boundary	▨	National park

208-215
0   100   200   300   400 km
0   100   200   300 miles

Streetplans

───	Main road	▣	Featured place of interest
───	Other road	▪	Important building
═══	Railway	✝	Church
●───	Metro light rail	[i]	Tourist information centre
●───	Metro monorail	▨	Park/cemetery
───	Tramway	☀	Viewpoint
●	Metro station	✉	Post office

216
Canberra
0   400   800 metres
0   400   800 yards

216
Melbourne
0   200   400   600 metres
0   200   400   600 yards

217
0   100   200   300 metres
0   100   200   300 yards

Atlas

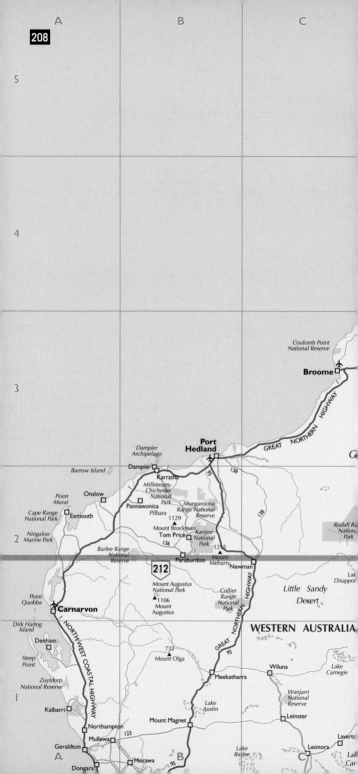

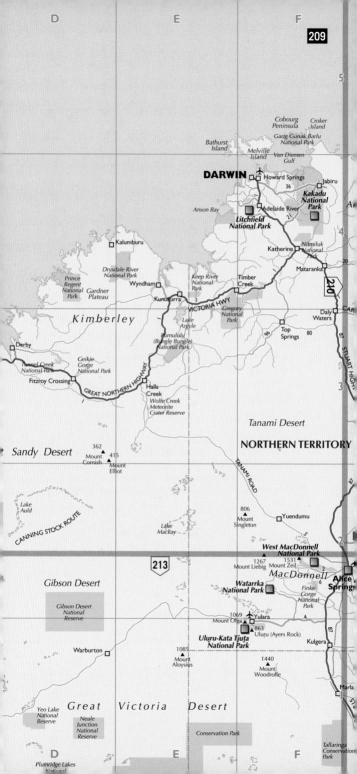

5

Cobourg
Peninsula
Croker
Island
Garig Gunak Barlu
National Park
Bathurst
Island
Melville
Island
Van Diemen
Gulf

DARWIN
Howard Springs
Jabiru
36
**Kakadu
National
Park**
Anson Bay
Adelaide River
**Litchfield
National Park**
Katherine
Nitmiluk
National
Park
4
Kalumburu
Mataranka
20
Drysdale River
National Park
Keep River
National Park
Timber
Creek
Prince
Regent
National
Park
Wyndham
VICTORIA HWY
Gregory
National
Park
Daly
Waters
CAR
210
Gardner
Plateau
Kununurra
Lake
Argyle
Top
Springs
80
STUART HIGHWAY
Kimberley
**Purnululu
(Bungle Bungle)
National Park**
96
Derby
Geikie
Gorge
National Park
GREAT NORTHERN HIGHWAY
87
Tunnel Creek
National Park
3
Fitzroy Crossing
Halls
Creek
*Wolfe Creek
Meteorite
Crater Reserve*
Tanami Desert
Sandy Desert
362
Mount
Cornish
415
Mount
Elliot
NORTHERN TERRITORY
TANAMI ROAD
Lake
Auld
87
CANNING STOCK ROUTE
806
Mount
Singleton
Yuendumu
2
Lake
Mackay
213
**West MacDonnell
National Park**
1267
Mount Liebig
1531
Mount Zeil
2
6
MacDonnell
**Alice
Springs**
Gibson Desert
**Watarrka
National Park**
Finke
Gorge
National
Park
Gibson Desert
National
Reserve
1069
Mount Olga
Yulara
**Uluru-Kata Tjuta
National Park**
863
Uluru (Ayers Rock)
Kulgera
87
Warburton
1085
Mount
Aloysius
1440
Mount
Woodroffe
Marla
Great Victoria Desert
Yeo Lake
National
Reserve
Neale
Junction
Nature
Reserve
Conservation Park
Tallaringa
Conservation
Park

Plumridge Lakes

Badu Island
Moa Island
Thursday Island
Horn Island
Prince of Wales
Island
Bamaga

Jardine River
National Park

Wessel
Islands

Elcho
Island

Nhulunbuy

Cape Arnhem

Weipa

Cape
York
Peninsula

Iron Range
National P...

Port Se...

Arnhem Land

Groote
Eylandt

Gulf of
Carpentaria

Mungkan
Kandju
National Park

Ngukurr

Lak...
Na...
Park

20

Wallaby Island

Mitchell and
Alice Rivers
National Park

Sir Edward Pellew
Group

CARPENTARIA HIGHWAY

209

Borroloola

Mornington
Island

Staaten River
National Park

Tjapuk...

Cape
Crawford

Forsyth Island
Bentinck Island
Sweers Island

87

STUART HIGHWAY

Karumba

Burketown

Normanton

Bulleringa
National Park

Mount Surpr...

Georgetown

Barkly
Tableland

Lawn Hill
National Park

Connells Lagoon
Conservation
Reserve

Burke & Wills
Roadhouse

66

Tennant
Creek

Barkly
Homestead

BARKLY HIGHWAY

Camooweal

A2

Mount Isa

Cloncurry

Julia
Creek

FLINDERS

White
Na...
HIGH...

RY

A6

Richmond

LANDSBOROUGH

A2

Gemtree

83

Boulia

Winton

Bladensburg
National Park

HIGHWAY

Alice
Ranges
prings

Diamantina Gates
National Park

QUEENSLAND

Longrea...

Lochern
National Park

Simpson
Desert
National
Park

Beclourie

Welford
National
Park

Simpson Desert

Windorah

Hell Ho...
Nationa...

Birdsville

Witjira
National
Park

Simpson Desert
Regional Reserve

Goyder
Lagoon

214

Sturt
Stony
Desert

Quilpi...

Marla

Innamincka
Regional
Reserve

STUART HIGHWAY

Oodnadatta

Innamincka

Noccundra
Thargomindah

Lake Eyre
North

Lake
Eyre
National Park

Strzelecki
Regional
Reserve

Curra...
Nationa...

...ringa
...servation

Coober Pedy

William Creek

Strzelecki   Desert

Sturt
National Park

A
B
C

5

4

Cape Melville National Park

Cooktown

Daintree
riginal Port Douglas
l Park Mareeba **Cairns**
Atherton Gordonvale
dara **Atherton Tableland**
a Tubes Innisfail Tully
Lumholtz National Park *Hinchinbrook Island National Park*
Ingham

3

Great Basalt Wall National Park **Townsville**
Ayr
Charters Towers Bowen Airlie Beach *Hook Island National Park*
Pentland Collinsville Proserpine *Whitsunday Islands National Park*
enden BRUCE
Eungella National Park Mackay
Beylando Crossing Moranbah Sarina
Muttaburra Dysart *Military Training Area* *Great Keppel Island*
Dividing Clermont *Goodedulla National Park* Yeppoon
Rockhampton
A4 **CAPRICORN** HIGHWAY Emerald *Curtis Island*
ford Barcaldine Alpha Blackwater A4 Mount Morgan Gladstone
Blackall Moura Miriam Vale
alia Tambo Biloela
ational *Carnarvon Gorge National Park* Monto *Bundaberg*
rk Theodore *Hervey Bay* *Great Sandy National Park*
Augathella Childers
Range Mundubbera **Fraser Island**
Expedition National Park Gayndah Maryborough
Charleville Roma A2 Murgon Gympie
Miles Kingaroy Noosa Heads
Surat Chinchilla Nanango *Sunshine Coast*
215 Dalby Caboolture Caloundra
Darling Downs **Toowoomba** *Moreton Island*
Wyandra St George Moonie **BRISBANE**
Bollon Millmerran Gatton Ipswich
Nindigully Goondiwindi Warwick *Gold Coast*
Lamington National Park Coolangatta
Hebel Mungindi Yetman Lismore Murwillumbah
Garah Tenterfield Ballina
Lightning *Washpool National Park*

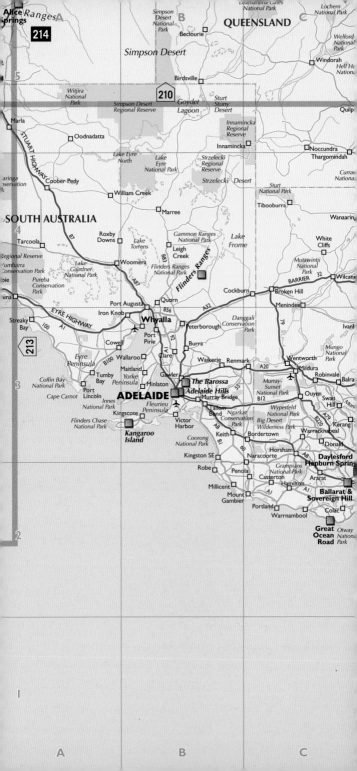

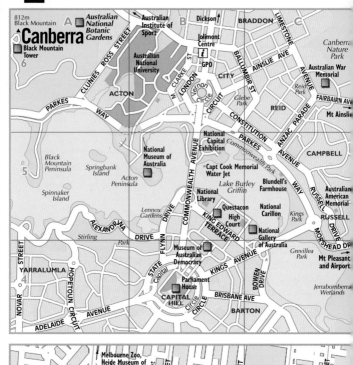

Canberra

812m
Black Mountain

Black Mountain
Tower

Australian
National Botanic
Gardens

CLUNIES ROSS STREET

Australian
Institute of
Sport

Dickson

BRADDON

LIMESTONE

Jolimont
Centre

GPO

BALLUMBIR ST

AINSLIE AVE

Canberra
Nature Park

CITY

London

Verna

Circle

Glebe
Park

Reid
Park

Canberra War
Memorial

FAIRBAIRN AVE

Mt Ainslie

CLARKE ST

ANU

ACTON

PARKES

WAY

LONDON

CIRCUIT

CONSTITUTION

REID

PARKES

Commonwealth Park

ANZAC PARADE

CAMPBELL

Black
Mountain
Peninsula

Springbank
Island

Acton
Peninsula

National Museum of
Australia

COMMONWEALTH AVENUE

National
Capital
Exhibition

Capt Cook Memorial
Water Jet

Lake Burley
Griffin

RUSSELL

Blundell's
Farmhouse

WAY

Australian
American
Memorial

Spinnaker
Island

National
Library

KING EDWARD
TERRACE

Questacon

National
Carillon

Kings
Park

RUSSELL

Lennox
Gardens

ALEXANDRINA

DRIVE

Stirling

FLYNN

Park

High
Court

National
Gallery
of Australia

MORSHEAD DR

Grevillea
Park

Mt Pleasant
and Airport

NOVAR

STREET

YARRALUMLA

HOPETOUN

CIRCUIT

STATE

Capital

Museum of
Australian
Democracy

Parliament
House

KINGS AVENUE

DRIVE

BOWEN

DRIVE

Jerrabomberra
Wetlands

ADELAIDE

AVENUE

CAPITAL
HILL

Circle

CIRCLE

BRISBANE AVE

BARTON

Melbourne

Melbourne Zoo,
Heide Museum of
Modern Art

Royal
Exhibition
Building

BRUNSWICK

STREET

GERTRUDE

Chetwynd

St

Rosslyn

William

Capel

PEEL

STREET

O'Connell

Leicester

Bouverie

SWANSTON STREET

Queensberry

Cardigan

LYGON

Drummond st

STREET

RATHDOWNE STREET

Carlton
Gardens

NICHOLSON STREET

Fitzroy

Young

St

VICTORIA

PARADE

DUDLEY

WILLIAM

Queen
Victoria
Market

VICTORIA

Therry

Franklin

STREET

Mackenzie
Street

Old Melbourne
Gaol

STREET

EXHIBITION

Lonsdale

Parliament
Gardens

GISBORNE

ALBERT

St Patricks
Cath

MACARTHUR

St Andrews
Pl

LANSDOWNE

 St James
Cathedral

Batman
St

Flagstaff
Gardens

Jeffcott

KING

LA TROBE

STREET

Flagstaff

A'Beckett

Melbourne
Central

Central
Mall

State
Library

Little

RUSSELL

ST

Bourke St

Parliament
House

Hotel
Windsor

Parliament

SPRING

Treasury

STREET

WELLINGTON PDE

SPENCER

STREET

Little Lonsdale

LONSDALE

Littte Bourke
Street

QUEEN

ELIZABETH

Mall

STREET

i

Town Hall

COLLINS STREET

Lane

St Michaels

STREET

Wellington
Parade Sth

SOUTHERN
CROSS

COLLINS

ST

Little Collins

Rialto
Towers

Flinders

Little Collins st

STREET

Lane

St Paul's
Cathedral

FLINDERS

Flinders

FLINDERS
STREET

Ian Potter Centre:
NGV Australia

i

Federation
Square

PRINCES
BRIDGE

Yarra

Birrarung
Marr

BATMAN
AVENUE

MCG

WURUNDJERI WAY

FLINDERS

STREET

KINGS
BRIDGE

Yarra Prom

Queens Wharf

QUEENS
BR

QUEENSBRIDGE ST

SOUTHBANK
BLVD

CITY RD

power

Eureka
Skydeck

Hamer Hall

Faulkner

ST KILDA

Southbank Blvd

ALEXANDRA
AV

QueenVictoria
Gdns

Alexandra
Gdns

National Gallery
of Victoria

ROAD

SWAN

BURNLEY TUNNEL

Kings
Domain

Royal
Botanic
Gardens

DOMAIN TUNNEL

Crown
Complex

CLARENDON
STREET

STURT

STREET

Moore

Grant
St

St Kilda

Domain

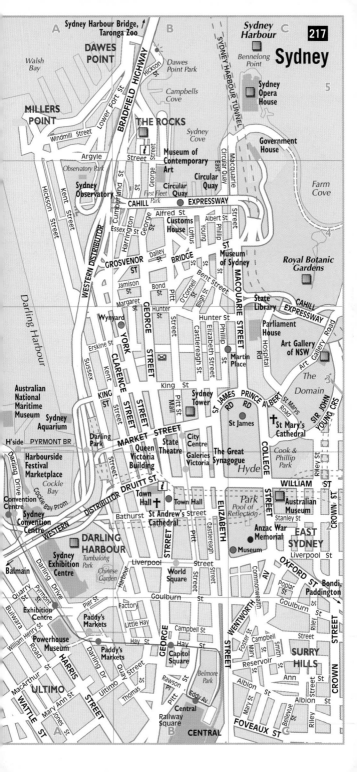

222 Acknowledgements

The Automobile Association wishes to thank the following photographers and organizations for their assistance in the preparation of this book.

Abbreviations for the picture credits are as follows – (t) top; (b) bottom; (l) left; (r) right; (c) centre; (cla) centre left above; (clb) centre left below; (AA) AA World Travel Library

2(i) Picture Contact/Alamy; 2(ii) Alamy/frank'n'focus; 2(iii) AA/S Day; 2(iv) Photo Library/Peter J Robinson; 2(v) Photo Library/David Wall; 2(vi) Photo Library/Nicholas Pitt; 3(i) Photo Library/Ken Wilson; 3(ii) Photo Library/Graham Monro; 3(iii) Photo Library/Chris Garnett; 3(iv) AA/S Richmond; 3(v) Tourism Australia/Jeff Drewitz; 5l Picture Contact/Alamy ; 5c Photo Library/Image 100; 5r Photo Library/Radius Images; 6-7 Robert Harding Picture Library/Laurent Grandadam; 8(i) Getty Images/Robert Harding Picture Library; 8(ii) Rex Features/Newspix; 8(iii) Robert Harding Picture Library/Hans Peter Merten; 8(iv) Photo Library/JTB Photo; 10l Photo Library/David Wall; 10c Photo Library/David Kirkland; 10r Photo Library; 11 Photo Library/RHPL/Claire Leimback; 12 The Bridgeman Art Library; 12-13 Corbis/Historical Picture Archive 13 Corbis/ Bettmann; 14t The Bridgeman Art Library/Ken Welsh; 14b The Bridgeman Art Library/ Samuel Thomas Gill/ Mitchell Library, State Library of New South Wales; 15 The Bridgeman Art Library National Library of Australia, Canberra Australia; 16 The Bridgeman Art Library/National Library of Australia, Canberra, Australia; 17 Photo Library/Julian Love 18t Photo Library/David Messent; 18c Photo Library/Jochen Schienker; 19 Photo Library/Ted Mead; 20l Photo Library/ OSF / Michael Fogden; 20r Photo Library/Anne Montfort; 21l Photo Library/Belinda Wright; 21r Photo Library/Bryan Reynolds; 22r Robert Harding Picture Library/Thorsten Milse; 23l Robert Harding Picture Library/James Hager; 23r Photo Library/Thorsten Milse; 24-25 Photo Library/Andrew Watson; 25ctl Photo Library/PeterWalton; 25cbl Photo Library/ David Hannah; 25bl AA/M Langford; 26l Photo Library/Otto Rogge; 26bc Corbis/Hannah Mason; 26-27c Photo Library/ Andrew Watson; 26-27b Photo Library/Robin Smith; 27cr Photo Library/Robin Smith; 28 AA/M Langford; 29l Alamy/ frank'n'focus; 29c Photos Library/Moodboard; 29r Robert Harding Picture Library/Robert Francis; 43l AA/S Day; 43c AA/S Day; 43r AA/M Langford; 44 Robert Harding Picture Library/David Jacobs; 46 AA/S Day; 47t Pictures Colour Library/Yann Guichaoua; 47b AA/S Day; 48-49 Photo Library/Peter Harrison; 49t Photo Library/Robert Francis; 50 Photo Library; 51 Photo Library/Don Fuchs; 52-53 Photo Library/Stewart Cohen; 54 Photo Library/Andrew Watson; 55 Robert Harding Picture Library/Fraser Hall; 56t AA/M Langford; 56-57 Photo Library/JTB Photo; 58 Photo Library/Pascal Deloch 59 Photo Library/Ingo Schulz; 61t Photo Library/Andrew Watson; 61b Photo Library/RHPL/ Fraser Hall; 62t AA/P Kenward 62b Robert Harding Picture Library/Timothy Winter; 63 Photo Library/Robert Francis; 69l Photo Library Peter J Robinson; 69c Photo Library; 69r Photo Library/Philip Quirk; 71 Photo Library/Claver Carroll; 72 Photo Library/ David Messent; 73t Photo Library/David Messent; 73b Photo Library/Claver Carroll; 74-75 Photo Library/David Messent 75b Photo Library/David Messent; 77 AA/P Kenward; 78-79 Photo Library/Andrea Robinson; 80 AA/S Day; 83 Photo Library/Geoff Higgins; 89l Photo Library/David Wall; 89c Photo Library/Pixtal Images; 89r Photo Library/Christian Riecke 92 Robert Harding Picture Library/Gavin Hellier; 93t Robert Harding Picture Library/Ken Gillham; 93b Robert Harding Picture Library/Jochen Schlenker; 94-95t Robert Harding Picture Library/Gavin Hellier; 94-95c Robert Harding Picture Library/Ken Gillham; 97 Photo Library/Japan Travel Bureau; 98 Corbis/Theo Allofs; 99 Robert Francis/Robert Harding; 100 Photo Library/Ken Stepnell; 102 Robert Harding Picture Library/eye ubiquitous; 104 Alamy/David Wall; 105 Photo Library/Wayne Fogden; 111l Photo Library/Nicholas Pitt; 111c Robert Harding Picture Library/Adina Tovy; 111r Corbis/ Doug Byrnes; 112 Photo Library/Geoff Higgins; 113 Robert Harding Picture Library/Fraser Hall; 114 Alamy/David Wall; 115t Photo Library/RHPL/ Amanda Hall; 115b Photo Library/JTB Photo; 116-117 Corbis/ Richard Eastwood; 117t Corbis/ Sean Davey; 118 Photo Library/OSF/Robin Bush; 119 Photo Library/Paul Thompson; 120-121 Photo Library/Corbis; 121c Photo Library/JTB Photo; 123 Photo Library/Ken Usami; 124-125 Photo Library/Geoff Higgins; 125t Photo Library/ Geoff Higgins; 126 Photo Library/Robin Smith; 127 Photo Library/David Messent; 128 Photo Library/Ted Mead; 133l Photo Library/Ken Wilson; 133c AA/S Watkins; 133r Photo Library/Pepeira Tom; 134 Photo Library/Corbis; 136c Photo Library/Andrew Watson; 136b Corbis/Patrick Ward; 137 Corbis/Larry Mulvehill; 139 Photo Library/Ted Mead 140-141 Photo Library/Botanica Botanica; 142 Photo Library/ RHPL/Sylvain Grandadam; 143 Photo Library/JTB Photo; 144-145 Corbis/Larry Mulvehill; 146 Photo Library/Imagebroker/Horst Mahr; 147 Photo Library/Andrew Watson; 148 Photo Library/Ted Mead; 151l Photo Library/Graham Monro; 151c Photo Library/Imagebroker/ White Star / Monica Gumm 151r Photo Library/Fresh Food Images/Steven Morris Photography; 152 Photo Library/Robin Smith; 154 Photo Library/ David Messent; 155t Photo Library/Gary Lewis; 155b Photo Library/Robin Smith; 156 Alamy/Jon Arnold Images Ltd; 157 Photo Library/Milton Wordley; 158 Photo Library/Wayne Fogden; 159t Photo Library/Ken Stepnell; 159b Photo Library Milton Wordley; 160 Photo Library/LOOK-foto/Don Fuchs; 161t Photo Library/Tips Italia/Bildagentur RM; 161b Photo Library/OSF /Konrad Wothe; 165l Photo Library/Christ Garnett; 165c Robert Harding Picture Library/Travellr 165r Photo Library/Oldrich Karasek/The Travel Library; 167 Robert Harding Picture Library/eye ubiquitous; 168 Robert Harding Picture Library/Peter Scholey; 169t Photo Library/Roel Loopers; 169b Photo Library/Radius Images; 170 Photo Library/RHPL/Gavin Hellier; 172 Photo Library/Radius Images ; 174 Robert Harding Picture Library/Gavin Hellier; 175 Photo Library/Ken Stepnell; 179l AA/S Richmond; 179c Photo Library/Imagebroker /Joerg Reuther; 179r Robert Harding Picture Library/Pete Oxford; 180 AA/A Baker; 182t Photo Library/John Warburton-Lee Photography/Julian Love; 182b Photo Library/Ken Stepnell; 183t Robert Harding Picture Library/G R Richardson; 183b Photo Library/John Warburton-Lee Photography/Julian Love; 184 Photo Library/age fotostock/Suzanne Long; 185 Photo Library/Virginia Star 186 AA/A Baker; 187 Photo Library/JTB Photo; 189 Photo Library/John Warburton-Lee Photography/Julian Love; 193l Tourism Australia/Jeff Drewitz; 193c Photo Library/Jochen Schlenker; 193r Tourism Australia/Dominic Harcourt-Webster; 195 Corbis/Michelle Chaplow; 200 Photo Library/Robin Smith; 201l Alamy/frank'n'focus; 201c Robert Harding Picture Library/Fraser Hall; 201r Tourism Australia; 205t Alamy/David Wall; 205c Alamy/Goplaces; 205b Alamy/ CulturalEyes-AusGS.

Questionnaire

Dear Traveler

Your comments, opinions and recommendations are very important
to us. So please help us to improve our travel guides by taking a few
minutes to complete this simple questionnaire.

Send to: **Spiral Guides, MailStop 64, 1000 AAA Drive,
Heathrow, FL 32746–5063**

Your recommendations...
We always encourage readers' recommendations for restaurants, nightlife or shopping
– if your recommendation is added to the next edition of the guide, we will send you
a FREE AAA Spiral Guide of your choice. Please state below the establishment name,
location and your reasons for recommending it.

_____

_____

_____

_____

_____

Please send me AAA Spiral _____
(see list of titles inside the back cover)

About this guide...
Which title did you buy?

_____ **AAA Spiral**

Where did you buy it? _____

When? m̲ m̲ / y̲ y̲

Why did you choose a AAA Spiral Guide? _____

_____

_____

_____

Did this guide meet your expectations?

Exceeded ☐   Met all ☐   Met most ☐   Fell below ☐

Please give your reasons _____

_____

_____

_____

_____

continued on next page...

Were there any aspects of this guide that you particularly liked?

_____
_____
_____
_____
_____

Is there anything we could have done better?

_____
_____
_____
_____
_____

About you...

Name (Mr/Mrs/Ms) _____

Address _____

_____

_____ **Zip** _____

Daytime tel nos. _____

Which age group are you in?

Under 25 ☐   25–34 ☐   35–44 ☐   45–54 ☐   55–64 ☐   65+ ☐

How many trips do you make a year?

Less than one ☐   One ☐   Two ☐   Three or more ☐

Are you a AAA member? Yes ☐   No ☐

Name of AAA club _____

About your trip...

When did you book? m m / y y   When did you travel? m m / y y

How long did you stay? _____

Was it for business or leisure? _____

Did you buy any other travel guides for your trip?   Yes ☐   No ☐

If yes, which ones? _____

_____

Thank you for taking the time to complete this questionnaire.